University Textbook Series

May, 1985

Especially Designed for Collateral Reading

HARRY W. JONES
Directing Editor
Professor of Law, Columbia University

ADMINISTRATIVE LAW AND PROCESS (1985)
  Richard J. Pierce, Jr., Dean and Professor of Law, University of Pittsburgh.
  Sidney A. Shapiro, Professor of Law, University of Kansas.
  Paul R. Verkuil, President and Professor of Law, College of William and Mary.

ADMIRALTY, Second Edition (1975)
  Grant Gilmore, Professor of Law, Yale University.
  Charles L. Black, Jr., Professor of Law, Yale University.

ADMIRALTY AND FEDERALISM (1970)
  David W. Robertson, Professor of Law, University of Texas.

AGENCY (1975)
  W. Edward Sell, Dean of the School of Law, University of Pittsburgh.

BUSINESS ORGANIZATION AND FINANCE (1980)
  William A. Klein, Professor of Law, University of California, Los Angeles.

CIVIL PROCEDURE, BASIC, Second Edition (1979)
  Milton D. Green, Professor of Law Emeritus, University of California, Hastings College of the Law.

COMMERCIAL TRANSACTIONS, INTRODUCTION TO (1977)
  Hon. Robert Braucher, Associate Justice, Supreme Judicial Court of Massachusetts.
  Robert A. Riegert, Professor of Law, Cumberland School of Law.

CONFLICT OF LAWS, COMMENTARY ON THE, Second Edition (1980)
  Russell J. Weintraub, Professor of Law, University of Texas.

CONSTITUTIONAL LAW, AMERICAN (A TREATISE ON) (1978) with 1979 Supplement
  Laurence H. Tribe, Professor of Law, Harvard University.

CONTRACT LAW, THE CAPABILITY PROBLEM IN (1978)
  Richard Danzig.

CORPORATIONS, Second Edition (1971)
  Norman D. Lattin, Professor of Law, University of California, Hastings College of the Law.

CORPORATIONS IN PERSPECTIVE (1976)
  Alfred F. Conard, Professor of Law, University of Michigan.

i

UNIVERSITY TEXTBOOK SERIES—Continued

CRIMINAL LAW, Third Edition (1982)
Rollin M. Perkins, Professor of Law, University of California, Hastings College of the Law.
Ronald N. Boyce, Professor of Law, University of Utah College of Law.

CRIMINAL PROCEDURE (1980) with 1984 Supplement
Charles H. Whitebread, II, Professor of Law, University of Virginia.

ESTATES IN LAND & FUTURE INTERESTS, PREFACE TO, Second Edition (1984)
Thomas F. Bergin, Professor of Law, University of Virginia.
Paul G. Haskell, Professor of Law, University of North Carolina.

EVIDENCE: COMMON SENSE AND COMMON LAW (1947)
John M. Maguire, Professor of Law, Harvard University.

EVIDENCE, STUDENTS' TEXT ON THE LAW OF (1935)
The late John Henry Wigmore, Northwestern University.

JURISPRUDENCE: MEN AND IDEAS OF THE LAW (1953)
The late Edwin W. Patterson, Cardozo Professor of Jurisprudence, Columbia University.

LEGAL CAPITAL, Second Edition (1981)
Bayless Manning.

LEGAL RESEARCH ILLUSTRATED, Third Edition (1985) with 1985 Assignments Supplement
J. Myron Jacobstein, Professor of Law, Law Librarian, Stanford University.
Roy M. Mersky, Professor of Law, Director of Research, University of Texas.

LEGAL RESEARCH, FUNDAMENTALS OF, Third Edition (1985) with 1985 Assignments Supplement
J. Myron Jacobstein, Professor of Law, Law Librarian, Stanford University.
Roy M. Mersky, Professor of Law, Director of Research, University of Texas.

PROCEDURE, THE STRUCTURE OF (1979)
Robert M. Cover, Professor of Law, Yale University.
Owen M. Fiss, Professor of Law, Yale University.

THE PROFESSION OF LAW (1971)
L. Ray Patterson, Professor of Law, Emory University.
Elliott E. Cheatham, Professor of Law, Vanderbilt University.

PROPERTY, Second Edition (1975)
John E. Cribbet, Dean of the Law School, University of Illinois.

TAXATION, FEDERAL INCOME, Fourth Edition (1985)
Marvin A. Chirelstein, Professor of Law, Columbia University.

TORTS, Second Edition (1980)
Clarence Morris, Professor of Law, University of Pennsylvania.
C. Robert Morris, Professor of Law, University of Minnesota.

TRUSTS, PREFACE TO THE LAW OF (1975)
Paul G. Haskell, Professor of Law, University of North Carolina.

WILLS AND TRUSTS, THE PLANNING AND DRAFTING OF, Second Edition (1979) with 1982 Supplement
Thomas L. Shaffer, Professor of Law, University of Notre Dame.

A CONCISE TEXTBOOK

ON

LEGAL CAPITAL

SECOND EDITION

. . . Being a General Exposition and Critique, for Law Students and Others, of Corporation Law Regulating Corporate Capital Accounts, Par and No Par Stock, Stated Capital, Distributions to Shareholders, Equitable Contribution by Shareholders, Promoters' Liability and Related Mysteries

By

BAYLESS MANNING

Partner, Paul, Weiss, Rifkind, Wharton & Garrison

Former Dean and Professor of Law, Stanford Law School
Former Professor of Law, Yale Law School

Mineola, New York
THE FOUNDATION PRESS, INC.
1981

COPYRIGHT © 1977 By THE FOUNDATION PRESS, INC.
COPYRIGHT © 1981 By THE FOUNDATION PRESS, INC.
All rights reserved
Printed in the United States of America

Library of Congress Cataloging in Publication Data

Manning, Bayless.
   A concise textbook on legal capital.

   (University textbook series)
   Includes bibliographical references and index.
     1. Corporations—United States—Finance.
2. Securities—United States. I. Title. II. Series.
KF1428.Z9M3   1981   346.73'0666   80-28464

ISBN 0-88277-020-9

ACKNOWLEDGMENTS

I have leaned on the knowledge, skill and good humor of a good many people in the course of writing this book. Among them were professors of law Gordon Scott and Junius Hoffman, who disciplined my legal analysis, Gordon W. Tasker, C.P.A., who weeded out my more egregious accounting gaffes, and Augusta McEachern, Shirley Wedlake, Judith Gustafson and Roberta Standish, who did more than a fair share of the real work. I am happy to say public thanks to them all.

But most of all I am indebted to, and dedicate this book to, Sam Cross, law practitioner and scholar, and Ernie Folk, scholar and law practitioner, who pushed me and helped me to climb up and over the high wall that separates an almost completed manuscript from a completed one.

BAYLESS MANNING

New York, New York
1977, 1981

*

PREFACE TO SECOND EDITION

I always read an author's preface. I have found that what authors have to say in their prefaces is often more consequential than what they offer in the main body of their works. Whoever reads these words will, by that act, have shown that he, too, is a Preface Reader. For that reader the following comments will prove helpful and perhaps even interesting.

First, the Preface to the First Edition of this book remains recommended reading and has been retained here in its entirety.

Second, in the original Preface appears the following passage:

> "But, whatever one's estimate of the efficacy of the statutory apparatus in this field, the apparatus is imbedded in our state corporation laws and cases, and lawyers have to deal with it, have to talk with accountants about it, and have to give opinions about it. Unfortunately, the worst charge that can be brought against these laws is that they are ineffective. No persuasive case can be made that the statutory provisions on par, stated capital and equity distributions are vicious, and no organized segment of American society is gored by them. As a result, the existing scheme shows prospects of great durability. American lawyers will have to continue to live and work with these provisions for a long time to come."

The last two sentences of that passage must now be modified. And in that modification lies the main impetus for the publication of this Second Edition.

Contrary to all expectation, the Committee on Corporate Laws of the American Bar Association's Section on Corporation, Banking and Business Law quietly and almost unnoticed has committed a full-scale revolutionary act as guardian of "the better view," the Model Business Corporation Act. In 1980 the Committee, on the basis of a particularly long and painstaking study by a subcommittee, calmly threw out of the window substantially all of the doctrinal propositions with which this book is concerned—if not lock, stock* and barrel then at least lock and barrel. To that event this author (who served as a member of the subcommittee) cheers "High time!" But the new amendments do raise a bit of a problem as to what should be done with this book.

However sound and bold the action taken by the custodians of the Model Business Corporation Act, unfortunately it does not

---
* See page 29.

PREFACE TO SECOND EDITION

make the problems discussed in this book go away. Nor will it do so, at least for a very long time.

–The Model Act is only a model; it remains to be seen whether many states will follow the lead of the 1980 revision.

–Many states, including some of the most important commercial states like Delaware, New York, and California, do not look to the Model Business Corporation Act as a guide at all.

–Ancient ways of thinking will not soon be laid aside by the courts.

–Perhaps most important of all, lawyers, accountants and corporate financial V-Ps who work daily with this material will find it very difficult to take seriously the effort of the Model Act revisions to obliterate their doctrinal learning at a stroke—and will doubtless keep on working in their old ways, even if the statutes are changed. The author's grandfather—a reflective and courtly member of the Kentucky bar—went to his grave at venerable years, declaring with undiminished conviction that the merger of law and equity was a terrible mistake, that rules of law and principles of equity remain immutably distinct, just as they have always been, and that the only consequence of the "merger" is that now there are no longer any good common-law lawyers or any good equity practitioners, either. Many experienced corporate practitioners are likely to react in similar vein to the 1980 revisions of the Model Act.

Yet the changes in the Model Act indicate a rate and magnitude of change in the law of "legal capital" that cannot be ignored. In these circumstances it appears that the only thing to do is to get out a Second Edition in a form that invites the reader's attention to these new happenings while retaining the material contained in the First Edition. A new edition affords the additional advantage of an opportunity to clean up some scattered goofs, glitches and garbles that somehow insinuated themselves into the First Edition.

Parts I and II of this Edition will therefore be found to remain much as they were in the First Edition, while Part III is entirely new.

BAYLESS MANNING

Paul, Weiss, Rifkind,
   Wharton & Garrison
New York, New York
January, 1981

PREFACE TO FIRST EDITION

Heretically, this is a legal textbook, though, it may be hoped, a modern one. It is not a case book. It is not a reference book. It is a textbook to be read by law students and other interested persons without the aid of an instructor.

The experienced corporate practitioner will probably find little in this book that is new to him, though its panoramic perspective may strike him as unique and interesting. The lawyer or judge who seldom deals with problems of corporate capital structure will find the book helpful when confronted with such a problem. Accountants and business school students can learn from the book something of the law in this field and its peculiarities. But every year in America's law schools, thousands of law students take, and scores of professors teach, a course in basic corporation law; this book is mainly written for them.

The subjects treated here include the development and current state of corporation code provisions and common law governing stated capital, par and no par stock, reductions of capital, statutory restrictions on distributions to shareholders, impairment of capital, the shareholders' problem of equitable contribution, stock watering and promoters' liability. Every person who has taught an introductory course in American corporation law knows the special frustration that attends the effort to deal with these topics. On the basis of fifteen years of law teaching experience at Yale and Stanford with this material, I have concluded that it is high time we admit that these subjects are simply not amenable to usual instruction methods.

Case law in the field is spotty and incoherent. Most of the relevant material is statutory and the statutes themselves display a considerable variety. Classroom discussion of the law in the field invariably comes apart at the seams as the instructor engages in a losing effort simultaneously to teach instant accounting to those members of the class who do not know a debit from a credit, to sophisticate those students who already know some accounting (the most difficult group), and to philosophize with those who have a strong and modern accounting background.

But awkward as these factors are, the basic pedagogical problem in this field lies elsewhere. The real problem is that the game is not worth the candle. The complexity and novelty of the

PREFACE TO FIRST EDITION

material involved require an investment of classroom time that is wholly incommensurate with the value of the educational return to the student. The usual law student in an elementary corporation course must first be introduced to the strange conceptual categories of par, capital, surplus and the like; he must then be shown how these concepts have been put together in our corporation codes in an effort to deal with certain problems; then he must be led to the higher plateau of perceiving that the statutory structures fail to solve the problems to which they were addressed.

In my experience in teaching advanced courses in corporation law and corporate finance, I have found that students who have endured this experience fall into three groups. The first group —recollecting weeks of classroom work devoted to par, stated capital, and the like—believes the subject is very real and very important. It is not. The second group remembers that the end product of the elementary instruction was the instructor's analytic devastation of the whole topic; this group sneers at the subject as trivial and not to be taken seriously. Later, as lawyers, they will get a client and themselves in trouble. The third group remembers only that the whole matter seemed terribly complicated at the time, they didn't understand any of it, and they haven't thought about it since. Each of these groups needs a brief, readable, inclusive and critical reading source to go back to. At present, however, there is no such source available.

This book is the author's attempt, based on a number of years of corporate law practice and a longer period of teaching corporation law, to provide a practical pedagogical tool for dealing with the special circumstances that inhere in this field. The book is not reverent in its attitude toward the law in this area for, as the author sees it, much of it is remarkable for its analytic naivete and want of policy content. But, whatever one's estimate of the efficacy of the statutory apparatus in this field, the apparatus is imbedded in our state corporation laws and cases, and lawyers have to deal with it, have to talk with accountants about it, and have to give opinions about it. Unfortunately, the worst charge that can be brought against these laws is that they are ineffective. No persuasive case can be made that the statutory provisions on par, stated capital and equity distributions are vicious, and no organized segment of American society is gored by them. As a result, the existing scheme shows prospects of great durability. American lawyers will have to continue to live and work with these provisions for a long time to come.

PREFACE TO FIRST EDITION

If this little book is successful, it should emancipate teachers of corporation law from the futile task of trying to deal in the classroom with regulation of capital structures and should release valuable classroom time for attention to matters of more substance. If the book is successful, it should give to student users in elementary corporation courses, whether or not trained in accounting, a reasonably sophisticated understanding of the legal capital area. If the book is successful, it should provide to advanced students and to lawyers a rapidly readable refresher on material they either never understood or have forgotten. Whether the book succeeds in these objectives, or any of them, must await the judgment of the readers.

BAYLESS MANNING

New York City
March, 1977

SUMMARY OF CONTENTS

	Page
ACKNOWLEDGMENTS	V
PREFACE TO SECOND EDITION	VII
PREFACE TO FIRST EDITION	IX

PART ONE. THE LEGAL CAPITAL STATUTES—ANALYSIS

Chapter
- I. The Problem—Corporate Creditor and Corporate Shareholder 1
- II. Legal Capital—Development of the Key Concept 16
- III. Regulating the Shareholder's Contribution 40
- IV. Statutory Regulation of Distributions to Shareholders 59
- V. A Preliminary Evaluation of Legal Capital Statutes 84
- VI. Creditor Protection Outside the Legal Capital Statutes 91
- VII. End Questions 108

PART TWO. THE LEGAL CAPITAL STATUTES IN ACTION

Introduction 109

Transaction
1. Loss 111
2. Small Profit 111
3. Large Profit 112
4. Asset Write-up—Appreciation Surplus 113
5. Elimination of Asset Write-up 115
6. Stock Issuance for Secret Process 116
7. Write-down of Asset 116
8. Stock Dividend 118
9. Stock Split 121
10. Reduction of Stated Capital 122
11. Reduction Surplus as Offset to Deficit 125
12. Paid-in Surplus 127
13. Stock Repurchase Agreement 128
14. Purchase of Stock for the Treasury 130
15. Sale of "Treasury Shares" 132
16. Retirement of "Treasury Shares" 133
17. Distribution in Kind 135
18. Increase of Stated Capital by Resolution 137
19. Issuance of Preferred Stock 138

SUMMARY OF CONTENTS

Chapter		Page
20.	Present and Future Stock Issuance (Issuance of No Par Stock; Convertible Debentures; Stock Subscriptions; Stock Warrants; Stock Options)	141
21.	Transactions between Corporation and Shareholders	148
22.	Corporate Combination; Purchase Accounting and Pooling of Interests Accounting	152
23.	Dissolution and Liquidation	162

PART THREE. FRESH WINDS BLOWING

I.	California, 1975	164
II.	Model Business Corporation Act, 1980 Changes	165
	A. The Shareholder's Pay-in Obligation	167
	B. Regulating Distributions to Shareholders	169
	C. Some Concluding Comments	179
Index		181

TABLE OF CONTENTS

	Page
ACKNOWLEDGMENTS	V
PREFACE TO SECOND EDITION	VII
PREFACE TO FIRST EDITION	IX

PART ONE. THE LEGAL CAPITAL STATUTES—ANALYSIS

CHAPTER I. THE PROBLEM—CORPORATE CREDITOR AND CORPORATE SHAREHOLDER 1
A. The Creditor's Perspective 1
  1. Creditors—General 1
  2. The Creditor of the Individual Proprietorship or Partnership 3
  3. The Creditor of the Corporation 5
B. The Shareholder's Perspective 8
  1. Payouts to Shareholders 8
  2. Equitable Contribution Among Shareholders—A Separate Problem 12
C. The Creditor's and Shareholder's Perspectives Combined .. 13

CHAPTER II. LEGAL CAPITAL—DEVELOPMENT OF THE KEY CONCEPT 16
A. The Standard of Equity Investment—What Amount of What Assets Must Shareholders Put Into the Corporate Pot? 17
  1. Minimum Pay-in Requirements 17
  2. The Prototypical Model and Par 18
  3. "Par," "Capital" and the Creditor 20
  4. The Going Enterprise: A Change in the Model 22
  5. Low Par Stock 24
  6. No Par Stock 25
  7. Legal Capital 26
B. Distributing Corporate Assets to the Shareholders 27
  1. *Wood v. Dummer*—The Classic Case 27
  2. The Key Proposition—"Legal Capital" as a Measuring Rod 29
  3. The Classic Example: High Par 30
  4. Legal Capital as a Bench Mark—Some General Observations 33
  5. The Classic Example Modified: Low Par 36
  6. The Classic Example Further Modified: No Par Stock 38

TABLE OF CONTENTS

Page

B. Distributing Corporate Assets to the Shareholders—Continued
    7. Changes in Capital Structure of the Ongoing Corporation ... 38
C. Legal Capital as a Concept: Conclusion ... 39

CHAPTER III. REGULATING THE SHAREHOLDER'S CONTRIBUTION ... 40

A. The Shareholder's Pay-in Obligation ... 40
    1. How Much Assets? ... 40
    2. What Kinds of Assets? ... 40
    3. Valuation ... 43
B. Qualifications on the Pay-in Obligation ... 45
    1. Transferees of Watered Shares ... 45
    2. Treasury Shares ... 45
    3. The *Handley* Doctrine ... 45
C. Enforcing the Pay-in Obligation—Creditor as Plaintiff ... 46
    1. Three Theories for Creditor Enforcement of the Obligation to Pay Par ... 46
        a. The Trust Fund Theory ... 46
        b. The Holding Out or Fraud Theory ... 46
        c. The Statutory Obligation Theory ... 48
    2. Two Other Theories for Creditor Enforcement of the Shareholder's Obligation to Pay In ... 48
        a. Stock Subscription ... 48
        b. Balance Sheet and Other Misrepresentation ... 48
    3. Hybrid Theories ... 49
    4. Procedural Pitfalls—The Significance of the Creditor's Theory ... 49
D. Enforcing the Pay-in Obligation—Shareholder as Plaintiff ... 53
    1. The Legal Capital Scheme ... 53
    2. Promoter's Liability ... 54
    3. Equitable Contribution Doctrine ... 55
    4. Disclosure and Securities Regulation ... 56
E. Enforcing the Pay-in Obligation—Corporation as Plaintiff ... 56
F. The Corporate Practitioner: An Ounce of Prevention ... 57

CHAPTER IV. STATUTORY REGULATION OF DISTRIBUTIONS TO SHAREHOLDERS ... 59

A. Insolvency Statutes ... 59
B. Balance Sheet Surplus Statutes: Stated Capital and Surplus ... 60
    1. Accounting, the Accountant, and the Law ... 61
    2. Computation of Stated Capital ... 64
    3. Reducing Capital ... 67
    4. Surpluses ... 68

TABLE OF CONTENTS

		Page
B.	Balance Sheet Surplus Statutes: Stated Capital and Surplus—Continued	
	a. Paid-in Surplus; (Capital Surplus)	69
	b. Reduction Surplus	70
	c. Appreciation Surplus and Unrealized Gain	71
	d. Earned Surplus	72
	e. Other Surpluses	72
C.	Earned Surplus Statutes	72
D.	Surplus or Net Profits Statutes	76
E.	Current Earnings Statutes: Nimble Dividends	76
F.	Share Reacquisition by the Issuer	77
G.	The Class Struggle: Classes of Shares	79
H.	Liabilities for Distributions Violating the Legal Capital Statutes	81

CHAPTER V. A PRELIMINARY EVALUATION OF LEGAL CAPITAL STATUTES ... 84

CHAPTER VI. CREDITOR PROTECTION OUTSIDE THE LEGAL CAPITAL STATUTES ... 91

A.	The General Trade Creditor	91
B.	The Finance or Institutional Creditor	94
	1. The Commercial Creditor	94
	2. The Investment Creditor and His Contract—The Corporate Indenture	96
	a. Structure	96
	b. Key Covenants	97
	(i) Covenant on Secured or Prior Debt	98
	(ii) Covenant on Unsecured or Funded Debt	98
	(iii) Covenant on Distributions to Shareholders	98
	(iv) Covenant on Informing the Trustee	106
	c. Contract and Statute Compared	106

CHAPTER VII. END QUESTIONS ... 108

PART TWO. THE LEGAL CAPITAL STATUTES IN ACTION

Introduction		109
Transaction 1:	Loss	111
Transaction 2:	Small Profit	111
Transaction 3:	Large Profit	112
Transaction 4:	Asset Write-up—Appreciation Surplus	113
Transaction 5:	Elimination of Asset Write-up	115
Transaction 6:	Stock Issuance for Secret Process	116

TABLE OF CONTENTS

		Page
Transaction 7:	Write-down of Asset	116
Transaction 8:	Stock Dividend	118
Transaction 9:	Stock Split	121
Transaction 10:	Reduction of Stated Capital	122
Transaction 11:	Reduction Surplus as Offset to Deficit	125
Transaction 12:	Paid-in Surplus	127
Transaction 13:	Stock Repurchase Agreement	128
Transaction 14:	Purchase of Stock for the Treasury	130
Transaction 15:	Sale of "Treasury Shares"	132
Transaction 16:	Retirement of "Treasury Shares"	133
Transaction 17:	Distribution in Kind	135
Transaction 18:	Increase of Stated Capital by Resolution	137
Transaction 19:	Issuance of Preferred Stock	138
Transaction 20:	Present and Future Stock Issuance (Issuance of No Par Stock; Convertible Debentures; Stock Subscriptions; Stock Warrants; Stock Options)	141
Transaction 21:	Transactions between Corporation and Shareholders	148
Transaction 22:	Corporate Combination; Purchase Accounting and Pooling of Interests Accounting	152
Transaction 23:	Dissolution and Liquidation	162

PART THREE. FRESH WINDS BLOWING

I. California, 1975 _____ 164
II. Model Business Corporation Act, 1980 Changes _____ 165
    A. The Shareholder's Pay-in Obligation _____ 167
        1. Consideration required _____ 167
        2. Equitable contribution _____ 168
        3. Procedural remedies _____ 168
    B. Regulating Distributions to Shareholders _____ 169
        1. "Distribution" _____ 169
        2. Insolvency _____ 170
        3. Balance sheet test _____ 171
            (a) Valuation _____ 172
            (b) Time of Measurement _____ 175
            (c) Redemption related debt _____ 175
            (d) Liability for improper distribution _____ 176
        4. Abolition of treasury shares _____ 178
    C. Some Concluding Comments _____ 179

Index _____ 181

A CONCISE TEXTBOOK

ON

LEGAL CAPITAL

Part One

THE LEGAL CAPITAL STATUTES—ANALYSIS

Part One of this book is an analysis of the central concepts of modern legal capital statutes and doctrine. Part Two surveys a sequence of typical corporate financial transactions to illustrate the legal capital statutes at work. Neither of these Parts is likely to be well understood without the other.

Part Three provides an updating of some recent developments in the field, and presupposes a grasp of the first two Parts.

Chapter I

THE PROBLEM—CORPORATE CREDITOR AND CORPORATE SHAREHOLDER

The interests of creditors of a corporation and the interests of shareholders of a corporation are likely to conflict whenever assets of shareholders are to be committed to the corporation's treasury and whenever assets are to be distributed to shareholders from the corporate treasury. The legal apparatus built by common law and statute around the concept of "legal capital" is fundamentally aimed at striking a partial accommodation of that conflict of interests.

A. THE CREDITOR'S PERSPECTIVE

1. Creditors—General

The legal term "creditor" implies a single basic proposition. Except in extraordinary circumstances (as when, for example, a debtor has received a bankruptcy discharge or holds a homestead exemption) a creditor has, subject to the special terms of the credit, a higher and prior claim to the assets of his debtor than the debtor has himself. When a loan or other class of creditor's claim has become due and payable, the creditor may, in normal course, enlist the engines of the law to compel his debtor to pay the debt, regardless of the consequent diminution of the assets that "belong" to the debtor. Though the term "priority" is usually reserved in the law to describe relationships among claimants other than the debtor, in a basic sense it may be said that the creditor's claim against the assets of his debtor is "prior" to the debtor's own claim to "his" assets. "Prior" in this sense has no relationship to the concept of time; it relates to hierarchy of claim. If the debtor has just enough assets to pay the creditor's claim, the creditor gets them all, i. e. his claim is "prior," and the debtor gets nothing.

General creditors are those creditors who are not secured creditors. A secured creditor is a creditor who, in addition to his creditor's claim, has a mortgage or other lien interest in particular assets of the debtor. Since all claims of all creditors to the assets of the debtor have priority over the debtor's claim, the secured creditor does not by force of his security interest in particular assets of the debtor gain in priority vis-a-vis his debtor. The purpose and effect of the mortgage or other lien interest obtained by the secured creditor is to achieve a preferred position as against, not the debtor, but other creditors. If, at the critical time for payment, the debtor has enough assets to pay all creditors, the secured creditor's security is irrelevant since he will be paid in any case. But if the debtor's assets are not sufficient to pay all the creditors' claims outstanding against him, some creditors will come out short. The creditor who has in some manner obtained a lien on particular assets of the debtor has, in effect, the opportunity to claim those assets for the full and complete payment of the debt owing to him, even if they are the only assets so that the dedication of the lien assets to his debt means that other creditors will receive nothing at all. Until paid, the secured creditor is "prior" to general creditors to the extent of the value of the assets that are subject to the secured creditor's lien.[1] The general creditors have no claim against the assets under the secured creditor's lien except to the extent that the value of the assets exceeds the secured creditor's claim.

---

1. The creditor, or class of creditors, may be persuaded, of course, to agree that its claim against the debtor's assets will rank below that of other creditors, or other particular classes of creditors, though still ahead of the debtor's claim to the assets. Such a creditor is said to be a "subordinated creditor," and his claim is called "subordinated debt."

Speaking generally, therefore, from the perspective of any single general creditor:

- he is more likely to be paid and is thus better off the more assets the debtor has on the payment date;
- he is adversely affected by an increase in the aggregate of outstanding claims of general creditors against the debtor since in any ultimate showdown, all the general creditors will share equally in the limited assets of the debtor; and
- he is more adversely affected still by the creation or existence of secured creditors, for in the showdown, the secured creditors will, to the extent of their security, be able to assert a claim prior to all general creditors.

2. The Creditor of the Individual Proprietorship or Partnership

When a creditor lends money to an individual, or allows him otherwise to become indebted to the creditor, the assets to which the creditor may generally look for payment of his claim are made up of the aggregate of the debtor's assets that have not earlier been placed under lien to some secured creditor. The creditor, may, of course, insist as a condition of his loan that he be empowered to pursue assets in addition to those owned by his debtor; he may, for example, require some device like a third party guaranty, a third party endorsement, or a third party pledge agreement. Occasionally, too, the law will step in to help a creditor reach assets beyond those of his debtor; thus a creditor may in some circumstances be able to reach the assets of a father for an indebtedness incurred by a child, or those of a husband for indebtedness incurred by a wife. But except for such special situations, (i) the creditor's *only* resort is the pool of unencumbered (unmortgaged) assets belonging to the debtor and (ii) *all* of the unencumbered assets of the debtor are at jeopardy for payment of the creditor's claim.

The second of these two propositions is more significant and less inevitable than may appear. Suppose B, a wealthy man, holds net unencumbered assets worth $1,000,000 made up of $950,000 in real property and a $50,000 sole proprietorship interest in a small suburban barber shop. Suppose, further, that the barber shop needs $20,000 worth of new furnishings and that, for whatever reason, B decides to borrow the money to pay for them. L, the lender, fully understanding that the money is to be used for the barber shop fixtures, and having satisfied himself that the profit potentials of the barber shop are such as to give promise that the loan can be paid off out of the proceeds of the barber shop business, thereupon lends B the $20,000.

In these circumstances, it might be argued that, when the time for payment comes, L should have no resort to B's assets beyond his property interest in the barber shop. But the law is to the contrary, and *all* of B's unencumbered assets—his "personal" as well as his "business" assets—will be held equally answerable to pay off L. L's claim is not limited to the assets of the enterprise for the use of which the loan was made. All of B's assets are at jeopardy. B is said to have "unlimited liability". The term is not a particularly apt one; B's liability is in fact limited in two ways—first by the size of the creditor's claim and second by the aggregate unencumbered assets that B has. But no matter. L, in considering whether to make the loan for purposes of the barber shop business, may assume that whatever unencumbered assets B may have when the loan becomes due (or, indeed, acquires thereafter) will be available to him (and other general creditors) for payment of his claim.

In substance, the same situation obtains, and the same results follow, if the borrower is a business enterprise conducting its affairs in the form of a partnership having partners P, Q, and R. Even though the loan be exclusively for the partnership enterprise, the law of partnership treats the loan as though each partner had been an individual borrower of the full amount of the loan. The lender may therefore, on the day of reckoning, look for his payment not only to the assets held in common in the business enterprise but to all unencumbered assets owned by each of the partners.[2] Again, the liability of each of the partners is said to be "unlimited".

In the case of a loan by L to B who has an individual proprietorship interest in an enterprise, or a loan by L to a partnership enterprise, L has an obvious and vital interest in seeing to it that the assets of the individual or of the partners are not dissipated before he is paid off. L will therefore not only investigate the asset condition of the individual, and of the partners, before he makes the loan, but he may seek to obtain a security interest in B's assets and/or seek to limit in some way his bor-

---

2. Of course, the lender who gave credit for the uses of the partnership enterprise may well, on maturity date, find himself locked in a struggle with personal creditors of the partners, where the sum of the partnership assets and the partners' assets is insufficient to meet both kinds of claims. Out of this situation arises the equitable procedure of marshalling assets and the principle that partnership creditors have prior claim to partnership assets, and personal creditors of the partners have prior claim to personal assets—embryonic recognition of the enterprise as an independent entity. See Uniform Partnership Act § 40(h), codifying the rule of *Rodgers v. Meranda*, 7 Ohio St. 180 (1857); see generally, Crane & Bromberg, Law of Partnership §§ 91 and 91A (1968).

rower's power to put assets beyond L's reach. L can do little or nothing to insure that B's investment portfolio will retain its market value, or that his other holdings will retain their value; but he may have at least a chance, by contract, to prevent B from engaging in certain transactions that could have the effect of leaving the creditor high and dry at the critical moment. L would like, for example, to prevent B from transferring all of his assets to his wife or children; and L will be very unhappy if B is left free to borrow more money from another lender or, worse, to pledge or mortgage his assets to another lender as security for another loan. Finally, L might like to try to keep B from living too high on the hog pending payment of the debt; enough yachts, trips around the world, and visits to casinos, and B's assets will have likely shrunk to nothing by the time L pounds on the door to collect his debt.

To generalize, there is a particular pot of assets to which the creditor L knows that he must look for payment. From his perspective, it is critically important that the assets in that pool be substantial when the loan is made and that, so long as the loan is outstanding, B's uses of the assets be limited in a way that will prevent their being dissipated, leaving L holding an empty bag. A prudent creditor will seek to protect himself by close investigation before the loan is made and by extracting from B some restrictions on B's power of disposition of his assets during the period of the loan. L cannot, and will not try to, protect himself against all the risks to which he subjected himself by making the loan; he accepts as inevitable what may be called the business risks inherent in the situation—the risk that the barber shop will go broke as young men around the world suddenly decide to let their hair grow long, like their ancestors, or the risk that the bottom will fall out of the real estate and other markets as people conclude that it is more pleasant to live in the sea, like their ancestors.

3. The Creditor of the Corporation

Much is usually made of the proposition that the hallmark of the corporate form of business enterprise is "limited liability." The statement is not untrue, but it deserves somewhat closer attention than is usually given to it.

As a matter of history, it is at least worth noting that the feature of limited liability to which so much importance appears to be attached today, played little or no part in the development of modern corporation law. The law of corporations grew up not out of law of commerce but as an offshoot from the public law area of municipal government. The device of the corporate charter, and of the implied separate corporate entity, found its appeal as a device for (i) providing a continuity of enterprise and of property ownership that would legally survive the death of individual participants in the enterprise, (ii) providing a semi-political vehicle for the grant of monopolies, such as the tobacco trade in a particular area, or a toll bridge, and (iii) providing a functional administrative structure that could simultaneously mobilize capital investments from many individual investors while offering a machinery for centralized decision making. Even when the corporate form had advanced so far as to be embodied in general corporation laws in the middle of the 19th century, limited liability for shareholders was not uniformly provided for in the general corporation laws in this country, and in England the Companies Act did not provide for generalized limited liability for corporate shareholders until 1862.

History aside, it is important to understand that modern corporation law does not "provide for" limited liability; what it does is provide that in the case of creditor claims against an enterprise in corporate form, *the corporation is the debtor* rather than those who hold claim to the proprietorship capital in the enterprise. Once that step is taken, the creditor law of the corporation exactly parallels the law of individual indebtedness and of creditors of individuals. As in the case of any debtor, the creditors of the corporation have a claim to the assets of the corporation that is prior to the corporation's own claim as "owner". The creditors' claim to the corporate assets is also axiomatically prior to the claim of the proprietorship investors— the shareholders. And the creditors' claim extends to *all* the assets of the debtor corporation. If necessary, the entire assets of the corporation must be devoted to payment of creditors of the corporation, even though nothing is left for the corporation and its proprietorship owners. Furthermore, as in the case of almost all debtors the creditors of the corporation must, in usual course, find their payment from the pool of assets that belong to the debtor corporation. If the assets of the corporation are insufficient to pay the claims, in the absence of some special guaranty a creditor can no more expect to pursue assets beyond the debtor corporation's assets than a creditor of an individual can expect that payment of a debt owed by that individual can be extracted from some other individual.

Thus, the creditor of a corporation has the same kind of economic interest as the creditor of a human individual and is subject to the same kinds of risks as the creditor of the individual. Similarly, the corporate creditor tries to resort to many of the same devices to enhance the likelihood that his corporate debtor will have sufficient funds in hand to pay off the debt when maturity comes. As a part of the bargain negotiated when the corporation incurs the indebtedness, the creditor may, of course, succeed in extracting from a shareholder (or someone else who wants to see the loan go through) an outside pledge agreement, guaranty, endorsement, or the like that will have the effect of subjecting non-corporate assets to the creditor's claim against the corporation. Such protective arrangements are common when the corporation is closely held and not well funded. But in the general conduct of corporate enterprises, the creditor cannot exact such extra protection. In the usual case, therefore, it will be a matter of major concern to the creditor of the corporation to seek four objectives—precisely as in the case of the lender to an individual debtor.

(1) The creditor will be happier if his corporate debtor has substantial assets in the corporate till at the time he extends credit and thereafter;

(2) The creditor will want to prevent the corporation from incurring debts to other general creditors with whom he may have to share the corporation's limited assets;

(3) The creditor will want the corporate assets to remain free and unencumbered of any lien interests by a prior (secured) creditor; and

(4) The creditor will want to preserve a cushion of protective assets, and will want to see to it that no claimants who rank junior to him (usually shareholders, but sometimes subordinated debt holders) make off with assets of the corporation while the creditor's claim is still outstanding and unpaid.

Note again that even if the creditor should happen to be so fortunate as to achieve all four of these protections—which he seldom does—still he has, by making the loan, put his funds at risk of the basic *commercial* vicissitudes of the debtor enterprise. If the market for the enterprise's product disappears, or the market value of the assets it holds drops through the floor, the creditor is apt to be left to whistle for his claim. Absent some special arrangement for recourse to assets lying outside the corporate enterprise, as through a shareholder's personal guaranty, the creditor has no protection against such commercial risks except his own skill in predicting whether an enterprise will or will not make enough return to pay out the loan with interest. In the long pull, there is no security for enterprise creditors (or any other investors) other than the profitability of the enterprise. This uncontrollable inherent commercial risk of the enterprise stands in marked contrast to the creditor's other risks—the risk that the corporate debtor might incur additional debt, or might distribute assets to the junior proprietorship investors, the shareholders. Those managers who control the business affairs of the corporate enterprise cannot determine what will happen to the general market, but they can determine whether indebtedness or distributions occur. Since the occurrence or non-occurrence of these events *are* amenable to managerial decision, they can be proscribed or limited by contract or by general law. And they often are.

To summarize the perspective of the lender to the corporation —he is willing to make the loan on the terms negotiated and assume the commercial risks that are inherent in it. But if he could have things all his way: the pool of corporate assets would be large; there would be no other creditors; the only other claimants to the pool would be the shareholders, whose claim is junior to his; the corporation would be forbidden from incurring later indebtedness, and especially secured indebtedness; and no assets of any kind would be permitted to be distributed out of the corporate pool to shareholder investors until the creditor had been paid off in full.

The legal doctrines revolving around the concept of "legal capital" developed as a partial response to, and was mainly attributable to, this perspective of the creditors of corporations. Before the accommodation reached by the legal capital system can be appreciated, however, it is necessary to take a look at the shareholder's perspective of the matter.

B. THE SHAREHOLDER'S PERSPECTIVE

1. Payouts to Shareholders

The ideal world as conceived by the creditor of the corporation is a world that is normally wholly unacceptable to the shareholder. The investor who buys shares of stock in the incorporated enterprise and the investor who lends money to the incorporated enterprise, are, as a matter of economics, engaged in the same kind of activity and are motivated by the same basic objectives. They are both making a capital investment; they both expect or hope to get their money back in the long run, either by liquidating pay-out or by sale of the security; and they both expect and hope to receive income from their investment in the interim before their capital is returned to them in full. In the stereotypic model transaction, the investor who chose to take a shareholder's position rather than a creditor's position in a particular transaction, simply made a calculated economic judgment that he could make more money by relinquishing to creditor investors a "prior" claim for interest and a fixed principal payment on maturity, and, by opting for uncertain "dividends" and the residual claim to the assets of the enterprise that would remain after all creditors, with their fixed claims, had been paid off.[3] The shareholder's willingness to admit the "priority" of the creditor's interest claim and claim for principal payment on maturity, does *not* imply, however, that the shareholder is willing to stand by chronologically until such time as the creditors have been paid in full. The shareholder will insist, in general, that if, as he hopes, the enterprise makes money (and perhaps even if it does not), the shareholders will receive some return on (or of) their investment from time to time, regardless of the fact that there are creditor claims outstanding. Such periodic payments to shareholders are characterized as "dividends"; and, in the usual and normal case of the healthy incorporated enterprise, it is assumed that some assets will be regularly paid out from the corporate treasury to the shareholder investors in dividend form.

---

3. This stereotypic model, like the other illustrative models used here, is grossly oversimplified.

In the first place, it groups together as a unitary interest all those characterized as "shareholders". Even as creditors may be arrayed along a spectrum of claim from secured to subordinated, shareholders are often divided among themselves into subclassifications of hierarchical claim by the creation of different classes of stock, each class having a differentiated claim to dividends, liquidation payments, voting rights, etc. In usual parlance these classes are spoken of as either "preferred" or "common", but the usage is misleading, since the various classes (or series) may be almost infinitely varied in their terms and still remain "stock" so long as their claim to liquidation payment falls hierarchically below the lowest ranking creditor's claim in liquidation. As a result, clashes of interest *among* shareholder classes may in some circumstances be as intense as, or even more intense than, the more generalized clash of interest between shareholders as a whole and creditors as a whole.

Second, the investor's choice as between the debt or equity position will be influenced as well by his tax position, marginal preferences as to growth potential versus current income, concern with voting power, estimates about inflationary or deflationary trends, equity-debt leverage, and many other considerations. Moreover, in the hands of sophisticated financial lawyers, the equity-debt difference itself blends into a grey continuum in the cases of convertible debt, debt with warrants, income debentures, etc.

Finally there is no necessary correlation in any case between the lawyer's characterization of the security and the economic deal that underlies it; for example, the "common stock" of the Carolina & Clinchfield RR Co. each year pays a dividend of $5 per share and the corporate structure is designed so that exactly $5 per share will be paid, no more and no less.

Simple as this observation may be, its implications are far-reaching. If all creditors had to be paid off before *any* payment could be made to shareholder investors, and if shareholders received nothing until ultimate liquidation of the enterprise when they would divide the residuum left after payment of all creditors—if, in other words, the terms "prior" and "before" were chronological as well as hierarchical—the creditor would not have to worry about assets being drained away into the hands of junior claimants and he would sleep better at night. But once it is conceded that *during the life* of the creditor's claim, assets may be passed out to an investing group that hierarchically ranks below the creditors, the question becomes unavoidable: How much of the assets in the treasury of the incorporated enterprise may be distributed to shareholders, when, and under what circumstances?

While "dividends" are the most common form in which distributions are made to shareholders out of corporate assets, the distributive process is potentially Protean. If it is decided that an incorporated enterprise should be broken up, or that some of its assets or separable operations should be sold for cash, extraordinary cash distributions may be made to shareholders; these will be referred to as liquidating distributions, or distributions in partial liquidation. Similarly, the decision-makers in a going economic enterprise may conclude that the company has more cash or other liquid assets on hand than it needs, that no interesting investment opportunities are visible, and that the best thing to do is to distribute the excess assets to the shareholders; such a transaction may be referred to as a partial return of capital. Substantially the same transaction may occur where, for one reason or another, it seems desirable to those who are making the decisions to transfer a major nonliquid asset (such as a parcel of land) to the shareholders, either by transferring to each shareholder a proportionate undivided interest in the asset, or by putting the asset into a subsidiary and distributing the subsidiary's shares to the parent's shareholders. Or those in control of an incorporated enterprise may decide to "buy in" some of the outstanding stock of the corporation—a transaction that pays assets out of the corporate treasury to shareholders but brings in to the corporation nothing but pieces of paper in the hands of the corporation. If, for example, a corporation has three shareholders, each of whom owns twenty shares of stock, and the corporation "buys in" ten shares from each of them at $1,000 per share, the consequence will be that each shareholder will continue to own and control ⅓ of the enterprise, but there is $30,000 less in the corporate treasury to meet the claims of creditors. Whether the stock bought in is said in lawyer's talk to be cancelled, or retired, or held as treasury shares, the result is identical as seen from the creditor's standpoint: $30,000 has been funneled off to the junior claimants, the shareholders.

These instances do not exhaust the numbers of ways in which assets can be transferred out of a corporate treasury into the hands of shareholders. Distributions of corporate assets to a shareholder may be denominated as "salary payments" though in excess of a compensation level that would be reasonable for the services performed for the corporation by the shareholder. Corporate assets can be sold to shareholders for less than their market value. Corporate assets can be loaned to shareholders, or leased to shareholders, on terms that in effect reduce the aggregate resources of the corporate treasury. If the corporation guarantees the debt of a shareholder to a third party, the corporation's credit is put in jeopardy to the benefit of the shareholder. Corporate assets can be pledged or mortgaged to shareholders through arrangements under which, upon nonpayment of the loan by the corporation (at the decision of the board), the assets will be forfeited to the shareholders.[4] These same transactions, with the same consequences, can be carried out through dealings between the shareholders of the corporation and subsidiaries of the corporation. In all these instances, and others, the problem of the creditor of the corporation is the same. Assets have left the corporate pot, have gone beyond his reach, and, worst of all, have been paid out to that group of investors whose claim to the assets of the corporation is junior to his.

Finally, it must be observed, there are two other factors that contribute to the creditor's unease. It is not just that there are many ways by which corporate assets *can* be channeled out of the corporate pot and into the shareholders' pockets. More worrisome is the shareholders' keen desire and incentive to do just that. The shareholder knows that so long as his money is at stake in the enterprise he will be the last one paid—or will not be paid at all—if the weather gets stormy. His instinct is to limit that risk by arranging for some kind of payout of at least his initial investment as soon as possible.

A closely related consideration is the dynamic known as "leverage". The creditor wants a thick equity cushion under him;

---

4. In addition, of course, one who is a shareholder can legitimately lend money to the corporation and thus become both a creditor and an equity owner. In that case, however, a payment made by the corporation on the loan is not, as an analytic matter, a distribution to shareholders, but a payment to creditors.

the equity investors tend to prefer a thick debt slice in the company's capitalization, up to the capacity of the enterprise to meet the carrying charges of the debt. The shareholder sees an obvious advantage in a funding plan under which he puts in $1 and the lender puts in $2, the lender agreeing to a fixed return of 5¢ for each dollar loaned; if the enterprise earns 10¢ on each of the three dollars invested, the end result is that the creditor's $2 investment yields him 10¢ while the shareholder's $1 investment yields him 20¢. Shareholders greatly relish such leveraged arangements under which the entrepreneurial harvest, if any, will come to them while the risk of capital loss is largely that of lenders.[5]

The second thought that disturbs the sweet slumber of the creditor is the knowledge that virtually all responsibility and power for the conduct of the enterprise is in the hands of the board of directors who are elected by and mainly interested in the shareholders, and of corporate officers selected by the board. As the creditor sees it, hungry goats have been set to watch the cabbages.

Out of the conflict between the creditor's desire to keep corporate assets from being distributed to shareholders, and the shareholder's insistence upon receiving asset distributions despite the existence of outstanding creditors' claims, arises the major problem to which the par and stated capital provisions—the legal capital provisions—of state corporation codes are directed.

2. Equitable Contribution Among Shareholders—A Separate Problem

Taken as a class, the shareholders of a corporation have in common a conflicting interest with that of creditors of the corporation. But within the class of those denominated "shareholders" clashes of economic interest also exist.

---

5. Again the real world proves more complex than the stripped down model. The desires of particular classes of investors will not always conform to the generalizations. Some creditors may, for example, have a view toward leverage that parallels that of the shareholder. A general creditor, though normally fearful that the corporate debtor might create senior debt ranking ahead of him, may see an advantage in the corporation's incurring new senior debt if the new money can be brought in at low cost so that the profits generated by the new capital will be greater than the cost of the new capital, the excess redounding to the advantage and payment of the junior creditor's claim. Moreover, if the enterprise is in sufficiently dire straits, the junior creditor may be happy to see senior debt created, regardless of the terms, where the new money may keep the enterprise going and where the only prospect for the enterprise in the absence of new investment would be bankruptcy.

Even in the simplest case of a corporation having a single class of stock, contention can arise between shareholder S1 and shareholder S2 as to whether each one made a fair and proportionate contribution of assets into the corporate pot in exchange for the share interest he received. Other things being equal, S1 will be very unhappy if he put up $2/3$ of the total assets invested by shareholders into the corporate till and received only $1/3$ of the total stock issued, while S2, who invested only $1/3$ of the total equity input, received $2/3$ of the stock issued.

It is easy enough to recite in black letter hornbook style: "The general principle is clear; shareholders should contribute equitably in proportion to their shareholdings." But this abstract principle is of little utility in dealing with any real situation. What is an equitable amount? What are equitable amounts when S2 buys his shares from the corporation at a different time from S1? What is an equitable amount for S2 to pay if he buys from the corporation an issue of shares of a class, or series, different from that held by S1? These, and many other related questions, constitute the problem of equitable contribution. Some of them are referred to in a later chapter and a number of illustrations are given in Part Two. For the present, it is enough to note the existence of the topic and to observe that one strand in the development of the law of par and stated capital has been an effort by the courts (often only dimly perceived or even unconscious) to develop a working solution to the problem of equitable contribution among shareholders.

C. THE CREDITOR'S AND SHAREHOLDER'S PERSPECTIVES COMBINED

It will now be seen that a corporate financial "model" has begun to appear. That model will be substantially elaborated in later pages. It is well to pause here, however, to emphasize again the point made in passing in two earlier footnotes—that the analytic corporate financial model discussed here is just that. The model does not purport to be fully descriptive of reality—of the actual way in which corporate creditors and shareholders go about their business of making investment decisions, and protecting their positions. Reality is much more complex, featuring detailed factors that are often determinative.

Moreover,—and this point deserves special underscoring—the whole model we are using here presents a fundamentally skewed picture because of its emphasis upon the creditor's concern about the *ultimate* payment of his claim out of his debtor's assets in liquidation or bankruptcy. Creditors *are* concerned about that of course. And debtors *do* sometimes wind up in liquidation proceedings that set all the claimants against one another in a Donnybrook over who gets what from the insufficient carcass. But such events are not normalcy in the conduct of business. They bear the same relationship to daily business as a train wreck bears to a train trip. It *could* happen; one may do well to carry some travel insurance against it, perhaps even sit in the middle of the car; but if one knows, or seriously suspects, that a train may wreck, he does not usually take extra protective precautions—he stays off the train. In the usual case, creditors expect to be paid, and are actually paid, on an ongoing basis out of the profitability of the enterprise—out of *earnings*. The depression of the 1930's and the repeated wipe-out of gold-plated "fully secured" bond issues of blue chip railroads drove the point home at last; enterprise debt is not ultimately paid out of balance sheet assets but rather out of operating profits. Security liens, liquidation preferences and the like, are disaster remedies —like emergency exits. When an enterprise asks to borrow money, the prospective lender's primary interest will be in the profit prospects of the enterprise—the *dynamics* of the enterprise—quality of management, markets for the product, competition, assembly of production components, labor relations, adequacy of financing, technological leads—to name but some. The model outlined here of creditors' concerns is thus distorted in its pervasive implication that balance sheet assets are foremost in the creditor's mind, and in the essentially static character of the model.

In defense of the use of the model employed here, one can say two things:

    (i) To a degree the creditor *does* look at static assets and consider the possibility of an ultimate liquidation Armageddon; to that degree the model is substantially accurate.

    (ii) We have no choice but to develop and understand this model if we are to understand the corporate code provisions on stated capital, for whatever its deficiencies, it is the model on which the statutes are based.

Accepting the model as given, how should corporation law, statutory or judge made, regulate the activities of businessmen and lawyers so as to deal with the combination of the corporate creditor's perspective and the shareholder's perspective—namely:

    (1) The creditor of the corporation desires that the enterprise have large quantities of assets against which the

Ch. 1 CORPORATE CREDITOR AND SHAREHOLDER

only other claimants are those who rank junior to him, i. e. the shareholders. Shareholders, by contrast, would like to have as little as possible of their own assets tied up in the enterprise and exposed to the jeopardy of creditors' claims.

(2) The creditor does not ordinarily welcome the creation of additional creditors' claims against the limited assets of the enterprise. The shareholder investor will often (not always) be willing for the incorporated enterprise to incur further debt in order to benefit from leverage, especially when his own equity investment position is small.

(3) The creditor would prefer that the junior investment claimant, the shareholder, receive nothing as a return on his investment for so long a time as the creditor's claim has not been paid. The shareholder, on the other hand, insists upon a concurrent return paid out to him as the enterprise earns profits.

(4) The creditor wants protection against all manner of asset distributions to shareholders. The shareholder wants maximum freedom to receive such distributions.

(5) Each shareholder wants assurance that each other shareholder has contributed to the corporate pot a proprietorship investment proportionate to his shareholdings.

The provisions of state corporation codes dealing with legal capital are addressed to resolving, or at least accommodating, these conflicts.

Chapter II

LEGAL CAPITAL—DEVELOPMENT OF THE KEY CONCEPT

This chapter is devoted to tracing the development of the concept of legal capital—the key concept that our corporation codes have evolved to deal with the problems outlined in Chapter I. The ways in which the concept is used by the statutes, and the consequences of that use, are reserved for discussion in later chapters.

The legal capital scheme contained in our modern corporation codes is the direct product of nineteenth century legal history. Legal capital provisions are comprehensible (to the extent they are comprehensible at all) only in the context of that history.

At the same time, one must not demand too much clarity or coherence from the record of the past in this field. During the latter half of the nineteenth century, when industrial capitalism was maturing in the United States and finance capitalism was beginning to emerge, the profession of accounting was in its infancy. Accounting concepts that seem both elemental and indispensable today had not yet been perceived or crystallized; terminology had not yet been settled upon; and, outside a very small group of emerging professionals, double entry bookkeeping had not penetrated the consciousness of the public, the bench, or the bar. Nineteenth century judicial opinions dealing with par values, stock issues, capital, and stock subscriptions, are nearly always analytically incoherent. But to harp on that point is unseemly; it is to shoot fish in a barrel. The field of corporate finance was too embryonic to have assumed shape, and the courts and advocates were not yet equipped with the conceptual tools required to deal with it. In large degree, therefore, it is an error to attempt a precise reconstruction of the way in which the nineteenth century looked at such matters. The truth is that there simply was no coherent view of these matters in the nineteenth century. And while each generation must write its own history of the past, we should not try to attribute to nineteenth century courts an integrated set of analytic theorems that they would have been incapable of understanding, much less inventing.

Ch. 2 *LEGAL CAPITAL—DEVELOPMENT OF CONCEPT* 17

A. THE STANDARD OF EQUITY INVESTMENT—WHAT AMOUNT OF WHAT ASSETS MUST SHAREHOLDERS PUT INTO THE CORPORATE POT?

1. Minimum Pay-in Requirements

As noted in Chapter I, a corporate creditor will be happiest if the corporation to which he extends credit has a substantial quantity of assets that are free of the claims of other creditors —assets whose only claimants are of the lowest priority rank, the shareholders.

The question of what amount of assets must be paid-in to an enterprise by its shareholders before it will be permitted to enter the market place has never been candidly addressed in American corporation law. For a governmental agency to prescribe minimum capital standards for particular enterprises or economic sectors has been considered wholly impractical as well as antithetical to the way in which we go about our economic process. There are exceptions to this statement, and they are significant ones; banks, insurance companies, and corporate trustees offer instances of enterprises where, as we have learned painfully, undercapitalization can be a public menace and in those instances a combination of statutes and regulations compels a minimum pay-in of equity assets. But the only fields of endeavor in which our law seriously undertakes to set minimum standards of capitalization are those we view as industries affected with a special public interest, and which we regulate in a number of other ways as well. Until very recently state corporation acts genuflected to the desirability of requiring a minimum amount of assets to be paid into a new enterprise as a prerequisite to achieving corporate status, or at least before commencing business. But these provisions were always *pro forma* only, typically requiring a *de minimis* pay-in on the order of $1,000 or less, and with no provision precluding an immediate return of this amount to the shareholders. In the last few years, however, most state statutes have eliminated even these *pro forma* requirements for initial pay-in by shareholders.[1] In general, therefore, the creditor has received little or no direct protection through legislative or regulatory prescription requiring an incorporated enterprise to have a minimum amount of assets at its inception.[2]

---

1. See 2 Model Business Corporation Act Annotated, § 54, Annot. ¶ 3.03(7) (2d ed. 1971).

2. Here and there a legal commentator or a judge will be found to say that shareholders may not enjoy the corporate shield of limited liability where the corporation is "grossly undercapitalized." And intuitively one wonders particularly about the situation of the tort vic-

2. The Prototypical Model and Par

Nonetheless, the corporate creditor's desire to have a well funded debtor has played a part in the development of the legal capital scheme contained in our corporation codes. To see the connection, it is necessary to reformulate the statement of the creditor's interest. To do so, it is necessary to run the statement through two transformations and, as a prototypical model, to consider a very simple business situation.

Consider a newly formed corporate enterprise at the stage of its initial financing by the issue of shares; the only assets in the corporate treasury are those which the shareholders have just put in for their stock, and the enterprise has done no business. If, at that time, a prospective lender asks the question, "How much assets does the corporation have free and clear after claims of creditors" the answer will be the same as the answer to the question, "How much did the shareholders put in?" Similarly, if a loan is then made to the corporation, the question, "How much assets did the corporation have at the time of the loan" has the same answer as the question, "How much assets have the shareholders put in over *all* time?" On this simplistic model, the statutory stated capital scheme is based. The scheme assumes that the key to protection of the creditor lies in the answer to these two questions which, taken together, become, "How much assets have shareholders put into the corporate treasury since the formation of the corporation?" Whether or not that question is one that really interests a creditor, it is the elemental question to which the statutory legal capital scheme is addressed.

The nineteenth century pattern of corporate financing provided a ready suggestion to judges and statutory draftsmen for a way to gauge the quantity of assets that shareholders had, at some time or another, put into the corporate treasury. According to that pattern of corporate practice, an entrepreneurial organizer, the "promoter" who had conceived of an idea for a new business would make the rounds of people who had money to invest ("capitalists" all, whether little grey widows or sturdy yeomen), and seek to persuade them to invest in stock of the proposed enterprise. If the idea had appeal, and if the promoter

tim of outrageous corporate negligence: would it really be possible to build a downtown culture center for bacterial warfare experiments and to immunize the equity investors from liability through formation of a corporation with an initial capitalization of $1,000? But, the concept of "gross undercapitalization" is too ill-defined a concept to afford creditors any predictable protection from the default of corporate enterprises capitalized on a shoestring, and actual judicial holdings on the point are, at most, scant.

was persuasive, he would succeed in obtaining commitments from them to buy stock. Such commitments called subscription agreements, had a number of features about them that were jarring to nineteenth century concepts of contract law and their assimilation into contractual jurisprudence proved very awkward. But its essence was simple enough: the subscriber agreed that if enough other subscribers were found, and if a corporation was formed for the purposes of the enterprise envisioned by the promoter, he, the subscriber, would, on call of the future board of directors of the corporation when organized, put in a set amount of money, or other assets, and would receive a set number of shares of the newly formed corporation. Given this practice, it was to be expected, and was perhaps inevitable, that in drawing up the subscription agreements for any single enterprise, a fixed mathematical relationship would be set between the amount of dollars to be invested by a subscriber and the number of shares he would receive: so many dollars to be put in for each share to be issued. That relationship produced the concept of the "par value" of the stock to be issued. In the normal situation, no equity investor could expect to obtain a share of stock for less than the par value of it, since presumably all other purchasers were paying that amount. Similarly, no share subscriber could be persuaded to agree to pay more than the par value for a share since other investors were receiving a similar share by paying in the par value.

If the promoter was successful in obtaining subscription commitments in an amount that appeared sufficient to provide the basic equity financing for the enterprise, he would then see to it that papers were prepared for obtaining a corporate charter under the local state law, often naming the subscribers (or a few of them) as the "incorporators".[3] The incorporators-subscribers were then brought together for an initial meeting, directors of the corporation were elected, by-laws were adopted, the board of directors made a call upon subscribers to ante up all, or a part of, the amount to which they had committed themselves under the subscription agreements, a corresponding amount of assets were paid into the corporate treasury by the subscribers, and stock certificates for an appropriate number of shares were delivered to the subscribers—now become shareholders. The stock certificates were formal and elaborate, and, in analogy to paper currency or banknotes, bore upon their face as the most dominant feature, the share's "par value" stated as

3. Sometimes the charter would have already been obtained, with only the earliest subscribers, or associates of the promoter, named as "incorporators."

a fixed number of dollars, typically $100. This number represented the amount the shareholders had agreed to pay for each share according to the subscription agreements. In time, by statute, the par value of the stock was required to be stated as a provision in the corporate charter.

The essentially arbitrary character of this number must be understood. If, for example, each of three investors agreed to invest $10,000 in stock of a new company, the number of shares to be issued, N, and the par value, $P, could be anything—could be any numbers that the promoters might set so long as N x $P = $30,000. Further, so far as the shareholders in this case were concerned, it was immaterial what "par" was so long as each one received the same number of shares for his $10,000 investment.

Against this familiar background of practice, however, it was easy for the courts—and legislatures—to take a next assumption, and it early became a matter of common understanding, that the "par value" was what the shareholder *ought* to have paid for his stock. Stock which was issued without a corresponding pay-in of assets valued at an amount equal to par was called "watered stock"—stock issued not against assets but against water. (The term also echoed an ancient sharp practice in another field, the aquatizing of livestock before weighing them in for sale.) The term "bonus shares" was reserved to describe shares that were issued to someone who had paid in nothing for them. Bonus shares and watered stock obviously gave the recipient shareholder a free, or cut-rate, ride, to the disadvantage of the other shareholders who had put more assets per share into the corporate pot.

It must be emphasized that concepts of watered stock and bonus stock, and the doctrines that came to surround them, were and are limited in application to the *issue* of stock, that is, sales by the *corporation* of its own stock. The doctrines do not in any way inhibit the *shareholder's* freedom to sell his stock at any price he can get, or to give it away if he wishes. Similarly, a corporation holding shares of another corporation may, like any other shareholder, dispose of them at any price it wishes or can get.[4]

3. "Par," "Capital" and the Creditor

It will be clear to the reader that the development of the "par" concept just described arose as a response to the problems of

---

4. See infra, as to resale of treasury shares.

Ch. 2 LEGAL CAPITAL—DEVELOPMENT OF CONCEPT

assuring equitable contribution among shareholders. But development of the shareholders' par payment obligation served, in a somewhat fortuitous and naive way, to further the corporate creditor's interest in seeing shareholder assets committed to the enterprise. One can spin at least a hypothetical argument as to why this should be and how it came to be.

If a creditor extends credit immediately after the incorporation of the new enterprise and if he has been informed that the par value of the shares is \$P and the number of shares that have been issued is N, it is not unreasonable for him to assume that the shareholders have collectively contributed into the corporate treasury an amount of dollars equal to the par value of the shares issued multiplied by the number of shares that were issued, or \$PN. In a kind of rough and ready way, assuming that there have been no other transactions, the creditor might infer that the number \$PN is an approximation of the total assets of the corporation, and on that basis might conclude that he could safely lend a certain amount of funds to the enterprise.

Did any rational creditor ever in fact act that way or extend credit on such a naive basis? The answer has to be "no." But two things did occur.

First, the number \$PN came in time to be called in legal discourse the corporation's "capital."

Second, if the enterprise ultimately went broke, and the creditor did not get paid, and he found out at that later time that some shareholder had *not* in fact paid into the corporate treasury an amount of assets equal to the par value of the shares he had received, the creditor's lawyer would certainly *argue* in a suit against the shareholder that: (i) Everyone knows that shareholders should pay into the corporate treasury assets equal to the par value of the shares issued to them; (ii) the defendant shareholder did not pay in that amount; (iii) the corporation is insolvent, creditors are unpaid, and the shareholders are not liable for the corporation's debts; (iv) therefore the court should require the defendant shareholder to pay over to this energetic suing creditor, to the extent of his claim against the corporation, the amount by which the defendant shareholder failed to pay into the corporation assets equal to the aggregate par value of the stock he received; and (v) if (iv) does not appeal to the court as the appropriate remedy, then the defendant shareholder should be required to pay into *the corporate treasury* now for the benefit of all corporate creditors, the full amount by which he failed earlier to pay into the corporate treasury assets of a value equal to the aggregate par value of the shares he received.

As will appear later, a number of serious analytic problems flaw this argument, as they do other approaches that litigants and courts tried in efforts to assert shareholder liability to contribute capital to the incorporated enterprise. And all sorts of remedial and procedural questions arose, as is discussed in Chapter III. But in time, this much became clear:

(i) The courts came to recognize that shareholders have some obligation to invest in the corporate enterprise;

(ii) It came to be understood (perhaps "assumed" is a better word) that the measure of the shareholder's liability was the number of shares issued to him times the par value of the shares; and

(iii) It came to be recognized that at least some creditors could in at least some circumstances enforce this obligation of the shareholder in some way.

Statements may be occasionally found to the effect that the *reason* why shareholders were held to pay in the par value of their shares is that that was the price exacted by the law for the corporate advantage of limited liability. While some such idea may have occurred to some nineteenth century court or legislative draftsman, the history of the matter will not bear out this theory. Limited liability arose in American corporation law as an almost incidental by-product of corporateness, and did so independently of the development of the par and stated capital scheme in the statutes.

4. The Going Enterprise: A Change in the Model

On the whole, the concept of par as a standard for shareholder investment did not work badly in the prototypical model of the corporate enterprise since par was nearly always the subscription price and since everyone agreed that a subscriber-shareholder should as a matter of contract be held to do what he had agreed to do. The system may not have helped the creditor very much, but at least it had a plausibility to it and could be made to work. But as the enterprise moved from the stage of initial financing to that of an ongoing enterprise, the system lost both plausibility and workability.

If an incorporated enterprise had navigated in the stream of commerce for ten years after its initial incorporation, and had undergone ten years of economic vicissitude, why would a prospective creditor in the company's 11th year consider it relevant to his credit decision to enquire whether subscriber-shareholders had, ten years before, paid fully for their stock? Perhaps the shareholders had invested heavily but the company had lost all its assets; perhaps they had paid nothing but the company had prospered. The passage of time destroyed the prototypical proposition that the assets in the corporation were the assets that had been put there by the subscriber-shareholders. Plausibility for that proposition had departed.

The problem of workability arose a little differently. Suppose that the original promotor, ten long years before, had set the par of the shares at $100 and the original subscriber-shareholders had paid in that amount per share. It is now the eleventh year, and the board of directors decides that it would be desirable—perhaps necessary—for the company to sell additional shares of stock in order to increase working capital and make it possible for the company to obtain additional lines of credit. Assume finally that the current market value of the stock is $52. What is to be done? The statute says that a purchaser of a newly issued share of stock with a par value of $100 must pay at least $100 for it; under that principle, any person who buys a share of the new stock from the issuing corporation for its fair market value of $52 may someday be held liable for an extra $48, an untempting prospect for a new investor. Something must give way in the face of economic reality. Of course, it turns out to be the principle of par payment.

In *Handley v. Stutz*[5] a company that was on the verge of bankruptcy managed to bail itself out for a while by attracting new money through the sale of bonds; to make the bonds saleable, the company gave a certain number of free shares of newly issued stock to each purchaser. Action was brought by a judgment creditor of the corporation to hold the new shareholders liable for payment of the par value of the shares they had received. With no support of any kind in the statute, the Supreme Court came out with the common sense answer fitted to the circumstances before it. It held that if a company is in a state of economic emergency it may, without generating risk of liability to new stock purchasers, issue stock at the best price it can get, whether or not below par. A legal prophet at the time would have predicted that because courts are by and large sensible, they would gradually expand the *Handley* concept of "economic emergency" to cover any situation where the going market value of the stock was below the par value. But in fact that proposition never fully developed, for other ways were found to deal with the problem.

5. 139 U.S. 417, 11 S.Ct. 530 (1891).

It will be recalled that though the par value of a share of stock appears upon the stock certificate its roots lie in the corporate charter. In the example given above, would it not be possible through the normal avenues of shareholder meeting and vote to amend the charter so as to reduce the $100 par of the company's stock to a figure below $52 and thereby make it feasible to issue shares on the current market and to do so compatibly with the requirement that the sale price must at least be equal to par? The answer was "Yes," and thus was opened another way by which the problem was—and is—handled under the corporation acts.

By this point, however, it is clear that concern about the economic worries of the creditor has moved to the edges of the universe and is receding at an ever-increasing speed. With par alterable by charter amendment, the switches, levers, and throttles are all in the hands of the very group whose interests conflict squarely with those of the creditors—the shareholders and corporate management.

5. Low Par Stock

In the nineteenth century pattern of corporate financing, it was simply assumed that good companies—respectable companies—solid investments—would have stock with a high par value. It is a tribute, indeed, to the power of mythology and folklore, that the buying market, the investment bankers who feed it, corporate managements, and their legal counsel all continue today to feel considerably more comfortable with a $50 par stock and cannot say "penny stock" without a sneer. And it remains true today that most "preferred" stocks continue to carry a high par value.[6] Nonetheless, eventually the practical argument prevailed and the invariable practice of using high par value common stock gradually gave way to the use of low par common stock as it came to be perceived that if the stock has a low par from the beginning, it might never be necessary to amend it or rely upon the vague license of *Handley v. Stutz*.

With this shift made, a typical transaction might see a promoter (i. e., his lawyer) set a par of $10 per share and a *higher* subscription agreement, say, $50 per share. What difference does it make to any shareholder that the par is lower than the

---

6. As Britain moved to the decimal currency system, a major question was whether to retain the pound as the basic unit or to adopt as the basic unit the shilling, a currency unit of a conveniently commensurate order of magnitude with the Swiss franc, the French franc, the German mark, the Dutch guilder, the Danish crown, etc. The decision, of course, was made in favor of the pound. Despite the awkwardness of its size, it had a more prestigious "par".

Ch. 2   LEGAL CAPITAL—DEVELOPMENT OF CONCEPT   25

purchase price, so long as each initial equity investor pays in the same amount per share? With this development, however, the prototype corporate model outlined earlier is reduced to splinters. If the subscription agreement calls for $50 per share for the $10 par stock, but the subscriber-shareholder pays in only $5 per share, should a subsequent unpaid corporate creditor be able at a later time to force an additional payment of $5 —to bring the shareholder's contribution up to the par value of $10—or should he be able to enforce a liability of $45—the balance the shareholder had agreed to pay under the subscription agreement? At this point it becomes conceptually critical whether the creditor is suing on a theory of statutory obligation of the shareholder to pay par, or on a contractual theory of enforcement of the shareholder's obligation to pay the corporation in accordance with the terms of the subscription. More important for present analytic purposes, the separation of par and purchase price has the effect of opening a chasm between the lawyer's perspective and the economist's concept of the entrepreneur's capital investment. If there are ten subscribers in a newly incorporated enterprise each of whom buys 10 shares of stock at a price of $50 per share, the economist, or the businessman, would say that the company's beginning "capital" is $5,000. But the lawyer (and later the accountant) will tell the economist or the businessman that the "capital" is determined by par, and in this case is the number of issued shares, 100, multiplied by the par value of each share, $10, for a total of $1,000; the other $4,000 is something else, about which we will hear more later. With the evolution of low par stock, came the evolution of that strange lawyer's convention, "legal capital"—the $1,000 in the example just given.

6. No Par Stock

If a corporation may have stock with a par value of 1¢, why not abandon the par concept entirely and permit the issuance of stock with no dollar amount printed on the share certificate? Why not have no par stock?

It was not until 1912 that analysis of the matter had reached a sufficiently wide circle to produce statutory authorization of no par stock. The advent of no par stock did not, however, have the effect of eliminating the concept of legal capital. It was, and still is, statutorily necessary to designate some dollar number on the corporate balance sheet as "capital". Since, with no-par stock, it is no longer possible to calculate what the "capital" is by multiplying the number of shares issued times the par value, a "capital" number can be arrived at for this purpose only by fiat—by declaration—by stating it. The responsibility for making that statement, and the power to make it, is placed by corporation statutes with the board of directors, and the dollar number declared by them made in the customary form of a board resolution, is the "stated capital" of the corporation. It remains so until such time as it is changed to something else by means set forth in the corporation act. The accountants accept this designation of "stated capital" and it appears on the lower right hand side of the corporate balance sheet as the corporate "capital".

Although no-par stock is common in the world of contemporary corporate finance, it is interesting that it has not preempted the field, and par stock continues to be in majority use. This is true for several reasons. For a long time, the computational method of the federal stamp tax on stock issuance favored par as against no par stock and some state franchise tax provisions still do. Additionally, for a careful lawyer concerned about such things, it is appealing that a low par value on a share of stock sets the outer limit of liability of a subscriber-shareholder as against a creditor's claim, whereas in the case of no par stock the subscriber's liability would appear inevitably—for want of any other criterion—to be measured by the full amount that he agreed to pay for each share of the stock.[7] More important than either of these factors, however, are the two points referred to in the discussion of par stock. To the market's ear, no par stock does not quite have the same ring of virtue as par stock (though it sounds better than "penny stock"). At the same time, the use of lower par values, and the ease of shareholder amendment to reduce par in situations where the par proved not to have been low enough, combined to make par stock a usable tool in the hands of the experienced corporate practitioner.

7. Legal Capital

The discussion so far dealing with pay-in requirements for shareholders has yielded the rudiments of the concept of "legal capital" or "stated capital", as it is more often called today. For further refinement of the concept, we turn to the other side of the coin, corporate pay-outs to shareholders.

---

7. Interestingly, the 1967 Delaware corporation law obliterated this longstanding distinction between par and no par stock, so that the subscriber to par stock is now also liable for the subscription price rather than the par. See Del.Gen. Corp.Law § 162(a).

B. DISTRIBUTING CORPORATE ASSETS TO THE SHAREHOLDERS

1. Wood v. Dummer—The Classic Case

What does the law do to prevent shareholders of a distressed company from pulling assets out of the corporate treasury just when the creditor needs them? The problem is not hypothetical. Indeed, from an historical point of view, the entire range of subjects to which this book is addressed may be seen to emerge from a single 1824 opinion of Justice Story, *Wood v. Dummer*.[8] The case could not be more elegant in its purity. The corporation was a bank that went broke. Just before the bank went under, the board of directors distributed most of its bank's liquid assets to the shareholders. Certain of the creditors of the bank sued some of the shareholders, claiming that in the circumstances the distribution of assets was illegal and that the shareholders should be made to pay the claims of the creditors. In an opinion that is simple, clear and wholly adequate for the particular problem with which he was confronted, Justice Story ordered the defendant shareholders to pay to the plaintiff creditors a proportionate share of the debt owed by the bank to the plaintiffs.[9]

---

8. 30 Fed.Cas. 435 (no. 17,944) (C.C.D.Me.1824).

9. Other aspects of this early bank case are interesting, foreshadowing the bank regulations of a later era. Not only did the directors pay out most of the current assets to the shareholders, thus precipitating insolvency, but it also appeared that at least some of the share subscription money had never been paid in by the shareholders and that the bank had used much of the money it had borrowed through its bank notes (from plaintiffs and others) to lend to the bank's own directors—who were at the time of the lawsuit also bankrupt.

As a pardonable digression, the reader may also wish to share the author's delight in the following passages from the learned justice's opinion in the *Wood* case, on which he sat while riding circuit in Maine; from these paragraphs, much can be gleaned about jurisprudence in action, about lawyering and about Justice Story, as an intellect and as a person.

"Bill in equity brought by the plaintiffs . . ., as holders of the bank notes of the . . . Bank, against the defendants, as stockholders . . . for payment of the same notes upon the asserted fraudulent division of the capital stock by the shareholders.

. . .

"The case is full of difficulties. The bill is drawn in a very loose and inartificial manner. It proceeds principally upon the grounds of a gross over issue of bank notes, and other violations of the charter, and of a fraudulent dividend by the stockholders with a knowledge of their insolvency; grounds, which are denied by the answers, and are not in the slightest degree established in the proofs. It does not directly proceed upon the ground, that the defendants hold a trust fund applicable to the payment of the debts of the corporation; but leaves this to be picked up in frag-

The eminent scholar-jurist's innovative legal theory underlying his decision—the so-called "trust fund" theory—and its subsequent fate are discussed in later pages. But a point of terminology in the court's opinion in *Wood v. Dummer* invites special attention. Throughout the opinion, the Justice talks of "the capital stock" of the corporation. It is evident that in his usage "capital stock" means the *assets* that had been put

ments by a minute analysis of the bill.

. . .

"The next consideration is, whether the bill makes out a case, which upon the facts proved or admitted, entitles the plaintiffs to relief. I have already adverted to the loose structure of the bill. It primarily charges the case, as a case of fraud; that is now abandoned. If it can stand at all, it must be simply on the fact, that the defendants have the funds in their possession. That alone could not entitle the parties to relief, without allegations of insolvency on the part of the corporation or of the non-existence of other funds. Now the bill does not allege, that the corporation is insolvent, nor that it is dissolved, nor that there is no other corporate property, out of which the debts can be paid. These are extraordinary omissions; and if there had been a demurrer to the bill, it would be difficult for the court to have strained hard enough to support it. But these defects are in some degree helped by the answers, which admit the insolvency of the corporation, and show, that in fact no sufficient funds for payment of its debts are in existence, independent of the capital stock. Then again the bill (notwithstanding the intimations thrown out by the court on a former hearing of the cause) does not charge, that the capital stock is a trust fund, appropriated by law and the charter to the payment of the debts, and that the surplus only, after such payment, belongs to the stockholders. Such an allegation was most fit to have been made upon the grounds, on which ultimately the plaintiffs concluded to rest their case at the hearing. The court is therefore compelled to thread it out by inference and intendment and exposition of the charter, as made part of the pleadings. Then again the bill charges the new Hallowell and Augusta Bank to be possessed of large funds of the old bank, which ought to be applied to the payment of the debts of the latter; and without attempting to bring the new bank to a hearing, the bill has, by the plaintiffs, been dismissed as against the new bank, leaving all the inferences, deducible from the charge in the bill, in full force against the plaintiffs. This ought to have been cured by an amendment of the bill.

"I advert to these defects, not in the spirit of censure, (for I am well aware, that an apology is found in the fact, that chancery proceedings have, hitherto, but in a slight degree engaged the attention of the bar in this district), but in a spirit of regret, because they have been most embarrassing to the court in every step of its progress, and distressed it by creating a perpetual struggle between the desire to do justice to the parties after so prolonged and expensive a controversy, and the difficulty of overcoming technical principles.

"The exception as to parties ranges itself under this head. There is no allegation in the bill, that the old corporation is defunct, so as to dispense with its being made a party. The answers do not deny, that it yet has a legal existence, and therefore afford no help to cure the defect. Now, if in existence, nothing can be more clear, than that it ought to have been made a party to the bill. It is the original debtor; its funds are to be applied in payment of debts, and it would be wrong to touch those funds without the most plenary proofs, that the debts were due, and the corporation had no defence." *Id.* at 435–6, passim.

One wonders how the lawyers for both parties explained these comments of the judge to their respective clients.

into the company by the stockholders, the "capital stock" that he held should not be withdrawn and returned to the proprietary investors until all creditors of the bank were paid.[10] Moreover, while the word "stock" in this phrase rings oddly to the modern ear, Story's use is the original etymological meaning of stock— the root of something growing, or a basic central supply. This meaning of "stock" continues today in many terms, such as "soup stock", "stockroom", "stock in trade", "gunstock" and "root and stock". But our concept of corporate stock has moved so far away from its original meaning that we are startled to hear Justice Story use "stock" as a synonym for the assets put in by the shareholders, and to hear him describe the events in *Wood v. Dummer* as an illegal return of the "stock" to the shareholders.[11] As perceived then by our most learned of judges in 1824, the terms "capital" and "stock" pointed to the upper left hand side of the balance sheet, close to the modern businessman's concept of current assets. But, as will appear in more detail subsequently, in the eyes of the law, both "capital" and "stock" were soon to slide over to the lower right hand side of the balance sheet.

Whatever the ultimate validity of Justice Story's theory in *Wood v. Dummer*, his decision on the facts in the case was unimpeachable. But it was certain to lead to a series of next questions that were much less susceptible to simple, or even sensible, answers. In *Wood v. Dummer*, the corporation was insolvent. It was easy to say that in such a case no assets should have been returned to the shareholders. But the *Wood* opinion gave only a general suggestion as to what limits there might be on distributions to shareholders if the bank had been a healthy ongoing enterprise.

2. The Key Proposition—"Legal Capital" as a Measuring Rod

As pointed out in Chapter I, there would be little or no problem about distributions to shareholders if corporate enterprises were periodically liquidated, creditors paid off, and only then the residuum or "velvet" returned to the equity investors. The problem of limiting distributions arises fundamentally out of the

---

10. E. g., "is the principal point argued in the cause, whether the capital stock in the hands of the stockholders is liable to the payment of the debts of the bank." Id. at p. 436.
11. Notice the similar usage in the 1784 newspaper announcement that led to the establishment of The Bank of New York:
    "It appearing to be the disposition of the Gentlemen in this City, to establish a BANK on liberal principles, *the stock to consist of specie only*; they are therefore hereby invited to meet Tomorrow Evening at six o'clock, at the Merchant's Coffee-House, where a plan will be submitted to their consideration."

    fm: New York Packet
    February 23, 1784
    (Emphasis added)

economic pressure to make some regular and ongoing distributions to shareholders while at the same time leaving creditor claims outstanding and unpaid. The condition is one that arises from the reality of the ongoing enterprise operating over time. The transaction in *Wood v. Dummer*, seen as a model, was a pathological case of an incorporated insolvent enterprise at the moment of dismemberment by its creditors. Similarly, the prototypical model transaction on which the nineteenth century conception of par value was predicated was also a static instant-of-time concept—the instant when the equity money was first put in and the stock certificates first issued. Nonetheless, probably inevitably, the courts and legislatures drew upon these static models as they sought to develop a standard by which to judge the legal propriety or impropriety of distributions of assets to shareholders by an ongoing enterprise.

Inevitably or not, the courts and the statutes did in fact combine the principle of *Wood v. Dummer* and the par value concept to produce an answer to their problems. Two basic propositions slowly emerged: (1) The measuring rod for judging the propriety or impropriety of distributions to equity holders is the corporation's "capital"; and (2) "capital" refers not to assets but to that abstract number that is obtained by multiplying the number of shares of stock oustanding by the par value assigned to each share. Following the emergence of low par and no par stock, the next step was, of course, to expand the second of these propositions to read that "capital" means "stated capital", or "legal capital".

3. The Classic Example: High Par

The most instructive way to see these propositions at work is to consider a simplified balance sheet of a hypothetical corporation with high par stock at three stages in its corporate life—immediately following its organization and funding; at the end of its first year of operations; and at the end of a second year of operations.

The general concept of the legal capital scheme is that no distribution may be made to shareholders unless there is a "surplus" —that is, sufficient assets in the corporation to pay off the creditors *plus* an additional amount of assets greater than the "stated capital". If the accounting entries representing the enterprise's assets do not total to a figure equal to the indebtedness of the enterprise plus the "capital", the capital is said to be "impaired" and the stock is said to be "under water". In such a condition (if one assumes that the figures on the assets side of the corporation's balance sheet are equal to their sell-off value), if all the

Ch. 2   LEGAL CAPITAL—DEVELOPMENT OF CONCEPT

assets were to be sold off for cash, and if all the creditors were to be paid off, the money that would be left for the equity investors, the shareholders, would be less than the "capital" they put into the enterprise in the first place. Where that is the condition, the statutory scheme forbids the distribution of assets to shareholders by dividend or otherwise.[12]

Assume that the shareholders of a new enterprise, Laminated Thumbscrew, Inc., pay in $50,000 in cash and take back 500 shares of $100 par common stock. The company's assets are $50,000 in cash; the corresponding entry on the right hand side of its balance sheet is the company's "legal capital", or "stated capital", the number of outstanding shares times the par value, $50,000. The balance sheet would read:

Balance Sheet of Laminated Thumbscrew, Inc.,
Immediately Following Organization and Funding

ASSETS		LIABILITIES	
Cash	$50,000		–0–
		SHAREHOLDERS' EQUITY	
		Capital: $100 par common, 500 sh.	$50,000
		Surplus	–0–
	$50,000		$50,000

In the circumstances of this balance sheet, there is no "surplus" and a distribution of assets to shareholders would be illegal.[13]

Now consider the same company's balance sheet at the end of a year of active business operations and a variety of transactions.

Balance Sheet of Laminated Thumbscrew, Inc.
Year End After One Year of Operations

ASSETS		LIABILITIES	
Cash	$20,000	Bank loan	$10,000
Accounts receivable	6,000	Accounts payable	2,000
		Liabilities	$12,000
Inventory	10,000	**SHAREHOLDERS' EQUITY**	
Land	5,000	Capital: $100 par common, 500 sh.	50,000
Patents	1,001	Surplus (Deficit)	(19,999)
		Shareholders' equity	$30,001
	$42,001		$42,001

12. This oversimplified introductory description assumes a so-called "balance sheet surplus test" statute. Other statutory variations are reviewed in Chapter IV and at length in the series of transactions in Part Two.

13. Deferred to Chapter III are all questions of who might be liable to whom for how much where an "illegal" distribution is made to shareholders.

This balance sheet shows that during its first year the corporation has incurred debt, that the accounting figures reflecting its assets have gone down and the enterprise suffered a loss during the year. The balance sheet in this condition shows—to use a common anomalous term—a "negative surplus". It will be observed that the corporation has far more than enough assets to pay off the $12,000 owed to its creditors and, indeed, the enterprise is in a position to pay them all off at once in cash. Nonetheless, distribution of any corporate assets to shareholders would be illegal where the legal capital figure of $50,000 is set as the bench mark of legality of the distribution.[14]

Suppose now the following balance sheet at the end of the company's second year of operations.

Balance Sheet of Laminated Thumbscrew, Inc., Year End After Two Years of Operations

ASSETS		LIABILITIES	
Cash	$16,000	Accounts payable	$ 3,000
Accounts receivable	8,000	Liabilities	$ 3,000
Securities	54,000	**SHAREHOLDERS' EQUITY**	
Inventory	15,000	Capital: $100 par common, 500 sh.	50,000
Land	5,000		
Patents	1,001	Surplus	46,001
		Shareholders' equity	$96,001
	$99,001		$99,001

As a result of the second year's operations, according to this accounting record, the company has acquired additional assets (most likely as a result of profitable operations during the year), has paid off the bank debt, overcoming the deficit it had at the end of the preceding year, and has generated a balance sheet sur-

---

14. While we speak of the inhibition as lying within the balance sheet, even the reader least familiar with accounting will be aware that the directors are not free to solve the problem by simply adding zeroes to the numbers representing assets, or removing zeroes from the figures representing debt. Accounting entries are made in accordance with so-called "generally accepted accounting principles" considered respectable and proper by the accounting profession and, in some respects, public agencies. These "principles" are often vague or conflicting or ambiguous, and the institutional sources of their legitimation are not yet fully identified. But the "principles" are sufficiently crystallized, sufficiently accepted as norms of behavior, and sufficiently recognized as a basis for fraud liability, that the accountant is not free to accept just any numbers the directors may wish. Application of the legal capital scheme inevitably entails a host of accounting problems, some of which are discussed later and especially in Part Two.

plus of $46,001 above its "capital" and debt. Under the general statutory scheme of the corporation codes, the company may now legally distribute to shareholders assets having a value of $46,001 or less (as valued how, and by whom?). Thus if the company should distribute all its cash ($16,000) to its shareholders, there would still be a surplus of $30,001, and the distribution would be in conformity with the statutory scheme. If the company sought to distribute to shareholders all its securities, however, the accounting effect would be to remove a $54,000 asset, wiping out the surplus, and generating a capital deficit of $7,999; distribution of all the securities would thus "impair" the capital, drive the stock under water again, and violate the statutory scheme.

4. Legal Capital as a Bench Mark—Some General Observations

Even at this preliminary stage of introduction to the legal capital scheme, several of its basic features have become visible and are worth underscoring.

1. As an analytical matter, the scheme is utterly dependent upon the way in which the assets of the enterprise carried on the books of the company are valued. Accounting decisions on write ups and write downs, on depreciation, on amortization, on cost or market valuation, and the like, will determine the total figure assigned to the asset side of the balance sheet, and in consequence the size of the balancing entry on the right hand side, and, in consequence the legality of the shareholder distribution. Inherently, the efficiency of the system can rise no higher than the level of consistency, objectivity, unanimity, enforceability, and (in some sense) verity that can be achieved within the accounting profession on questions of asset value accounting in particular, and "generally accepted accounting principles" in general.

2. One result of the perspective adopted by the legal capital scheme is that lawyers and judges often speak of making a distribution "out of surplus", or of "paying out the surplus" to shareholders. There is no special harm in this manner of speaking so long as the speaker and all their listeners are fully conscious that the statement is hash. "Surplus" and "deficit" are concepts invented by lawyers and accountants. They refer to an arithmetic balancing entry on a balance sheet, to the number that is the resultant of all the other numbers on the balance sheet and that is dictated by the basic mandate of the double entry bookkeeping convention—that the left side and the right side must at all times balance. Distributions are never paid "out of surplus", they are paid out of assets; surplus cannot be distribut-

ed—assets are distributed. No one ever received a package of surplus for Christmas. A distribution of assets will produce accounting entries that reduce assets and also reduce something on the right hand side of the balance sheet—often surplus—but that is quite another statement.

The enterprise that wishes to make a distribution to its shareholders must use assets to do it. It will usually find that only a small fraction of its total assets are in a form suitable for the purpose. Dividends are typically paid in cash. Occasionally, distributions are made in kind, as by parceling out security holdings or, to recall a famous World War II instance, through the distribution of warehouse receipts for whiskey.[15] In special circumstances, a distribution may sometimes be made by distributing fractional undivided interests in a major asset, such as an oil well working agreement. But, to take the example of Laminated Thumbscrew, the directors would find it difficult as a practical matter to distribute the patents, the land, the inventory or the accounts receivable; only in unusual circumstances would it wish to distribute the securities; and it cannot distribute all the company's cash since it needs cash for running its operations. The practical choices that will face the Laminated board of directors are, therefore, to make no distribution, or to make a small cash distribution, or to sell off some of the securities to generate cash for distribution, or to borrow cash for the purpose of distributing it to shareholders, the last being a transaction that usually has little appeal for either lender or borrower. Except for an enterprise that is unusually cash heavy, or an enterprise that is in liquidation, the form and character of the assets (plus, of course, the need of the enterprise for working cash) will usually be much more of an inhibition on shareholder distributions (assuming that the management *wants* to make such distributions)[16] than the arithmetic statement on the right hand side of the balance sheet called "surplus".

3. It is obvious that "legal capital", or "capital" as used by the law, has little or no relationship to the word "capital" as the economist, or even the businessman, knows it. Nor is it the block of assets that Justice Story had in mind.

---

15. See *In the Matter of Ira Haupt & Company*, 23 S.E.C. 589 (1946).

16. Retained earnings are today the largest source of new capital investment for American business enterprise. Dividend payments tend to be held to about ⅓ of net profits after taxes, the other ⅔ being committed by management to growth and research. Institutional Investor, Study Report of the Securities and Exchange Commission, Vol. 1, Ch. III at pp. 72, 80 (Table III–5) (1971); Standard & Poor's Trade and Securities Statistics, Security Price Index Record at p. 132 (1976).

Ch. 2   LEGAL CAPITAL—DEVELOPMENT OF CONCEPT   35

The following statements may now be made about "legal capital".

    a. Legal capital is a number expressed in dollars.

    b. That number is initially the product of par value—itself an arbitrary dollar amount printed on the stock certificate and recited in the certificate of incorporation—multiplied by the number of shares "outstanding".[17]

    c. Legal capital is a number that appears on the *right-hand*, or claimant's side of the balance sheet, *not* on the left hand asset side. "Legal capital" is *not* an asset, a fund, or a collection of assets. And it does not refer to an asset, a fund, or a collection of assets. (The same is true of "surplus.")

    d. Legal capital is a number that can at best be read to convey a message by implication—a message about an historical event. It can be read to imply that a valuation of at least that amount was placed upon some indeterminate assets that were transferred to the corporation at some indeterminate past time in exchange for shares then issued.

Legal capital is entirely a legal invention, highly particularized in its meaning, historical in reference, *and not relatable in any way to the ongoing economic condition of the enterprise.* For most purposes, it is best thought of simply as a dollar number—a number having certain consequences and derived by specified statutory procedures, but just a number.

4. The law makes use of the concept of "legal capital" in two ways:

    a. It is the maximum number of dollars up to which someone might in certain circumstances be able sometime to hold some shareholders liable if the implied statement in 3d above could be proved to be false.

    b. It is a datum line, or water table, or bench mark, or nock on a measuring stick laid alongside the total number on the asset side of the balance sheet, on the basis of which lawyers will—or will not—sign an opinion that a proposed distribution of corporate assets to shareholders is valid, legal, and generates no liabilities either

---

17. Legal capital where no par stock is involved is discussed later, as are situations in which the stated capital may be higher than the product of par times shares outstanding.

for the board of directors that declares it or the shareholders who receive it.

And here is the real bite. In the world of corporate finance, transactions are utterly dependent upon opinions of legal counsel. If the financial lawyers are unwilling to opine favorably upon the legality of a corporate transaction, or a subcomponent of it, the transaction will usually not go through. Whenever a corporate financial transaction requires the lawyers to inquire into a company's legal capital position, the impact of the statutory schemes of legal capital is enormously magnified by the Go/No-go function performed by opinions of counsel. The lawyers, in turn, are compelled to develop an understanding of the statutory scheme and of its application. From that state of affairs "legal capital" draws its vitality, and this small book draws its functional relevance.

5. The Classic Example Modified: Low Par

As described earlier, in the typical corporation financing of the nineteenth century, the stock had a high par value, such as $100, and the subscribers did not agree to pay in more per share than the par value printed on the certificate. As promoters and investors became more sophisticated, however, low par stock came into use with the end in view of lowering the liability exposure of shareholder investors and of simplifying later issuance. If Laminated Thumbscrew was to receive $50,000, and was to issue 500 shares, as in the earlier examples, but the stock was to have a par value of $10 rather than $100, how then would its legal capital structure operate and with what consequences?

*Balance Sheet of Laminated Thumbscrew, Inc.
Immediately Following Organization and Funding*

ASSETS		LIABILITIES	
Cash	$50,000		$ –0–
		SHAREHOLDERS' EQUITY	
		Capital: $10 par common, 500 sh.	5,000
		Paid-in surplus	45,000
	$50,000		$50,000

Since on this balance sheet the "capital" is only $5,000, there is, in some sense of the term, a "surplus" of $45,000. If the only limitation on distributions to shareholders is the aggregate of debt plus legal capital, it is apparent that this company could lawfully distribute to its shareholders up to $45,000 of the cash that has just been put into the enterprise treasury. If, for some

Ch. 2   LEGAL CAPITAL—DEVELOPMENT OF CONCEPT

reason it is thought desirable that the statutory scheme prohibit such a distribution, the statute can do so only by going beyond the concept of capital as a restriction and by differentiating between one group of surpluses that may be properly charged when shareholder distributions are made and another group of surpluses that may not. The more modern accountant would characterize the particular surplus here as "paid-in surplus" or "contributions in excess of capital" or "amount paid in in excess of par"; older terminology, and most statutory provisions on legal capital, would call it "capital surplus". The status of such paid-in surplus, or capital surplus, under various alternative statutory schemes is discussed later.

The possible significance and impact of the use of low par stock and the creation of paid-in surplus may be seen by returning again to the Laminated Thumbscrew balance sheet at the end of its first year of operations, but with $10 par rather than the $100 par stock assumed earlier. Making that one change, the balance sheet at the end of the first year would look like this:

Balance Sheet of Laminated Thumbscrew, Inc.
Year End After One Year of Operations

ASSETS		LIABILITIES	
Cash	$20,000	Bank loan	$10,000
Accounts receivable	6,000	Accounts payable	2,000
		Liabilities	$12,000
Inventory	10,000	**SHAREHOLDERS' EQUITY**	
Land	5,000	Capital: $10 par common, 500 sh.	5,000
Patents	1,001	Paid-in surplus	25,001
		Shareholders' equity	$30,001
	$42,001		$42,001

The difference in the par, the capital accounting and the statement of the legal capital has changed a $19,999 negative surplus to a $25,001 surplus. If a paid-in surplus account is legally chargeable for equity distributions under the law of the state of the company's incorporation,[18] Laminated Thumbscrew, which with $100 par could pay no dividends, may, with $10 par, pay up to $25,001.

---

18. All matters of legal capital, shareholders' distributions and the like are governed by the law of the corporation's state of incorporation.

As Laminated Thumbscrew begins to make money in its second year of operations to an extent that would permit it lawfully to pay dividends with $100 par stock, a number of accounting options are legally available to deal with the paid-in surplus account that was generated by the issuance of the $10 par stock at a price of $50 per share. Those options need not be explored here, but the principle should be clear; the paid-in surplus may, depending upon the applicable statute, provide the company greater latitude of choice and a greater capability for making distributions to equity holders than it would have had if it had used $100 par stock.

6. The Classic Example Further Modified: No Par Stock

Statutory provisions authorizing the use of no par stock, and a corresponding sophistication of the money market making no par stock acceptable, pulled one of the pintles out of the statutory scheme for controlling corporate capital and equity distributions. If "capital" was supposed to be the par value of the shares multiplied by the number of shares outstanding, what was capital to be if there was no par to multiply by? The only available answer was to say that the "capital" was whatever the board of directors "stated" it to be. The removal of the "par" printed on the stock certificate brought to visibility the arbitrary character of the process by which the number called "capital" was arrived at.

No other changes in the operation of the statutory machinery were required by the advent of no par stock, and no analytic problems were solved by it. If the capital account of Laminated Thumbscrew was to be made up of 500 shares of no par stock, the board of directors at the time of the issue would simply assert by resolution that $X of the $50,000 entry on the right hand side of the balance sheet should be allocated as "capital" and $50,000 minus $X as capital surplus. From there on, the matter would be handled as in the case of low par stock.

7. Changes in Capital Structure of the Ongoing Corporation

The simplified models examined so far have assumed that Laminated Thumbscrew has a static capital structure that was set once and for all at the time the company was organized and funded. In fact, of course, the capital structure of a corporation is altered from time to time to conform to the evolving needs of the enterprise in response to the business conditions in which it finds itself. Additional stock may be issued; stock may be bought in by purchases out of the corporate treasury, after which it may be cancelled, or retired to the status of authorized but unissued stock, or, as is said, "held in the treasury"; so-called stock dividends may be paid out, or the stock outstanding may be split; reverse splits are not unknown through which, for example, each two outstanding shares are converted into one; stock options may be granted and subsequently exercised; new stock subscription agreements may come into being; stock or debt instruments with convertible privileges may be turned into newly issued shares; new classes of stock may be created; by amendment of the certificate of incorporation, the par value of one or more classes of stock may be altered; the board of directors may wish in a particular circumstance to increase the stated capital or reduce it without altering the par of the outstanding class; or a merger may eliminate, or radically alter any existing capital structure.

Every one of these transactions, and others, can have the effect of altering the stated capital figure on the company's balance sheet. The effects of these changes, and the corporate procedures required to bring them about, are considered in more detail later, especially in Part Two. For the present it is enough to note three points. First, changes in the capital structure of a company are commonplace and may be frequent. Second, the procedures required for particular changes are usually specified in detail in the applicable corporation code. Third, almost any change affecting the number of shares "outstanding", or altering their particular characteristics of par, will require an adjustment in the stated capital account and will, therefore, have direct repercussions upon the legality, in accordance with the applicable corporation code, of distributions to its shareholders.

C. LEGAL CAPITAL AS A CONCEPT: CONCLUSION

The purpose of this chapter has been to develop a general understanding of the concepts of par value and legal capital. With the general concepts in hand, the next two chapters consider the way in which these concepts are used by the law to regulate shareholder investment and corporate pay-outs to shareholders.

Chapter III

REGULATING THE SHAREHOLDER'S CONTRIBUTION

It is generally agreed that shareholders have an obligation to pay for their shares, and everyone knows that bonus shares, discount stock and watered stock are Bad Things frowned upon by the law. But the corporation statutes and the courts have had great difficulty in translating that general notion into practical terms. There are few cases and most of them are old. The statutes are not well worked out. In this untidy field, many more questions are open than are resolved, not only as to procedural pragmatics but as to basic theory as well.

A. THE SHAREHOLDER'S PAY-IN OBLIGATION

1. How Much Assets?

As earlier observed, state corporation laws make no effort to require that an incorporated enterprise be funded adequately for the business operations contemplated. Until recently the corporation statutes typically gave a general mandate to the effect that a corporation may not commence business until a minimum amount of assets have been paid in; but the minimum was always trivial ($500 or $1,000) and it was seldom clear who would be liable to whom for what if the assets should not in fact be paid in. Today, even this token requirement has been abandoned in most states. As a practical matter, therefore, the shareholder's only general legal obligation to contribute to the corporate pot is that he pay in assets in an amount equal in value to the par value of each share issued to him. Where no par stock is involved, his obligation is to pay in assets in an amount equal to the "stated capital" attributed on the balance sheet of the corporation by the board of directors in respect of each share of the newly issued stock.

Let it be emphasized that the topic at hand is the shareholder's obligation imposed by general corporation law; a shareholder may, of course, incur additional enforceable obligations to pay in assets to a corporation through stock subscription or other contract.

2. What Kinds of Assets?

Apart from the question of amount, what *kind* of asset payment will be considered effective to discharge the shareholder's obligation to pay in to the corporate treasury? What kinds of assets will qualify for the purpose?

Cash poses no problem. Real property and chattel property also may be used by the shareholder to discharge the obligation. Similarly, contract rights such as a lease, or patent license will do. If the shareholder has performed services for the corporation prior to the issuance of the stock, those services, too, are a medium of payment that effectively discharges the pay-in obligation.

But beyond these common garden varieties of marketable "property" the courts and statutes have had trouble. Payment for stock made in forms of "property" that involve an element of future performance or future return has been viewed with suspicion by the courts. To the economist or businessman, the agreement of a high-powered executive or other talented performer that he will go to work for the corporation may be an enormously valuable asset which will command a high price on the market. But the courts and statutes have taken the view that an agreement to perform services in the future is not acceptable as a medium of payment to discharge the shareholder's obligation to pay for his shares; stock issued in exchange for such an agreement for future services is watered stock.[1] Similarly, the economist or businessman will readily attach economic value to a promissory note signed by John D. Rockefeller, III, or to a General Motors bond. But the courts have said that if X Corporation issues stock to Rockefeller for his note or to General Motors for its bond, neither will qualify as "property" for purposes of meeting their shareholder's pay-in obligation since Mr. Rockefeller's note, if delivered to the issuer by Mr. Rockefeller, is not payment but only his promise to pay and the General Motors bond, if delivered by General Motors, is not payment but only its promise to pay. In Mr. Rockefeller's hands, of course, a General Motors bond would be "property", and he could pay for the newly issued X Corporation stock with it; and in the hands of General Motors, Mr. Rockefeller's note is "property" with which GM could pay for its X Corporation stock. Indeed, from an economist's point of view, the value of most goods is made up precisely of a present market valuation of a future return, the patent license, the lease, and the bond being fundamentally like the contract for future services in this respect. But in the

---

1. This is overwhelmingly the prevailing American view, although an occasional jurisdiction takes the contrary position. E. g., *Petrishen v. Westmoreland Fin. Corp.*, 394 Pa. 552, 147 A.2d 392 (1959).

strange land of legal capital, the law has, for reasons none too clear, sought to distinguish the sheep from the sheep.[2]

Particularly foggy has been the use of capitalized future earnings of an enterprise as a basis for meeting the shareholder's obligation to pay for his stock. Suppose a board of directors wishes to issue stock to acquire a going enterprise which has substantially no physical assets but has large annual earnings. Setting aside the question of the rate that should be used to capitalize the earnings in arriving at a valuation, may the capitalized earnings be considered at all as a medium for effective discharge of the shareholder's obligation to pay for the newly issued shares?[3] In the well-known New Jersey case of *See v. Heppenheimer*,[4] decided in 1905, creditors of an insolvent corporation sought to hold defendant shareholders liable for the debts of the corporation, arguing that they had not paid for their stock since the valuation of the property they had transferred to the corporation in exchange for their stock was based upon a capitalization of future profits. The court held the shareholders liable, and in the course of the opinion stated that the word "property" must evidently be construed by its context which refers to something visible and tangible. A later New Jersey case looks the other way as do other cases,[5] and it is hardly conceivable that a modern court would take quite so unsophisticated and non-economic a view. But the *Heppenheimer* case serves as a reminder and illustration of the literal-minded, antique flavor that besets much of the law of legal capital and, more specifically, the difficulty that courts have had in this field with share payments that explicitly identify a future element in the valuation of the property paid in.

---

2. The once inflexible bar to promissory notes as satisfying the pay-in requirement for issued shares is starting to yield.

   The Delaware statute now permits promissory notes for any part of the consideration in excess of the par value of par stock or the stated value of no par stock—an obvious incentive to attribute as little of the consideration as possible to "stated capital." Del.Gen.Corp.Law § 152 (as amended in 1974). California's 1975 statutory revision forbids promissory notes of the purchaser "unless adequately secured by collateral other than the shares acquired" or unless the shares are issued through a stock option plan. Calif.Gen.Corp.Law § 409(a)(1).

3. As the example grows slightly more complex, it may be well again to note that the only matter under discussion here is the application of the legal capital provisions in a corporation law. As a matter of contract or sales law, of course, the corporation is free to issue its stock for whatever kind of consideration, in whatever amount, it wishes or can command.

4. 69 N.J. 36, 61 A. 843 (Ch.1905).

5. *Railway Review et al. v. Groff Drill & Machine Tool Co.*, 84 N.J. Eq. 321, 91 A. 1021 (Ch.1914), aff'd mem. sub nom. *Sloan v. Paul*, 84 N.J.Eq. 508, 96 A. 1103 (Err. & App. 1915).

On the other hand, another aspect of the peculiar non-economic character of the law of legal capital may be seen in the courts'· (and statutes') unquestioning acceptance of the practice of issuing stock "against surplus". If a corporation with a stated capital of $50,000, representing 500 shares of $100 par value each, declares a stock "dividend" of an additional 50 shares, issuing one new share to each shareholder for each 10 shares he already holds, it is uniformly assumed by courts, practitioners and commentators that the demands of the legal capital laws will be fully met if the stated capital account is raised from $50,000 to $55,000, representing now 550 shares of $100 par value each, and the surplus account is correspondingly reduced by $5,000. While it is true that that procedure generates a satisfactory looking balance sheet conforming to the statutory par scheme, it is also true that the new stock was issued without any new property of any description being paid in to the corporate treasury. To argue that the transaction is permissible under the statute because the "surplus" is "property", and to say that the accounting entry is a "pay-in", is ridiculous on so many levels that it betrays the truth that the concern of modern legal capital law is frequently no more than formal in character.

3. Valuation

If the shareholder who buys a new issue of shares pays cash for them in the legally required amount, and there is an appropriate record of the transaction, he runs no risk of later assessment or liability. But when the payment is in the form of other property, or services rendered, an issue of proper valuation is inevitably introduced. Many of the old cases that disqualified certain kinds of assets as a medium of exchange for newly issued stock in fact involved problems of valuation—situations in which it could be seen in hindsight that the consideration paid in had been overvalued. The *Heppenheimer* case offers an example: the capitalized prospective earnings had never materialized. Case law in the field typically arose from situations in which the corporation had become insolvent, and creditors were pursuing shareholders whose pay-in had been in the form of overvalued speculative real estate, contract rights, or services purportedly performed. From these cases there developed, as would be expected, varying doctrinal pronouncements as to the proper way to judge the propriety of the valuation.

Some courts declared themselves in favor of the "true value" rule, under which the value of the shareholder's contribution would be judged with the wisdom of judicial hindsight; [6] others

---

6. See *Clinton Mining & Mineral Co. v. Jamison*, 256 F. 577 (3d Cir. 1919).

opted for a "good faith" or "reasonable prudence" rule under which the shareholder was safe from later attack if the valuation put upon the property was one that a reasonably prudent man would have put upon it in the light of the facts known at the time of the valuation.[7]

Eventually, however, pressures for certainty and predictability led most state legislatures to add provisions in the corporation codes declaring that "in the absence of fraud" the valuation placed on the property by the board of directors at the time of the pay-in is conclusive and determinative of the valuation question. These provisions have virtually eliminated the valuation problem today as a subject of litigation. As assets are paid in and stock issued, the well advised board of directors adopts a resolution prepared by counsel valuing the assets at a level that at least matches the par value of the stock being issued for them; once that is done, the shareholder can cease to worry about the risk of later suit by creditors, "in the absence of fraud," whatever that may be.[8] Thus, again, the statutory legal capital scheme that was born out of an impulse to protect creditor claimants has arrived at a state of affairs in which the stock purchasing shareholder and the board of directors of the issuing corporation are in a legal position to head off any potential objection by creditors.

Experienced counsel will give a special twist to the valuation question where no par stock is being issued. Since the shareholder-purchaser's only statutory obligation in the case of no par stock is to pay in whatever he agreed to pay in, the board resolution authorizing the issue will be drafted to state simply that the company will issue N shares of the no par stock for particular described assets and will make no mention of any valuation for the property. If the share purchaser then delivers the assets described, he has, by definition, fulfilled his obligation in full. The board (or at least the company's accountant) will eventually have to assign a value to the assets to enter them on the balance sheet, and the board will also have to set some dollar number for entry as the "legal capital" attributable to the newly issued no par shares. But the shareholder who paid in the assets is safely out of the controversy once he turned over the assets he agreed to turn over—whether or not they have significant value.[9]

---

7. *Coit v. Gold Amalgamating Co.*, 119 U.S. 343, 7 S.Ct. 231 (1886).

8. E. g., Model Act § 19; Del.Gen. Corp.Law § 152 ("in the absence of actual fraud in the transaction . . .").

9. If the assets paid in are worth less per share issued than the value

B. QUALIFICATIONS ON THE PAY-IN OBLIGATION

1. Transferees of Watered Shares

Does the shareholder's obligation to pay in run with the shares, so that subsequent transferees of watered shares risk later suit by creditors? Absent complicity, the courts and statutes have said no.[10] The creditor's remedy, if he has one at all, must be against the initial stock purchaser who underpaid—if the creditor can find him.

2. Treasury Shares

But what if the subsequent transferee of the watered shares is the issuing corporation? If shares are issued for less than par, then "reacquired" by the corporation, "held in the treasury," and later sold by the corporation, should the resale be treated as a transfer from one shareholder to another, and thus free the purchaser from worries about the legal capital provisions, or treated as an "issue" by the corporation and therefore subject to the pay-in rules? The law has historically been consistently baffled by the mirror of treasury shares, and once again on this question the cases and almost all the statutes have opted for the conceptual instead of the sensible answer. As a result, the corporation that has reacquired a block of its shares, and held them "as" treasury shares rather than "retiring" or "cancelling" them, is free under the statutes to sell those shares for whatever it can get for them and can at the same time assure the purchaser that he runs no risk of later claims by creditors.[11]

The law governing treasury shares has very recently begun to move sharply, as is discussed in Part Three, infra.

3. The Handley Doctrine

Earlier reference has been made to the doctrine announced by the Supreme Court in *Handley v. Stutz* that shareholders will be exempted from the obligation to pay in assets equal to the par value of newly issued stock where the corporation is in financial trouble and the market value of the stock at the time of issue is less than par.[12] It is difficult to assess the continuing vitality of the *Handley* doctrine under modern corporation statutes. The statutes never refer to it. And the courts have not been called upon to pinpoint the implications or scope of the doctrine because

---

per share of the shares already outstanding, the transaction, of course, dilutes the interest of the preexisting shareholders. Their remedy, if any, is discussed infra.

10. E. g., Model Act (1979) § 25; Del. Gen.Corp.Law § 162(c).

11. E. g., Model Act (1979) § 18; Del. Gen.Corp.Law § 153(c).

12. 139 U.S. 417, 11 S.Ct. 530 (1891).

modern techniques of corporate financing give rise to simpler and more reliable ways to predetermine the scope of the shareholder's obligation. Nonetheless, no general statement of the shareholder's obligation to pay par is complete without noting that the *Handley* rule may, in some situations, be invokable to qualify the absoluteness of that obligation.

C. ENFORCING THE PAY-IN OBLIGATION— CREDITOR AS PLAINTIFF

How, and to what extent, can the creditor make avail of the shareholder's statutory obligation to pay for his shares? At least *five* approaches may be found in the cases!

1. Three Theories for Creditor Enforcement of the Obligation to Pay Par

a. The Trust Fund Theory

Justice Story in his landmark opinion in *Wood v. Dummer* [13] said that shareholders are not permitted to take their assets out of a corporation, thus rendering the company insolvent, because the shareholders' equity (the "capital stock") is in the nature of a "trust fund" for creditors. Later creditors' lawyers and courts took up the term "trust fund" and sought to build from it a basis for a judicial remedy requiring shareholders to pay assets into the corporation to the extent of the par value of their shares.

Though one still hears occasional reference to the "trust fund" theory, the idea spawned an inconsistent and unsatisfactory jumble of case law. The fault cannot be laid at the door of the learned Justice Story. In his opinion in *Wood v. Dummer*, he had been talking of assets that had been paid in, while the later "trust fund" cases were addressed to an asserted obligation to pay in funds that had not. Part of the problem lay in the difficulty of applying the notion of a "trust fund" where there was no "fund," and where there were none of the usual concomitants of a trust. And part of the problem lay in the fact that Justice Story's reference to a 'trust fund" had been addressed to corporate assets while later usage was addressed to the emerging new concept, "legal capital", on the right hand side of the balance sheet.

b. The Holding Out or Fraud Theory

In 1892 the Supreme Court of Minnesota in *Hospes v. Northwestern Mfg. & Car Co.*[14] boldly announced that the "trust fund" theory was a shambles and proclaimed as a substitute a "holding out" theory of shareholder liability. Though foreshadowed by

---

13. 30 Fed.Cas. 435 (No. 17,944) (C.C.D.Me.1824).

14. 48 Minn. 174, 50 N.W. 1117 (1892).

Ch. 3 REGULATING SHAREHOLDER'S CONTRIBUTION 47

some earlier decisions purporting to follow the trust fund theory, the *Hospes* case was the first to make explicit the idea that the basis of the shareholder's liability to pay in the par of his shares was grounded in tort and misrepresentation. The basic rationale of the *Hospes* court was that the creditor had somehow received a representation from the corporation to the effect that the shares had been fully paid for; if in fact the shares had not been paid for, and if the company later became insolvent the creditor could claim that he had been misled and could compel the shareholders to pay up the par value of their shares.

The most immediate effects of this beautifully representative expression of late 19th century jurisprudence were to make it absolutely clear that (i) the creditor had no cause of action against shareholders unless the company became insolvent (since no damage had been shown to the creditor) and that (ii) any creditor who extended credit to the corporation *before* the relevant stock was issued was barred from complaining.

There are obvious problems with the opinion of the Minnesota court in the *Hospes* case. On its face, the opinion shows itself as less than serious in its talk of misrepresentation and reliance as the gravamen of the action, for the court explicitly says that the creditor need not show that there were any representations made to him about the paid-in equity, or that he knew anything about the balance sheet, or that he had in fact relied on such statements; these are all simply "presumed" by the law. Moreover, like other earlier courts, the Minnesota court in the *Hospes* opinion continued to be confused, and confusing, by its failure to perceive the elemental difference between the question whether the shareholder had originally paid for his shares when they were issued and the question whether the corporation had assets in that amount in its treasury at the time the creditor made his loan.[15]

But whatever the difficulties in the analysis, the holding in the *Hospes* case was clear: the shareholder will not be held liable unless the company is insolvent and unless the complainant is a

---

15. "The capital of a corporation is the basis of its credit. It is a substitute for the individual liability of those who own its stock. People deal with it and give it credit on the faith of it. *They have a right to assume that it has paid in capital to the amount it represents itself as having*; and if they give it credit on the faith of that representation, and if the representation is false, it is a fraud upon them; and, in case the corporation becomes insolvent, the law, upon the plainest principles of common justice, says to the delinquent stockholder, 'make that representation good by paying for your stock.'" *Hospes v. Northwestern Mfg. & Car Co.*, 48 Minn. 174, 197, 50 N.W. 1117, 1121 (1892). (Emphasis added). Note, too, the court's shifting uses of the word "capital."

creditor who extended credit after the issuance of the shares. The *Hospes* case has exerted great influence in other courts and it states the rule followed in many jurisdictions.

c. The Statutory Obligation Theory

A smaller group of jurisdictions has in recent years taken another approach—one that, not surprisingly, has a more modern jurisprudential ring to it. Abandoning both the trust fund theory and the holding out theory, a few courts have held that creditors of an insolvent corporation may compel shareholders to pay in full for their shares because the applicable corporation statute says so.[16]

2. Two Other Theories for Creditor Enforcement of the Shareholder's Obligation to Pay In

a. Stock Subscription

One way to approach a legal characterization of the shareholders' pay-in obligation is to view it as a matter of contract law. In this perspective, the shareholder should be held to the terms of the subscription agreement he entered into with the corporation, and an unpaid corporate creditor should be able to pursue satisfaction for his debt by enforcing through the locally available third party procedure the corporation's unpaid claim against the subscriber. When shareholder subscriptions were a common method for financing corporations, and when the subscription price was the par value of the stock (which was the usual case) a creditor's action based on the contractual theory of subscription enforcement was substantively (though often not procedurally) the functional equivalent to an action to compel the shareholder to pay the par value for his shares under one of the three theories just reviewed.

b. Balance Sheet and Other Misrepresentation

In rare circumstances, a creditor might successfully contend that the facts in his case gave rise to a classic action for actual misrepresentation. Suppose a creditor, before making his loan to a corporation, had asked the board whether certain shares had been paid for; they had not, but the board answered untruthfully. Or suppose the prospective lender had requested and been

---

16. Probably this is the best way to interpret the 1979 Model Act, but in fact it is not clear that the Act adopts any particular view. Unhelpfully, it says only that a stockholder or subscriber "shall be under no obligation to the corporation or its creditors with respect to such shares other than the obligation to pay to the corporation the full consideration for which such shares were issued or to be issued." Section 25, par. 1.

Ch. 3 *REGULATING SHAREHOLDER'S CONTRIBUTION* 49

given the corporation's balance sheet and that, as the shareholders knew, the balance sheet listed properties which the shareholders had not in fact paid in to the corporation. In such rare cases, the classical action of common law fraud would be available and could, depending upon the misrepresentations involved, provide the creditor with an action against a shareholder participating in the fraud that would be substantially equivalent to an enforcement of the shareholder's obligation to pay in the par value of his stock.

3. Hybrid Theories

It must not be thought that the five theories separated and isolated here for identification have been scrupulously thought through by the courts, or that the cases in the field (there are not very many) can be neatly stacked into five piles. As often as not, a judicial opinion in this field will be found to have adopted some hybrid theory, and it would not be startling for a court in a single opinion to refer dimly to a "trust fund", to advert to the shareholder's subscription contract, and to suggest that creditors may have relied, or may be presumed to have relied, upon the fulfillment by the shareholders of their statutory obligation.[17]

4. Procedural Pitfalls—The Significance of the Creditor's Theory

With five theories and their permutations to work from, the courts and corporation statutes have not been notably successful in solving the procedural problems that are inherent in the legal capital exercise upon which corporation law embarked a century ago. On the whole, the legal capital statutes themselves have been of little help, for they merely assert that shares shall not be issued except upon the payment designated, and are silent as to who may do what to whom if that mandate is not followed. The discussion that follows is illustrative—but surely not inclusive—of the kinds of procedural problems encountered.

---

17. For example, the former California Corporation Code on its face laid down an absolute statutory prescription for shareholders to pay in at least the par value of their shares, and commentators on the code, including the draftsman, Ballentine, had identified California as a statutory obligation jurisdiction. The Supreme Court of California, however, when called upon to apply the statute interpreted it as being for the benefit of creditors who had actually relied on a representation about the shareholders' pay-in—thus blending the statutory obligation theory, the holding out theory, and the balance sheet misrepresentation theory, *Bing Crosby Minute Maid Corp. v. Eaton*, 46 Cal. 2d 484, 297 P.2d 5 (1956). (The case and its underlying statutory provisions were superseded by California's new corporation code in 1975). See Part Three.

In the first place, the statutes do not usually even make it clear that creditors may invoke the legal capital scheme for their benefit at all. The courts have simply assumed that they may—reasonably enough, if the engine is to have any function whatever. In developing that assumption, however, the courts have added another—equally without statutory basis—namely, that the corporation must be insolvent before the creditors may pursue the purchasers of the watered or bonus stock. The point is not insignificant. It means that the apparent injunction to the shareholder to pay in assets equal to the par value of his shares is in reality only a statement of a risk that may be remote. Insofar as the liability under legal capital provisions are concerned, the shareholder may hold back the pay-in of his own funds until insolvency comes—which, he hopes and believes at the time he acquires the stock, will be never.[18]

Assuming that "insolvency" is a prerequisite to suit by a creditor, by what standard shall insolvency be judged—by the equity criterion or by the bankruptcy criterion?[19] Through what procedure is "insolvency" to be determined? Before pursuing the shareholder, must the creditor first receive judgment against the corporation and obtain a return *nulla bona*? May he proceed immediately upon the institution of some form of voluntary or involuntary insolvency proceeding?

Then there is the question of *what* creditor has standing to enforce the shareholder's pay-in obligation. As noted earlier, the holding out theory of the *Hospes* case eliminates as possible complainants those creditors who became such before the issuance of the watered stock. As noted, the California Supreme Court managed to come to the same conclusion even in a state that had been thought to subscribe to the theory of statutory obligation. On the whole, the courts have not been sympathetic toward the role of the creditor as avenging archangel or as policeman undertaking to enforce the general obligation imposed by the corporation codes upon the shareholders; the courts' tendency has been to think in terms of tort and injury (real or assumed) to the individual creditor plaintiff.

Division of creditors into those who may pursue (some) shareholders, and those who may not, increases the procedural complexity of the situation enormously. Since the corporation must be "insolvent" to ground the action at all, there will typically be

---

18. In such a situation, however, if the corporation's legal counsel is called upon at any time to opine whether the outstanding shares are validly issued and non-assessable, he will have to decline to do so; and that may trigger off some corrective action.

19. Most statutes prescribe the equity criterion. See Model Act, (1979) Section 2(n).

Ch. 3 REGULATING SHAREHOLDER'S CONTRIBUTION 51

a receiver for creditors or other creditors' representative in the driver's seat. If the receiver is thought of representing "the corporation" rather than creditors he will have no action at all under a *Hospes* analysis. Even if he is thought of as an agent representing and acting in the place of creditors, the misrepresentation or holding out approach compels the creditors' representative to discriminate among his principals and, correspondingly, determines which shareholders may be sued, how much they may be sued for, and what shall be done with the proceeds of the suit. The creditors' representative will obviously be much happier with a theory of the action that will enable him to force all shareholders who have not met their pay-in obligation to do so, and to add the proceeds to the assets available to all creditors.

Then there is the question of who may be sued. Each of the five theories outlined above will, if logically carried out, produce its own characteristic group of potential defendants as, over the course of the life of the corporation, shares will have been issued at different times to different shareholders under different arrangements at different prices while many shareholders who took originally issued shares will have disappeared from sight in favor of transferees who are not liable.

Through what kind of proceeding shall a creditor, or a representative of a creditor, pursue the shareholder defendants? Must each one be sued individually? Will some kind of class action be possible? May all of the actions be consolidated into some sort of plenary insolvency proceeding? What about service of process? And the jurisdiction of the court? Res judicata? Collateral estoppel? Notice to other creditors? Settlement? Collusive settlement?

What is the measure of the amount for which the shareholder may be sued? Again different theories of the action will produce different answers. Consider the case of the creditor who is owed $100 by the corporation and who sues a shareholder whose liability under the local prevailing theory is $1,000; assuming that the plaintiff's judgment will be limited to $100, may other creditors in successive suits pursue the shareholder up to the remaining $900?

If judgment is obtained against a shareholder, to whom does he make payment? To the complaining creditor alone; does the race go to the swift? To the corporation for the benefit of all creditors similarly situated; if the recovery will be shared by all creditors of the bankrupt corporation, what incentive has the individual creditor to bear the costs of pursuing the delinquent shareholder? May the shareholder defend on the ground that the plaintiff creditor is a junior creditor whose claim against the corporation would not have been collectible in any case because of the prior claims of higher ranking creditors? What is the effect of the intervention of bankruptcy proceedings or state insolvency proceedings?

How about actions over? If a shareholder has been compelled by creditors' action to live up to his pay-in obligation, may he then turn to other shareholders similarly situated and compel contributions from them?

The statute of limitations is likely to impose a problem and, again, the characterization of the shareholder's pay-in obligation as being essentially contractual, or tortious, or statutorily prescriptive, will point to a choice among the potentially applicable statutes of repose and determine the time when the statutory period starts, ends, and is tolled.

Efforts by creditors to pursue shareholders on the theory of enforcement of their stock subscriptions became hopelessly snarled in the theology of 19th century contract law. Suppose the board of directors of a corporation simply refused to make the call on the subscriptions; was not the call a necessary precondition to the subscribers' contractual liability? Or, suppose the directors had, for a trivial consideration, waived or cancelled the subscriber's liability? Was that not a defense for the subscriber? Finally, how could the corporation, after it had become insolvent, perform its part of the subscription bargain—that is, the issuance of shares in accordance with the subscription agreement; would the subscriber be getting what he bargained for, i. e., shares of a viable business enterprise, and if not, was the subscription agreement enforceable against him?

Out of these and similar problems, the courts amassed a doctrinal slag pile of subscriptions, subscription agreements, stock purchase agreements, agreements to purchase stock, options, estoppels, constructive conditions, and the like. This jumble will never be sorted out for, with the development of different forms of corporate financing, the subscription agreement largely faded away, the law took another turn, and today the pile molders, forgotten and decreasingly visible under the green cover of time.

So much for procedural problems of the creditor. They are seldom relevant anyway, it must be reemphasized. In the real world, the creditor will almost always find that he has no basis under the legal capital provisions to pursue shareholders since the stock issuance will usually have been carried out in formal compliance with the statute. It is so easy to comply with the legal capital requirement that only the most careless lawyering

Ch. 3 *REGULATING SHAREHOLDER'S CONTRIBUTION* 53

will botch the stock issuance in a way that will leave the purchaser open to risk from this source. But in the unusual circumstance in which the shareholder *has* been left open to risk, the creditor who seeks to take advantage of that delinquency will find his way beset by one procedural pitfall after another, and almost no statutory or judicial chart to guide him.

D. ENFORCING THE PAY-IN OBLIGATION— SHAREHOLDER AS PLAINTIFF

1. The Legal Capital Scheme

Development of the concepts and procedures of legal capital machinery is traceable entirely to a judicial and legislative concern with the problem of creditor protection. In some situations, however, the shareholder may have benefited from the legal capital scheme.

The interest of a shareholder in having other shareholders make a contribution to the corporate pot equitably commensurate with his own has already been noted in earlier discussion. In the days when high par value stock was commonly used, and when the mores of corporate financing did not contemplate purchase of initially issued shares at a price higher than the par value, the par machinery at least tended to produce an incidental equitableness of contribution. Of course, once the enterprise is underway, the par value of the stock is irrelevant to its economic value and is therefore useless as a standard for measuring the equitableness of subsequent shareholder contributions. And, as low par and no par stock came into common use, the fortuitous protective effect of the par scheme largely disappeared even in the context of an initial stock offering.

What of the possibility that a shareholder might be able to rely upon the par payment obligation to implement his interest in equitable contribution in a case where bonus, discount or watered shares had been issued to the shareholders? There is apparently only one case on the books in which a shareholder has been able to invoke in his own behalf the statutory par scheme. In *Scully v. Automobile Finance Co.*,[20] the enterprise had prospered. An original shareholder who had not fully paid for his stock was sued by other shareholders, not to compel him to pay in the par value of the shares he had received, but to cancel the shares he had received, a remedy that would have immediately and dramatically raised the value of the other shares outstanding. The Delaware court gave judgment for the

---

20. 12 Del.Ch. 174, 109 A. 49 (1920).

plaintiffs, but, at the request of the *defendant* refused to cancel the shares and instead permitted the defendant to pay in the full par value and retain his fractional share of the enterprise.

2. Promoter's Liability

There was once, and in a sense there still is, a substantial body of law grouped together under the rubric "promoter's liability". Enough cases were litigated in the vocabulary of "promoter's liability" to generate, if not justify, treatises in the field.[21] Though the courts of the day almost never perceived it, the main problem that gave rise to this litigation (other than simple misrepresentation and fraud) was the problem of equitable contribution among shareholders. Corporate promoters in these cases had put little or nothing into the corporate pot except their "services", often of dubious value, while other shareholders had paid in the par value of the shares in cash or property; the promoters wound up owning a substantial fraction of the corporate shares, and the other shareholders' proportionate share in the corporate assets was correspondingly diluted.

The courts were either unable or unwilling to embark upon the development of a jurisprudence spelling out the obligations of promoters to individual purchasing shareholders (including *later* shareholders) or to tackle the problem of developing economic standards for determining the fair price of newly issued shares. Instead, the judges tried to deal with the question in terms of a breach of fiduciary relationship between the promoter and "the corporation." The essence of the courts' theory was that the promoter was some kind of special fiduciary vis-a-vis "the corporation" and, as such, owed "the corporation" a duty not to obtain secret or "unconscionable" profits. This theory may have been better than nothing in a day that was innocent of securities regulation. But the effort could not possibly succeed. In the "promoters liability" cases, the problem was not one of injury by the promoter to an abstract "corporation" but dilution of the economic and political power of full paying shareholders by the issuance of cheap or free shares to other shareholders—i. e. the promoter. Inter-shareholder conflicts cannot be resolved in legal categories that treat the "corporation" as a collective unity. When Shareholder group A and Shareholder group B of the same corporation are at odds, neither the promoter, nor the board, nor counsel, nor a court will find guidance for behavior in pronouncements about someone's duty to "the" corporation. Intra-corporate factional dispute called for

21. E. g. M. Ehrich, *The Law of Promoters* (1916).

Ch. 3 REGULATING SHAREHOLDER'S CONTRIBUTION

molecular corporate jurisprudence to be supplanted by atomic, or even smaller-particle, jurisprudence.

Sometimes the promoter's transactions with the corporation involved the issuance of shares for overvalued property, in which case there would be an overlap between the theory of the promoter's general fiduciary duties and his obligation as a shareholder to pay the par value of the shares. To that extent situations giving rise to promoter's liability might also have given rise to liability under the requirement for the payment of par value; but the theory of the action, the measure of damages, the legal qualifications required of the plaintiff, and the legal requirements of corporate insolvency would be wholly different in a promoter's liability suit from those that would inhere in a suit to compel payment under the par value requirement.

In many other situations, however, there would be no such overlap of theory. For example, the promoter may not have taken stock but rather received money from the corporation in payment for alleged property or services. Or he might have made an undisclosed profitable sale of properties to the corporation. Development of a rational law of promoter's liabilities was stunted by the conceptualistic decision made by Justice Holmes in *Old Dominion Copper Mining and Smelting Co. v. Lewisohn* [22] that shareholders could not recover from a promoter on grounds of fiduciary violation if the promoter at the time of the sale of overvalued property to the corporation owned all the shares of the corporation, since "the corporation" had full "knowledge" of the inflated value of the land it had received from the promoter.

Though the promoter's fiduciary theory may have been of some help in restraining the most spectacular excesses of promoters, the doctrinal structure was a weak one and of little assistance to those who most needed help, subsequent purchasing shareholders. The field has today been taken over almost entirely by disclosure requirements under state and federal securities laws, and by the development of modern securities fraud law.

3. Equitable Contribution Doctrine

With the doctrines of legal capital largely inoperable to protect shareholders against dilution through underpriced issue of shares, there has been some small modern tendency to develop specific doctrinal tools to deal with the matter. In a few states, the corporation code vaguely requires that a corporate issuer

---

22. 210 U.S. 206, 28 S.Ct. 634 (1908).

receive consideration for its stock in an equitable amount.[23] Some courts are developing a jurisprudence condemning sale of stock at less than "fair" value as a breach of the board of directors' fiduciary obligation to "the corporation",[24] though that of course is not the real problem. And occasionally a court appears accurately to perceive the issuance of stock at too cheap a price not as a problem of abstract "corporate waste" but as a dilution transaction that reallocates political power and economic return among shareholders.[25]

4. Disclosure and Securities Regulation

But by far the greatest protection the shareholder has today against stock issues at improper prices lies in the disclosure and filing requirements of state Blue Sky laws and of the federal Securities Acts. As a result of developments in securities law over the last fifty years, the stock purchaser and the stock owner who cares enough to enquire can today usually ascertain what fees were paid to promoters and how and what securities have been or are about to be issued by a corporation to whom, when, and for what. When the statutory stated capital machinery is contrasted with live, developing, economically oriented, and continuously current disclosure requirements and with the rapidly evolving rules of security fraud under modern securities laws, the former is seen to be an obsolete and seldom relevant mechanism for protecting shareholders threatened with dilution.

E. ENFORCING THE PAY-IN OBLIGATION—CORPORATION AS PLAINTIFF

As a matter of contract law, a corporation may by suit compel a stock subscriber to make payment to the corporation, on call, in accordance with the terms of the subscription agreement. But may the recipient of bonus, discount, or watered stock of a corporation be sued later by the corporation, while it is still solvent, to compel him to pay in the full par value of the shares?

---

23. E. g., Minnesota Bus.Corp.Act § 301.16(1) ("Shares . . . shall not be allotted for a cash consideration which is unfair to the then shareholders nor for a consideration other than cash upon a valuation thereof which is unfair to such shareholders; . . .").

24. Cf. *Schoenbaum v. Firstbrook*, 405 F.2d 215 (2d Cir. 1968) with *Popkin v. Bishop*, 464 F.2d 714 (2d Cir. 1972), and with *Schlick v. Penn-Dixie Corp.*, 507 F.2d 374 (2d Cir. 1974), and with *Blue Chip Stamps v. Manor Drug Stores*, 421 U.S. 723, 95 S.Ct. 1917 (1975).

25. *Bodell v. General Gas & Electric Corp.*, 15 Del.Ch. 119, 132 A. 442 (Ch.1926), aff'd 15 Del.Ch. 420, 140 A. 264 (Sup.Ct.1927). See also *Atlantic Refining Co. v. Hodgman*, 13 F.2d 781 (3d Cir. 1926).

Under the holding out theory, there would obviously be no such liability, since there is no creditor even presumptively injured. While it would be arguable under the statutory obligation theory that the corporation should be able to pursue the shareholder to enforce the statutory requirement, such a suit would obviously be met by the defense that the corporation had with knowledge consented to the issuance and thereby specifically waived all right to collect the full par value. Except for one case in which one shareholder brought a *derivative* action against other shareholders who had not paid in full for their stock, there has been no implication in the judicial opinions that the corporation may sue a shareholder to compel him to pay up the par value of the shares he received.[26]

As noted earlier, the corporation's legal incapacity to enforce the shareholders' pay-in obligation has also proved an embarrassment to a corporate receiver where the receiver has been viewed as "standing in the shoes of" the corporate debtor.

F. THE CORPORATE PRACTITIONER: AN OUNCE OF PREVENTION

The perspective of the corporate practitioner is prospective. Litigation is usually the result of failure to perceive trouble in advance and to take appropriate steps at an earlier date. The corporate lawyer and the corporate accountant can have almost no excuse for letting a situation develop where there is any question about shareholder liability for violation of legal capital provisions. The statutes place within the hands of the board, and their counsellors, almost unlimited opportunity to set par, or eliminate par, to prescribe the consideration paid, to value it, and to control the corresponding accounting entries. The issuance of stock can, of course, raise genuine and difficult problems; "fairness" of price and appropriate disclosure under developing doctrines of federal securities fraud are difficult to determine, as are assessments of the equitableness of the terms of mergers and exchanges of stock. But the statutory legal capital provisions, as such, are almost invariably manageable in advance through the application of rudimentary skill and attention in the design of the transaction. If there is an exception to this statement it arises not from the legal capital provisions of the statutes but from the annoying unreal doctrines that still prohibit the issuance of stock in exchange for contractual commitments for future performance.

---

26. *Scully v. Automobile Finance Co.*, 12 Del.Ch. 174, 109 A. 49 (1920).

Given the vagueness and uncertainties that attach to all procedural aspects of the legal capital provisions, it is well worth the time required for the corporate practitioner to invest the energy needed to comprehend the legal capital provisions under which he must work, however fossilized they may be, and to include in his prescription for a corporate transaction the ounce of prevention that will ward off trouble from this source. Part Two of this text provides an assist in that endeavor, as it sets out a series of transactions involving stock and capital readjustments, with corresponding accounting entries under the legal capital provisions. The main focus of Part Two is upon regulation of pay-outs to shareholders, discussed in Chapter IV, but the examples also provide representative guidance in the application of the statutes to share issuance and pay-ins.

Chapter IV

STATUTORY REGULATION OF DISTRIBUTIONS TO SHAREHOLDERS

The statutory legal capital scheme seeks to regulate the flow of asset distributions to shareholders. The provisions differ from state to state, and when dealing with a specific problem, the lawyer must examine the applicable statute carefully. For purposes of description, however, the statutes regulating such distributions may be conveniently divided into five general groups: insolvency statutes; balance sheet surplus statutes; earned surplus statutes; surplus or net profits statutes; and current earnings statutes.[1]

A. INSOLVENCY STATUTES

No one has contested the basic proposition of *Wood v. Dummer*. If the hierarchical relationship of creditor to shareholder is to have any meaning at all, then the management must not be left to shovel all the assets in the corporate treasury out to the shareholders when the corporation has insufficient assets to pay its creditors or when the shareholder distribution itself renders the corporation unable to pay its creditors.

In Massachusetts, the only limitation on distributions of assets to shareholders is that the corporation not be rendered "insolvent or bankrupt" by the distribution.[2] The statutes in most other jurisdictions contain a similar provision as a supplement to other restrictions of the character discussed later. In jurisdictions which do not provide for a specific insolvency standard by statute, the principle is likely still to be found operative as a common law inheritance. Further, the Uniform Fraudulent Conveyance Act may be interpreted to produce the same result, since it provides that a conveyance without a fair consideration by a person who is rendered insolvent thereby is fraudulent as to his creditors.[3]

"Insolvency" has, of course, long had a recognized duality of meaning. The test of insolvency in the equity courts was whether the debtor was unable to meet his obligations as they became

---

1. The 1975 California Corporation Code and the 1980 amendments to the Model Business Corporation Act are discussed in Part Three.

2. Mass.Bus.Corp.Law, Ch. 156B, Section 61.

3. Uniform Fraudulent Conveyance Act § 4. At least one court has specifically held that the U.F.C.A. applies to a corporation paying a dividend which triggers insolvency. *Powers v. Heggie*, 268 Mass. 233, 167 N.E. 314, 317 (1929).

due. The test for purposes of bankruptcy in the law courts was whether the aggregate dollar amount of the debtor's assets was less than the total dollar amount of his liabilities. The difference between these two conceptions can be very great. Solvency in the equity sense is concerned with liquidity; a debtor may be able to cope with his bills as they roll in month by month even though the market value of all his assets is only a fraction of the aggregate of his liabilities maturing over time in the future. The emphasis of the bankruptcy sense of solvency is upon liquidation; a debtor might not be sufficiently liquid to meet his current obligations but still hold unliquid resources having a value far in excess of the total of his obligations. In jurisdictions which use insolvency as the, or a, critical standard for determining the legality of a distribution to shareholders, the definition of insolvency employed by the statute may often be vital. Today, most statutes employing an insolvency standard define it in an equity sense.[4] The Massachusetts approach is generally considered the most lenient of the statutory schemes for restricting distributions to shareholders. It should be noted, however, that in jurisdictions that provide for regulatory restraints in addition to the insolvency standard, it is quite possible for a corporate debtor to comply with those other restraints and still find itself in violation of the insolvency standard if the statute uses insolvency in the equity sense.

The insolvency rule for governing equity distributions obviously has the merits of simplicity, ready comprehensibility and economic sense. It dispenses entirely with concepts of capital, legal capital, surplus or any other accounting terms. And there is no evidence to suggest that creditors of Massachusetts corporations fare any worse—or any better—than creditors of companies incorporated in states having more elaborate statutory schemes for inhibiting distributions to shareholders.

B. BALANCE SHEET SURPLUS STATUTES: STATED CAPITAL AND SURPLUS

The discussion in Chapter II developed the general history and concept of stated capital, and the simple model transactions reviewed there illustrate the way in which the concept of stated capital could be used as a device for inhibiting distributions to equity holders. The examples shown there illustrate the working of a balance sheet surplus test. Under this test, one deducts the liabilities shown on the balance sheet from the assets shown on the balance sheet, and then deducts from that difference

---

4. See, e. g., Model Act (1979) § 2(n).

Ch. 4 REGULATION OF DISTRIBUTIONS 61

the amount of the stated capital; if the result of that operation produces a positive dollar figure—a balance sheet surplus—then distributions may to that extent be legally made to shareholders. A number of state corporation laws today use the balance sheet surplus test, usually in conjunction with an independent insolvency test.

New York is a typical balance sheet surplus jurisdiction. Under the New York Business Corporation Law, the substantive restraint on equity distributions reads as follows:

> "Dividends may be declared or paid and other distributions may be made out of surplus only, so that the net assets of the corporation remaining after such declaration, payment or distribution shall at least equal the amount of its stated capital." [5]

The New York Business Corporation Law then provides a statutory definition of stated capital, reading:

> ". . . the sum of (A) the value of all shares with par value that have been issued, (B) the amount of the consideration received for all shares without par value that have been issued, except such part of the consideration therefor as may have been allocated to surplus in a manner permitted by law, and (C) such amounts not included in clauses (A) and (B) as have been transferred to stated capital, whether upon the distribution of shares or otherwise, minus all reductions from such sums as have been effected in a manner permitted by law." [6]

Balance sheet surplus statutes have an appearance of simplicity about them. In application, they turn out not to be so simple, as will now be seen.

1. Accounting, the Accountant, and the Law

A balance sheet will show a surplus, or not show a surplus, depending upon the numbers entered upon it. The interplay of law and accounting that determine these numbers is exceedingly complex, subtle and difficult. Whether or not clearly perceived, several kinds of questions arise out of the relationship. Should statute and court undertake to prescribe a corpus of accounting principles? Should legislatures and courts instead refer all questions to the accountants' own evolving common

---

5. N.Y.Bus.Corp.Law § 510(b).

6. N.Y.Bus.Corp.Law § 102(a)(12) Cf. Model Act (1979) § 2(j).

law—"generally accepted accounting principles"?[7] Or just refer some questions, and if so, which ones? Assuming that the guide is to be "generally accepted accounting principles", has the accountant in the particular situation followed those principles, or made an appropriate selection from among an array of different but equally permissible principles? And, finally, has the accounting principle in question been properly applied to the facts at hand?

A balance sheet surplus scheme for restricting distributions to shareholders would, if seriously pursued, require the development of a full scale judicial jurisprudence of accounting. Nearly everyone agrees that that would be wholly impractical and a disaster. Courts do not have and do not claim to have the technical training to sit as accounting tribunals; the accounting profession would far prefer to be its own law generator through opinions of the Financial Accounting Standards Board and the development of "generally accepted accounting principles"; and the corporate lawyer has no desire to submit technical questions of this kind to a court. As a result, there is virtually no litigation in the field. And when there is occasional litigation, there is a strong tendency for the court to find that when the accountant created the surplus by the entries he decided to make, he was acting in accordance with *some* generally accepted accounting principle, and, with that, the mandate of the statute has been met.

After embarking bravely upon the adventure of regulating shareholder distributions in the interest of creditors, both court and legislature recoiled from actively carrying through with that enterprise as they came to realize, more or less consciously, the enormity and complexity of law building that would be necessary to make the system really work. That second judgment was undoubtedly a wise one; perhaps, too, it suggests that it was a mistake to embark upon the endeavor in the first place.

Generally accepted accounting principles have a reality, and do provide a usable general guidance. The professionally responsible accountant is not free to write down any number that

---

7. The North Carolina Business Corporation Act is unique in incorporating into the statute the concept of what it calls "generally accepted principles of sound accounting practice." See, e. g., N.C.Gen. Stat. § 55-2(2), (7) (definitions of "assets" and "liabilities," respectively); § 55-49(b) (in determining legality of dividends, distributions, or "withdrawals of corporate assets," assets may "be carried on the books in accordance with generally accepted principles of sound accounting practice applicable to the kind of business conducted by the corporation"); § 55-49(d) (definition of "earned surplus"). Those interested in the interplay of law and accounting practice will find the financial sections of the North Carolina statute a challenge, N.C.Gen. Stat. §§ 55-43 to -52.

occurs to him. But laymen who are neither trained nor experienced in accounting tend to assume that these principles have a certainty, precision and exclusivity which they do not in fact have. Financial statements are inevitably a composite of a myriad of judgmental decisions made by the accountants, or some combination of accountants, lawyers, and business management. What expenditures should be expensed and which ones "capitalized"[8] as an asset? When should the accountant's convention of carrying assets at cost be modified so as to write up or write down the figure at which the assets are carried? What allowances should be made for potential bad debts, and when? When should losses be recognized and written off? How should depletion, amortization, and depreciation be treated? To what extent and when should capitalization of anticipated earnings—so called "goodwill"—be carried or not carried on the balance sheet? On these, and similar questions of asset accounting arising in particular circumstances, accountants and industry practices will differ, and will claim support of generally accepted accounting principles.

On the liability side of the balance sheet similar questions will arise. When should contingent liabilities be recognized and entered as liabilities? The same question for bilateral contracts requiring future payments by the corporation. When should they be footnoted? How shall unliquidated liabilities be quantified? How about long term pension liabilities? Indebtedness (and assets) held in fluctuating foreign currencies?

And what, if any, adjustments should be made for inflation?

More fundamentally still, it must be recognized that in most ongoing business situations, there is only a fractional relationship between the concerns of the creditor and the figures that show up on a corporate balance sheet. In part this is true because the creditor's primary concern is with his debtor's ability to pay the debt when and as it matures. In part, however, it is because the focus of the accountant's art is not to present a continuous picture of the "value" of the enterprise (whatever that may mean) but to apply with consistency a series of accounting conventions (which are recognized to be conventions) on a periodic basis and to achieve at least a satisfactory degree of disclosure of selected kinds of transactions and elements in the economic life of the enterprise. By force of the limitations of his function and his tools, the accountant offers a picture that is incomplete, is differently focused from that of the creditor, and is of a highly stylized character.

8. Note this, the nth, variant meaning for "capital."

The reader will find it instructive in reading Chapter VI of this text to compare the statutory stated capital protection scheme, utterly dependent as it is upon formal accounting, with the techniques that creditors and their lawyers have handcrafted for their protection.

2. Computation of Stated Capital

One factor that must be used in the computation of "surplus" is a dollar figure designated as the corporation's stated capital. More than any other components of the balance sheet, "stated capital" is a lawyer's concept rather than an accountant's and a modern corporation statute will usually provide more guidance for its computation than for other balance sheet elements. But most statutes leave many questions open, and some questions are not answered by any of the statutes.

Computation of stated capital is simple if the situation is simple. Following the statutes, and history, an entry must be carried as "capital" in the shareholders' equity portion—the southeast corner—of the issuing company's balance sheet with regard to all shares "outstanding." To determine the amount of this entry one multiplies the number of shares "outstanding" times the par value prescribed in the certificate of incorporation for each share; if there is no par value, a "stated value" of each issued share is substituted by resolution of the board of directors. When additional shares are issued, if the company's existing stated capital is equal to the number of shares theretofore outstanding multiplied by their par value, stated capital is increased by an amount equivalent to the par value of the new shares times the number of new shares being issued. So far, so good. But after that point, matters begin to become a little more difficult and uncertain.

For any number of reasons, the stated capital of a company may at any particular time be higher than the product of the par value of the shares multiplied by the number of shares outstanding. Most statutes permit the board of directors, acting without shareholder vote, to increase the company's stated capital and that step is sometimes taken.[9] Suppose a corporation has on its books an aggregate stated capital of $750 attributable to an outstanding issue of 10 shares of $50 par stock, or an average of $75 per share, and that the corporation now issues one new such share for a price of $60. Should the issue of the new share be reflected in the stated capital account by an in-

---

9. See e. g. Model Act (1979) § 21 paragraph 4. See also discussion infra on "reducing capital."

crease of $50 (the par), or $60 (the issue price), or $75 (the preexisting average stated capital per share), or some other arbitrarily assigned number greater than $50; or is *no* increase in stated capital needed to reflect the issuance of the new share since the existing stated capital of $750 is greater than the product of all shares outstanding including the new share (11), multiplied by the par value ($50)? Similar questions arise in the case of a so-called "stock dividend" where the preexisting stated capital is greater than the par value per share times the number of shares outstanding; when the new shares are issued *pro rata* to existing shareholders, by what measure, if at all, must stated capital be increased, and surplus (of some kind) be correspondingly charged?

If there are outstanding subscriptions to shares, should the stated capital be increased to reflect the stock subscribed for at the time the subscription agreement is entered into, or when the directors call for payment, or when payment has been made in part, or when payment has been made in full? A similar question is raised where, as is specifically authorized by some corporation statutes, shares may for some purposes be considered to be "issued" though they are only partially paid for and the balance owing is expected to be received in installments? Current accounting practice regarding stock subscriptions would tend to write-up the stated capital as soon as a subscription is entered into and correspondingly create an account receivable on the asset side, but that result is not inevitable; it is quite reasonable to argue that there should be no account receivable at least until the directors have called the subscription, and it is also possible that the statutory provision governing the stated capital might be based upon a legal concept of "outstanding" shares that is independent of and different from accounting practice i. e., is the subscribed for share "outstanding" for some purposes but not others?

How should stock warrants and stock options be handled in the stated capital account? Contemporary accounting practice would probably not enter a stock option as part of the stated capital until the optionee exercised his option. But it is a separate question whether that practice, to the extent followed, should govern the statutory concept of stated capital.

How about convertible shares? Suppose an outstanding share of preferred stock with a par value of $100 is convertible into two shares of common stock each having a par value of $100: should the stated capital of the outstanding preferred be $100 or $200? Or take the example of a $1,000 convertible debenture that may be converted into three shares of common stock with a par value of $100 each. Should the accountant at the time of exercise of the conversion privilege reduce liabilities by $1,000 and increase stated capital by $300, thereby increasing surplus by $700? If this example is slightly modified, a peculiar by-product of the system becomes visible. If a $100 debenture is convertible into three shares of $100 par value common stock, the effect of the conversion is to reduce liabilities by $100 and increase stated capital by $300, thus further restricting shareholder distributions to the extent of $200; but why should the general creditor need extra protection as a result of a transaction that is entirely to his benefit, namely, the elimination of an outstanding creditor claim and the substitution of a lower ranking shareholder's claim?

And then, what of acquisitions by the corporation of its outstanding stock? If the company "buys in" a share of its $10 par stock and pays $40 for it at a time when the average stated capital per share attributable to that class is $20, what happens to the stated capital account? Analytically there are at least the following options: the treasury share is considered still to be "outstanding", and no change is made in the stated capital account; or the share is considered no longer to be outstanding and the stated capital account is reduced by $10 (the par), or $20 (the average stated capital per share), or $40 (the price). Consider how the answers should be affected by the lawyer's distinctions between "holding the reacquired share as a treasury share," "retiring the reacquired share to the status of authorized but unissued stock," and "cancelling" the share thereby eliminating it from the aggregate of authorized shares. Consider then what legal capital entry should be made when "the share" that has been "reacquired" by the corporation is not retired or cancelled but is "resold" for $30.

Finally, is stated capital to be thought of as an aggregate concept, or should one instead think of separate stated capitals for each class of shares? This point is discussed subsequently in connection with limitations on distributions to shareholders and the differing interests of differing classes of shareholders, but it should at least be noted here. Where a company has a complex capital structure involving several classes and series of shares, and where stock dividends, stock splits, conversions, options, warrants, exchanges, new issues and other sophisticated corporate transactions are routine events, this matter of the aggregate or componential character of stated capital can become very complex—and often indeterminable.

All of these transactions, and others like them, are discussed with illustrative examples in Part Two of this book.

3. Reducing Capital

At this point the concept of "reduction of capital" must be addressed, though the discussion may entail a modest digression.

Frequent reference may be found in cases, statutes, and texts, to "reducing capital". Unfortunately, "reducing capital" has had, and still has, at least three wholly different meanings:

   (i) In the era of *Wood v. Dummer*, and occasionally still today, "reduction of capital" referred to a distribution of corporate assets to shareholders. The assets—the "capital"—put at stake by the shareholders is reduced when a part of those assets is returned to them. This sense of the term is that of the economist or the businessman.

   (ii) In its second meaning, reduction of capital takes "capital" to refer to the outstanding shares, and a reduction to mean a decrease in the number of shares outstanding. The focus of this meaning is not upon an asset distribution but upon a legal step whereby the corporation by purchase, retirement, conversion, exchange, or cancellation cuts back on the number of shares that are legally characterized as "outstanding".[10]

   (iii) Finally, reduction of capital in its modern statutory sense refers neither to an asset distribution nor a decrease in the number of outstanding shares, but to a downward revision in the stated capital account on the lower right hand side of the balance sheet. The most direct way to bring about such a downward revision is, of course, through a lowering of the par value of the outstanding shares; this is usually achieved by a simple resolution adopted by directors and shareholders amending the certificate of incorporation to lower the dollar figure prescribed as the par value of the shares of a particular class, and filing with the state corporation authority a suitable certificate of such amendment. If, for example, a corporation has outstanding 100 shares of $100 par value each, and the certificate of incorporation is amended to provide for a par value of $5 per share, the minimum stated capital is thereby changed from $10,000 to $500, and so, by appropriate corporate procedure

---

10. Once in a while, but fortunately not often, one also hears reduction of capital used to refer to an amendment to the certificate of incorporation reducing the number of shares *authorized* to be issued by the corporation.

the stated capital can be written down on the corporation's books to $500. This reduction in the stated capital produces a corresponding increase in a surplus account, sometimes denominated "reduction surplus". If and to the extent that such reduction surplus may, under the governing statute, be charged in conjunction with a distribution of assets to shareholders, the reduction of capital that creates the reduction surplus bears a potentiality for a threat to creditors; but that risk is a potentiality only, and the reduction of capital itself affects no one economically in any way. It is simply an accounting entry. But the hangover effect of the older meanings of reduction of capital continues to tincture the atmosphere and in statutes, judicial opinions and legal commentary, it is usual to find that "reduction of capital" is viewed as a drastic event with ominous overtones.

It is not uncommon to find two or more of these wholly different meanings of "reducing capital" used within a single statute, judicial opinion or commentary. This practice does not bring added clarity to a topic already technical and confounding.

Reduction of capital in its sense as a downward revision of stated capital can obviously be brought about by a number of ways in addition to lowering the par value of shares. A conversion of $100 par value convertible preferred stock into three shares of $10 par common could lead to such a reduction, as noted above. Different avenues for reducing stated capital typically call for different voting and filing procedures under the applicable corporation statute. In this connection, see the later discussion of reacquisitions of shares by a corporation, and of distributions in liquidation.

For a sampling of "reduction of capital" provisions, see the statutory sections collected below.[11]

4. Surpluses

Given a balance sheet on which assets, liabilities, and stated capital are designated by specific dollar figures, deducting the latter two from the first yields the "surplus". When the total of corporate assets is decreased by a distribution to shareholders the left hand side of the balance sheet is reduced and the amount of surplus shown on the right hand side goes down correspondingly.

---

11. Model Act (1979) § 69; Del.Gen. Corp.Law §§ 244 and 242(b); N.Y. Bus.Corp.L. § 516; N.C.Gen.Stats. § 55–48.

Under the simple balance sheet surplus statutes, assets may lawfully be distributed to shareholders up to the point where the decline in assets consequent upon the distribution reduces the surplus account to a zero balance. Under many statutes, however, analysis must not be permitted to stop at this point.

When corporate accounting was in its infancy, accountants customarily used only one surplus account. They did not seek to explain *how* the surplus had come to be there. Statutes following a strict balance sheet surplus test approach have not moved past that stage in accounting analysis. Over the last twenty or thirty years, the accounting profession has, however, moved steadily in the direction of sub-categorizing surplus in an effort to have the balance sheet identify the way by which the surplus was generated. A modern balance sheet may therefore show many kinds of surpluses, and in turn a modern corporation statute may declare some kinds of surplus ineligible for purposes of charging an asset distribution to shareholders.

a. Paid-in Surplus; (Capital Surplus)

If stock with a par value of $10 is issued for $25, and the stated capital is correspondingly increased by $10, as it normally would be, some kind of surplus has been created to the extent of the $15 difference. In older usage, this $15 difference was called a "capital surplus"; today it is typically denominated a paid-in surplus. Or if the corporation "buys in" a share of its outstanding stock for $10 and then later sells "that share" for $15, the $5 difference may show up on the balance sheet as a paid-in surplus item. Paid-in surplus can be generated in other ways. When, for example, no par stock is issued, the directors are required by the statutes to designate all or some portion of the proceeds as stated capital; if they so designate less than the full amount received, the balance is entered on the balance sheet as paid-in surplus.[12]

Where a corporation has a paid-in surplus, and no other surplus, may it legally distribute assets to shareholders and charge the paid-in surplus account? On this key point, the statutes are divided, some specifically providing that paid-in surplus may be a basis for equity distributions, some providing that it may not, and some providing nothing. Where the statutes do not dis-

---

12. Some statutes, for reasons that are unfathomable, require the directors in such a case to allocate a designated minimum fraction, such as one-quarter or one-third, of the proceeds as stated capital. E. g. Va. Code Ann. § 13.1–18 (par. 2).

tinguish among surpluses, the courts have declined to read in a distinction.[13]

A few statutes provide that paid-in surplus may be used as a basis for distributions to preferred stock but not common stock.[14] The argument in favor of permitting the paid-in surplus to be used as a basis for dividends to preferred shareholders is that it is a more serious threat to the corporation's general financial standing to build up arrearages on preferred stock dividends than to skip common stock dividends and that the restraints on payment of preferred dividends should therefore be more relaxed.

b. Reduction Surplus

"Reducing capital" and "reduction surplus" are described earlier. May such reduction surplus, under a balance sheet surplus test statute, provide an appropriate basis for a dividend or other distribution of assets to shareholders? Some statutes say no, but most, including the Model Act, say yes.[15] If the statute countenances this usage, one can readily see the appeal that capital reduction has to a corporate management that is facing a negative surplus and that would have to skip a dividend payment unless something is done. Directors do not like to skip dividend payments. Shareholders grow restive or even rebellious, unfavorable comment is aroused in the press, on the street and in the lunch clubs, and the management nearly always loses points on the scoreboard of managerial competition—the stock market.

---

13. An argument is available that even in states that generally forbid the use of paid-in surplus as the basis for a dividend distribution, an exception to that prohibition should exist in the case of so-called "equalization surplus". Assume the case of a corporation that has ten shares of $10 par stock outstanding, a stated capital of $100, an earned surplus account of $100, assets of $200 in cash, and no liabilities. The book value, liquidation value and (probably) market value of each share is $20. If now the corporation issues one additional share, the purchaser may be expected to have to pay $20 for it, and the entries on the corporate books will be $10 additional to stated capital and $10 to paid-in surplus. But in this case, $10 was paid above par because each of the other outstanding shares had a claim to $10 of prior earnings. Before the issuance of the new share, the corporation could have declared a $10 dividend on each share based on earned surplus; why should it not be in a position after the issuance of the new share to pay a dividend of $10 on each of the eleven outstanding shares, even though $10 out of the total of $110 distributed would have to be charged against the $10 paid-in surplus created by the equalization payment made by the new shareholder? Neither statute nor court has thrown light in this corner, but some commentators have argued for recognition of the special situation of equalization surplus.

14. E. g., Model Act (1979) § 46 (last par.) (any "capital surplus" may be so used.)

15. Model Act (1979) § 46.

Ch. 4   REGULATION OF DISTRIBUTIONS   71

The reduction device has often been used to accommodate a dividend and the courts have not sought to prevent it.

c. *Appreciation Surplus and Unrealized Gain*

Is it permissible for a corporation's directors to revalue its assets upward, thereby increasing the surplus account, and then charge to the appreciated surplus a distribution of assets to shareholders? Surplus created through such a revaluation of assets is known as "appreciation surplus" or "revaluation surplus."

Almost all the statutes are silent on this question.[16] According to "generally accepted accounting principles," fixed assets are carried at historical cost less depreciation, and the usual accounting view is that no increment in market value should be recognized until the property is disposed of—until the gain is "realized." In general, the income tax laws proceed on a similar basis. Nonetheless, in some situations a failure to reflect an increased market value may be more dangerously misleading than the "conservative" practice of continuing to carry the purchase price.[17] And it appears increasingly that we are on the brink of developing new techniques for indexed accounting, or replacement cost accounting, to cope with the reality of inflation. To stay with simple fixed dollar accounting in an inflationary world is to measure with a shrinking yardstick.

But again, it is not inevitable that the attitude of the accounting profession is determinative for purposes of determining the legality of a shareholder distribution. If the board of directors of a corporation, or corporate counsel, decides that it would be misleading to the investing public to continue to carry assets on the balance sheet at cost after they have radically increased in value, and instructs the company's bookkeeper to write the assets up to the market value as judged by the board, the mere fact that the company's outside auditors are unhappy about the entry or even qualify their audit certificate, does not necessarily force the conclusion that the surplus created by the write up may not be legally used under the applicable corporation code as a basis for a dividend or other distribution of assets to shareholders.[18]

---

16. An exception is North Carolina, Section 55–49(e), which recognizes that there may be such revaluations.

17. Compare *Zahn v. Transamerica Corp.*, 162 F.2d 36 (2d Cir. 1947).

18. In *Randall v. Bailey*, 288 N.Y. 280, 43 N.E.2d 43 (1943), which arose under an earlier New York statute, the New York Court of Appeals upheld the legality of a shareholder distribution charged to an undivided surplus account that was

At the least, it may be expected that a present-day accountant would insist that the surplus created by a write up of assets be specially designated in the surplus accounts as "appreciation surplus" so that there is at least disclosure of the method by which the corporation put itself into compliance with the statutory legal capital scheme before making the distribution of assets to shareholders.

d. Earned Surplus

The next section discusses legal capital statutes that prescribe earned surplus as the standard for determining the legality of shareholder distributions. Earned surplus as a concept is discussed there.

e. Other Surpluses

Many kinds of transactions involving changes in the capital structure of a corporation have an impact upon the stated capital and upon surplus accounts. Surpluses created by these transactions and adjustments may either be viewed generically as "surplus", or they may be fitted into the sub-categories of surplus just reviewed, or may be further sub-classified; or, increasingly it is observable that accounting usage on the balance sheet is simply to describe the way in which the surplus was created, without seeking to categorize it. Accounting refinements have today moved far beyond the gross and clumsy conceptual tools of the legal capital statutes. The legal capital provisions are attempting to work on a watch movement with a one-inch wide screwdriver. Eventually the question must be asked whether it should either make a large investment in a set of watchmaker's tools—a dubious investment for a dubious purpose—or give up the job.

C. EARNED SURPLUS STATUTES

As accountants and other analysts have brought closer focus to bear upon the concept of balance sheet surplus, and have further asked themselves what kinds of transactions should provide a basis for distributing corporate dividends, the view has emerged increasingly that, in general, corporate dividends should be the product of enterprise earnings and, therefore, the statutory regulatory system should limit asset distributions to shareholders to situations in which the enterprise has accumulated earnings. Development of this viewpoint is in part attributable

attributable in part to a write-up of appreciated corporate assets. Both the lower court and appellate court opinions are less than satisfactory, however, and the statute involved was unusual in that it explicitly referred to the "value" of the corporate assets as a factor in determining the propriety of a distribution.

to a perception of the analytic limitations of the balance sheet surplus test. In part the argument in favor of an earned surplus test has arisen out of an increasing awareness that there are interests at stake other than those of the creditors, mainly the interest of one class of shareholders against another and the general interest of all shareholders and the market place to be accurately informed. And finally, the turn of focus from the general concept of surplus to the more restricted conception of earned surplus coincides with and is associated with a major change in perspective in the world of finance that has taken place during this century; affecting lawyers, accountants and bankers alike, earlier concentration upon static, balance sheet, asset accounting has been overtaken by a more sophisticated concern with the dynamic, ongoing, profit and loss statement, earnings flow of an enterprise. Balance sheet analysis is important, particularly when liquidity is a major concern. But sad experience with gilt edge bonds in the 20's and 30's drove home the point that ultimately enterprise debt will be paid off, if it is paid off, out of enterprise earnings. What good does it do bond holders to foreclose on several hundred miles of unprofitable rusting railroad track?

With the emergence of these newer attitudes, state corporation codes tended to move away from the general balance sheet surplus test and adopted a new approach restricting distributions to shareholders based upon earnings. In general, such statutes permit shareholder distributions only to the extent of available earned surplus and only in the absence of insolvency.

Dramatic changes were made in the Model Business Corporation Act in 1980. Those changes are reviewed in Part Three of this book. But so far no state has adopted those changes and the M.B.C.A. in substantially its 1979 form is now in effect in approximately 35 states; it is that Act which is discussed here and referred to as the 1979 Act.

The 1979 Model Business Corporation Act, as now widely adopted, purports to be an earned surplus statute of this character. In fact, however, the restraints imposed by the Act are much weaker than that term would imply. Section 45 appears to limit dividends to unreserved and unrestricted earned surplus of the corporation. But the exceptions are nearly as large as the rule.[19]

19. See Hackney, *The Financial Provisions of the Model Business Corporation Act*, 70 Harv.L.Rev. 1357 (1957). Note, however, that changes in the Act have been made in the years intervening.

The draftsmen of the 1979 Model Act felt that the earned surplus criterion could not prudently be adhered to in the special cases of distributions by extractive industry companies. Absent insolvency, corporations engaged in exploiting natural resources and holding wasting assets are permitted by the 1979 Model Act to make dividend distributions as they turn their natural resource into liquid assets.[20]

The 1979 Model Act's earned surplus standard is more fundamentally undermined by the provision authorizing "distributions from capital surplus."[21] This is a procedure for capital contraction—a reality more evident when the earlier version of the Model Act described the analogous procedure as a "distribution in partial liquidation." Distributions of corporate assets may, under the Act, be charged against a capital surplus account, if the company will not thereby be made insolvent, if it is current on its dividends on any cumulative preferred stock outstanding, if there is enough surplus (of some kind) remaining to cover the liquidating preference of the preferred stock, and if the recipients are informed that the distribution is being charged against a capital surplus account. The certificate of incorporation may grant to the board of directors the authority to make such payments, so that no shareholder approval need be sought for the distribution; otherwise, a shareholders' vote is needed. There is no requirement that the corporation exhaust its earned surplus before turning to the device of charging capital surplus; as a result, the board can, while reducing the creditors' cushion through pay-outs to shareholders, hoard a favorable earned surplus balance against the day when it might have a special use for it. There is no requirement of notice to creditors. The fact is, at this point, that the 1979 Model Act has completely forgotten about creditors, those for whom the whole statutory legal capital scheme was built.

Further, all companies subject to the Act may use capital surplus to support dividend payments on cumulative preferred stock if they have no earned surplus, assuming again that the distribution does not precipitate insolvency.[22]

Then, the 1979 Model Act explicitly makes place for the so-called "quasi-reorganization." This strange term requires a little explanation. If the only permissible statutory basis for dividend payments is earned surplus, the management has a considerable incentive to avoid making other kinds of charge against

---

20. Model Act (1979) § 45(b).

21. Model Act (1979) § 46.

22. Model Act (1979) § 46 (last par.).

"earned surplus" and, where some surplus charge must be made, to try to arrange for the charge to be made against some subcategory of "capital surplus" as defined in the statute. It would be nice, for example, if an uninsured fire loss could be charged against a paid-in surplus account, leaving the earned surplus account intact. That particular instance is denied by generally accepted accounting principles and met by the Model Act, for the definition of earned surplus makes it clear that the management will not be free to protect and immunize its earned surplus account in this fashion. But after having taken this step, Section 64 of the 1979 Act provides:

> "A corporation may, by resolution of its board of directors, apply any part or all of its capital surplus to the reduction or elimination of any deficit arising from losses, however incurred, but only after first eliminating earned surplus, if any, of the corporation by applying such losses against earned surplus and only to the extent that such losses exceed the earned surplus, if any. Each such application of capital surplus shall, to the extent thereof, effect a reduction of capital surplus."[23]

What this means is that a corporation that has distributed assets to shareholders to the full extent of its earned surplus and later develops a negative earned surplus, may then apply a portion of its capital surplus to the deficit to bring the deficit up to zero and thereafter pay out additional assets to its shareholders as soon as there are any earnings. As has been described earlier, capital surplus is not difficult to generate; a simple reduction of par or other reduction of stated capital will do it.[24] The net result of these provisions of the 1979 Model Act, therefore, is that in addition to permitting direct distribution of capital surplus a corporation may, through use of capital surplus as an offset to deficit, pay out all current earnings to its shareholders despite a deficit in the earned surplus account prior to the offset. Thus, by going through the right moves, capital surplus, *or even stated capital,* can be set off against a corporate deficit. That is a so called "quasi-reorganization." The operational consequence is precisely antithetical to the creditor protection purposes of the stated capital scheme in general—and to the earned surplus standard in particular.

See also the discussion below of reacquisition of shares. And once again, note that the Model Act has recently been radically revamped, as discussed in Part Three.

23. Model Act (1979) § 70 (third par.).   24. Model Act (1979) § 70 (first par.).

D. SURPLUS OR NET PROFITS STATUTES

A corporation law provision adopted in New Jersey in 1904 provided that "the directors of a corporation shall not make dividends except from its surplus, or from the net profits arising from the business, nor shall it divide, withdraw, or in any way pay to the stockholders, or any of them, any part of the capital stock of such corporation, or reduce its capital stock except as authorized by law." [25] To the extent that this language is comprehensible at all, it appears to draw a distinction between surplus and net profits arising from the business. The New Jersey court accepted the distinction and sought to provide meaning for both.[26] Statutory variants in other states have included "surplus profits . . . [nor] . . . divide capital stock"; "surplus profit, nor divide . . . capital stock"; "surplus or net profits . . . nor divide . . . capital stock". It is very difficult to tell what any of these statutes may mean and very little judicial gloss has been put upon them. On the whole, these statutes bear with them all the problems of the balance sheet surplus statutes, compounded by their own special verbal obscurity.

E. CURRENT EARNINGS STATUTES: NIMBLE DIVIDENDS

The law of stated capital and dividend restriction is the product of a continuing conflict between an urge to protect creditors by a simplistic mechanical rule, on the one hand, and, on the other, the pressures of business reality. Business reality won a big round in the development of the concept of so-called "nimble dividends".

As a practical business matter, a corporation that has accumulated large deficits and has a heavy burden of unpaid debt has no prospect of obtaining further credit unless new equity capital can be attracted to the enterprise. In turn, there is no hope of attracting additional equity capital unless there is some prospect that dividends will be paid. The old deficits must not, therefore, be allowed to block future dividends. The obvious—

---

25. Note here again the classical use of "capital stock" to mean "assets" in the statutory phrase "to pay to the stockholders . . . the capital stock." Is the meaning the same in the following line?

26. *Goodnow v. American Writing Paper Co.*, 73 N.J.Eq. 692, 69 A. 1014 (Ct.Err. & App.1908). The revisers of the recent New Jersey corporation law intended to eliminate the possibility of declaring dividends from "historical" net earnings while there is a capital deficit. Comment to N.J.Bus.Corp. Act § 14A:7–14, noting that such a practice was possible under the old statute, N.J.Rev.Stat. § 14:8–19.

perhaps the only—way out is to arrange matters so that dividends can be paid if the enterprise earns a current profit from its operations, even though the deficits piled up in previous years have not yet been eliminated. The Delaware corporation statute in 1927 took the lead in authorizing that result. As recently amended, the Delaware act permits a corporation to pay dividends "either (1) out of its surplus", as defined, "or (2) in case there shall be no such surplus, out of its net profits for the fiscal year in which the dividend is declared and/or the preceding fiscal year." [27]

The effect of the Delaware approach, followed in several other states as well, is thus to go even further than the 1979 Model Act provisions just described. Under the Delaware act, dividends—aptly called "nimble dividends"—may be paid out in any fiscal year in which, or in the year following a year in which, there are earnings, in spite of the presence of a deficit and without the Model Act requirement that the deficit first be written off against available capital surplus. The Delaware act makes it possible for a deficit company, deeply under water, to distribute its earnings to equity holders with respect to a fiscal year in which they are earned and thereby to continue indefinitely the deficit condition of the balance sheet. The statutory authorization of nimble dividends makes overt and explicit the usually unadmitted reality—the abandonment of all effort to protect creditors through stated capital machinery. The Delaware provision does, however, nod in the direction of protecting the preferred shareholder by forbidding distribution of current earnings to common shareholders if the value of the corporation's net assets is not at least equal to the stated capital of the outstanding preferred shares.[28]

Accounting problems are to be expected under nimble dividend provisions, since the privilege extended by these sections is wholly dependent upon the determination of net income for a specific one year period.

F. SHARE REACQUISITION BY THE ISSUER

It must be recalled that the creditor's desire to restrict asset distributions to shareholders is very much broader than keeping down dividend payments. *Any* transfer of corporate assets to equity holders, if not matched by an equivalent pay-in of other assets, has the effect of reducing the total corporate asset pool available for the payment of creditors. Therefore a purchase by the corporation of its outstanding stock, or a retirement of pre-

---

27. Delaware General Corp., § 170.

28. Why not the liquidating preference instead of the stated capital?

ferred stock, or a bargain sale of corporate assets to shareholders, or a cancellation of indebtedness owing by shareholders, or a payment of assets to shareholders as compensation is equally objectionable from the creditor's standpoint.

Earlier discussion dealt with the appropriate way to handle entries to stated capital and surplus accounts to reflect share reacquisitions and "treasury share" transactions. Still to be considered is whether under the applicable statute the purchase by the issuing company of its own outstanding shares, and corresponding distribution of corporate assets to a shareholder, is itself restricted by the statutory restraints on dividends, and with what results. The entire topic of share reacquisition, treasury shares, resale, retirement and the like is technical and sorely vexed under the legal capital statutes, and generalization is not reliable. But it is important that the character of the problems be recognized.

Some older statutes do not cover the matter at all, and seem to restrict "dividends" only. More modern statutes, such as the 1979 Model Act, are at least clear in requiring that the pay-out to the shareholder to buy in his shares can only be made if there is an appropriate surplus account available to be charged. But then what happens?

Suppose a corporation has assets of $2,000 in cash, $500 in liabilities, 10 shares outstanding with a par value of $100 each, a stated capital of $1,000 and a surplus account (earned, to make it easy) of $500. It now buys in one share for $100 and pays $100 out to the selling shareholder, the board of directors directing that the share be carried as a "treasury share". The company's cash is reduced to $1,900; stated capital is unaffected; an accounting entry restricts the surplus account by $100, but leaves its total at $500; and a separate line item reading "Less shares held in the treasury $100" is deducted from the shareholders' equity part of the balance sheet. Then, at a later time, the board by resolution retires the share to the status of authorized but unissued stock, or cancels it. Upon the retirement or cancellation, the share is obviously no longer "outstanding", and the stated capital is changed by (in this case) the stated capital attributable to it, $100; the restriction of $100 on the surplus account is removed, the total remaining at $500; and the line item on treasury shares disappears. The end consequence of these steps is that $100 has been paid out to a shareholder, yet the company's surplus account is just where it was at the beginning, available to buy in other shares or pay out dividends. Expressed another way, stated capital has been reduced by direct payment of assets to shareholders—precisely the result the stated capital engine was supposed to avoid as a protection to creditors—and this reduction has been effectuated without even the shareholder vote or notice to shareholders usually prescribed by the statutes for reducing capital. Insolvency, of course, always remains as a legal barrier to further pay-out to shareholders.

The transaction just outlined is, of course, greatly simplified. As an exercise, it is worth considering under various kinds of statutes the effects of the introduction of elements such as these: The aggregate stated capital is greater than par times the number of shares outstanding. The price paid for the share is less (or greater) than the par (or the stated capital attributable to it). The company has other surpluses besides earned surplus. The company later "reissues" the treasury at a price less (or greater) than the par (or than the stated capital attributed to it) (or than the price at which it was purchased). The company has several classes of shares outstanding with (without) separate stated capital and surplus accounts. Etc., etc.

From a technical standpoint the legal capital statutes are a shambles in their treatment of share reacquisitions. From a substantive standpoint, share reacquisition creates another major perforation in the protective wall supposedly built for the creditor by the legal capital statutes.

Intellectual command of reacquisition procedures is of frequent practical importance to the practicing corporate lawyer in dealing with closely held corporations where it is common for shareholders to enter into share repurchase agreements effective upon the death or retirement of a major shareholder.[29]

See particularly in Part Three the effort of the 1980 changes to Model Business Corporation Act to eliminate completely the concept of treasury shares.

G. THE CLASS STRUGGLE: CLASSES OF SHARES

Reference has several times been made here to the special problems raised by legal capital statutes where a corporation has two or more classes of shares outstanding. As a simple illustration of the problem, consider the case under a balance sheet surplus statute of a corporation that, having a zero surplus, issues 100 shares of $10 par preferred stock for $15 per share, thus creating a stated capital attributable to the preferred of $1,000 and a paid-in surplus of $500. If the board of directors now undertakes to pay out a $500 dividend to the common shareholders, based on

---

29. See Part Two, Transactions 13, 14, 15 and 16.

a charge against the newly created paid-in surplus, it can be readily seen that the preferred shareholder will not be happy to see the money he has just paid in go out to the common shareholders. The same kind of problem would also arise if the par value of one class of shares were reduced, thus creating a reduction surplus, and the board then charged that reduction surplus as the basis for a dividend payment to another class of shares.

In point of fact, a little reflection will reveal that separate classes of shares can be put at loggerheads by almost any transaction that involves adjustments of stated capital accounts and surplus accounts. An interesting aspect of the evolution of stated capital machinery is that the modern statutes have gradually come to recognize this conflict of interests among classes of shares. For example, some statutes require that shareholders vote by class to reduce capital. A New York court has held that a reduction of stated capital attributable to common shares was such a serious event that it gives rise to an appraisal remedy in favor of an objecting preferred shareholder under a statute that provided appraisal rights to preferred shareholders who are "adversely affected" by an amendment to the certificate of incorporation.[30] Delaware, as mentioned earlier, restricts the availability of nimble dividends to situations where the corporation's net assets are at least equal to the stated capital of the preferred. The Model Act permits assets distributions to common shareholders but only so long as the company's net assets exceed the aggregate liquidating preference of the preferred—which is sensible enough, but which drops entirely the facade that par has any real significance.

Still, even the most modern legal capital statutes have only started to enter upon the problem of interclass conflict and have not gone far in specifying the accounting procedures to be followed in multi-class capital structures. Balance sheets carry separate stated capital accounts for separate classes, but treatment of surplus accounts is varied and uncertain. If a stated capital scheme were to be rigorously worked out so as to be coherent intellectually (whatever its substantive desirability) it would maintain a careful separation in the capital and surplus accounting for each class of shares. The point is faintly recognized in a few statutes, such as those of North Carolina and Ohio, but no statutory draftsman has carried the analysis through with determination and consistency—so complex does it become, and so inconsequential are the marginal returns. But it may be hazarded that litigation under legal capital statutes today is more

30. *Matter of Kinney*, 279 N.Y. 423, 15 N.E.2d 645 (1939).

Ch. 4   REGULATION OF DISTRIBUTIONS   81

likely to arise at the instance of a discomfitted shareholder of a multi-class corporation than at the instance of a creditor.

H. LIABILITIES FOR DISTRIBUTIONS VIOLATING THE LEGAL CAPITAL STATUTES

What are the consequences if an asset distribution of some kind, whether by dividend or other technique, is made to shareholders in violation of the applicable statutory restriction?[31]

As a generalization, the statutes now specifically impose liability upon directors who vote for or assent to a dividend or other distribution or stock repurchase if the action violates the statute or restrictions in the articles of incorporation. In the Model Act prototype, the liability runs to the corporation. In particular jurisdictions, statutory or case law may identify other possible plaintiffs. There are few reported cases, however, and the statutes generally provide little or no guidance on questions of remedial procedure.

Also, the statutes usually contain significant limitations on the directors' liability. Generally, a director's reliance upon the corporate financial statements, figures provided by an accountant, or reports of the chief executive or the financial officers of the corporation exonerates him from liability. Directors who are required to make payment to the corporation ordinarily have a statutory right of subrogation against shareholders who received the distributions knowing of their illegality; such directors also have rights of contribution from their guilty confreres.

What of the measure of liability? Older statutes sometimes provided that the directors should be liable for all debts to creditors of the corporation if improper distributions were made to shareholders.[32] But modern statutes typically narrow the liability to the amount of the illegal distribution, or to the amount of the unpaid debt, whichever is lower.

The question of who, if anyone, has a remedy against the directors raises another cluster of questions unsatisfactorily handled by the statutes. Is the remedy limited to creditors? If so, to what kinds of creditors? That is, must the creditor's claim be liquidated and matured, must he be a judgment creditor whose

---

31. No doubt, absent statute, a director's general duty of care includes a duty not to declare unlawful dividends. However, the Model Act some years ago codified the director's duty in this area, Model Act (1979) § 48, and this provision has been widely adopted in most new corporation law revisions.

32. See, for example, former Del. Gen.Corp.Law § 172.

execution against the corporation has been returned *nulla bona*, must he have been a creditor at a time prior to the illegal distribution to shareholders, etc. May the complainant bring an action to enforce the full liability of the director (whatever it may be) or may he sue only for the amount of his personal debt claim? May a trustee in bankruptcy of the corporation enforce the remedy, and if so, is he acting on behalf of all the creditors or in his capacity as successor to the rights of the corporation? What kinds of releases or waivers from whom would constitute a defense to the director? May a shareholder, or a shareholder of a particular class, pursue the director, either directly, or on the theory that the director's action has placed the shareholder in jeopardy of having to respond to creditors. And if a shareholder may bring such a suit does he do so in derivative form on behalf of the corporation, or is the action a personal action of the shareholder? Most of these questions have never been answered, nor indeed even publicly asked.

Apart from the director's liability, what about the liability of the shareholder who receives the illegal distribution? Most of the remedial questions just raised in connection with enforcement of the director's liability reappear—and in a more complex form—in the case of an effort to enforce liabilities against shareholders. How, for example, does a qualified plaintiff, whoever that may be, obtain a judgment of liability against shareholders that is binding upon all shareholders of the company or, at least, provides a basis for collateral estoppel in subsequent lawsuits against other shareholders? What now of the question of contribution as among shareholders? May the corporation sue the shareholders to recover the assets improperly distributed? Does the liability for the illegal distribution run with the stock or remain attached to the person who received the dividend? And his estate? Typically, of course, the recipient shareholder has no way to know at the time he receives the dividend check whether the dividend was properly declared or not. Does that make any difference to his liability? It is an interesting line of speculation to contemplate what would be involved in unwinding the tax consequences of an illegal dividend payment to thousands of shareholders in a large publicly held company.[33]

Viewed as a whole, one is forced to conclude that the enormously complex and technical machine of legal capital goes through an extraordinary amount of grinding and clanking to produce, at the end, very little. It is difficult not to be reminded of the

---

33. And recapturing from the government the portion of the distribution it collected as tax?

popular Black Box toy that features a switch which when turned on, activates a motor, that powers a small mechanical hand, that emerges from the Box, and turns off the switch.

Nonetheless the almost complete absence of cases imposing liability on directors or shareholders does not mean that the question of possible liability is a dead issue. Boards of directors do not wish to undertake personal risks needlessly and it is normal therefore for them to look to the corporation's legal counsel to design a distribution transaction in a way that removes all doubt of its legality. Despite the absence of litigation attesting to the reality of the risk, lawyers who do corporate work must continue to have a working knowledge of the way in which the statutory scheme operates—and how to thread his way through the maze to the desired result. As a practical matter, virtually any distribution to shareholders can be done legally by the experienced practitioner so long as the company is not insolvent. But it may not be legally possible without an expensive formal shareholders' meeting, a delaying notice procedure, or a sometimes risky exposure to the blackmailing propensities of a cranky shareholder who has a statutory right to demand a vote by class.

This chapter will be considerably clearer to the reader who later works his way through Part Two of this book. Part Two sets out a sequence of illustrative corporate financial transactions, discusses the related accounting entries and reviews the permissibility of shareholder distributions under different types of statutes. An earnest attempt has been made to present the examples there in a way that is comprehensible to the reader who has not had a prior exposure to accounting. Part Two provides an avenue to a practical understanding of the material in this chapter and of the way in which the statutes actually work.

Chapter V

A PRELIMINARY EVALUATION OF LEGAL CAPITAL STATUTES

What has preceded has been largely descriptive of the legal capital scheme. It is now both possible and in order to ask how well it works.

First, the legal capital machinery makes only the most marginal effort to protect groups or classes of shareholders from each other despite their often conflicting interests.

As for creditors, the system makes no attempt to ward off two of their main worries—incurrence by the corporation of additional debt liabilities and creation of secured or senior debt claims. The system does purport to guarantee that shareholders have put something into the corporate pot and that they will not redistribute corporate assets to themselves without first protecting the corporate creditors. Does it work at all?

We have no systematic empiric studies. It is a safe generalization, however, that the statutory legal capital machinery provides little or no significant protection to creditors of corporations, and that they, knowing this, do not rely upon it. They instead seek to achieve their protection through other means, some of which are discussed in the next chapter. The legal capital schemes embedded in the nation's corporation acts are inherently doomed to a low level of effectiveness (perhaps even zero). Some of the reasons are:

1. The system is analytically incomplete in the same sense that a protective encircling wall is useless if not closed throughout its perimeter. A balance sheet surplus figure, and even an earned surplus figure, is the product of dozens of judgmental accounting decisions. If one were seriously interested in using surplus accounts as an on-off switch for certain transactions, he would inevitably find himself involved in full scale regulation of corporate accounting systems, just as state utility commissions have found that pursuit of the goal of fair rate regulation has inexorably transformed them into legislatures of accountancy and tribunals of bookkeeping. Without the development of a jurisprudence of accounting to support the statutory legal capital scheme, the system is inherently incomplete and haphazard in its operation.
2. Given that the original purpose of the legal capital scheme was to protect creditors from transactions that

benefit shareholders but prejudice creditors, it is at least odd that the statutes should hand over all the control switches and levers to the shareholders and those whom the shareholders elect, the board of directors. The statutes are detailed and explicit about the procedures and steps to be taken in order to effect changes in the capital structure of a corporation, but the decision-making power is always vested in the board or the shareholders, or the two together; in no case do the statutes provide for participation by the creditors, consultation with the creditors, or even notice to the creditors.

3. A corporation's "legal capital" is a wholly arbitrary number, unrelated in any way to any economic facts that are relevant to a creditor. No one who is considering whether to lend money today to General Motors Corporation is interested in knowing what, or whether, a shareholder paid for his shares 50 years ago, or what was the par value that was stamped on the stock certificate that he received at that time. Given the existence of the legal capital system, the creditor would prefer to see a high stated capital figure rather than a low one, but from his standpoint the stated capital is simply a fortuitously derived number that could as well have been taken from a telephone directory as from a series of unconnected and irrelevant historical events.

4. Similar to the next preceding point is the fact that the entire system has no fundamental "why" to it. There is no reason why a reasonable man would take the number called stated capital and use it as a measure for limiting distributions to equity investors. At the same time, the kinds of things the creditor is interested to know and does want to police—some of which are mentioned in the next chapter—are left unasked and unattended by the legal capital system.

5. The statutory legal system is inherently deficient for want of a time dimension. Ancient, present and future economic events are all scrambled together without regard to their differing current economic significance. In computing the availability of "surplus", a debt due in twenty years is treated no differently from a debt due next week; to a lender it makes a lot of difference. For purposes of the statute, cash and other quick assets are treated exactly the same as assets that would

take years to liquidate for purposes of paying debts; a prospective creditor sees it differently. It is assumed by the statute that creditors of today and tomorrow care about sales of stock made years before. They don't. And so forth.

6. Efforts to apply the system in context of sophisticated modern corporate finance produce appalling, even revolting, conceptualistic debate. In the manner of medieval theologians at their worst, lawyers and accountants hold up (and are forced to hold up) sensible economic transactions while they wrangle over the appropriate stated capital treatment for stock subscriptions, agreements to purchase stock, mergers, treasury share cancellation, retirement conversions, stock warrant purchases, option exercises, stock discounts, liquidation preferences, allocation of "capital" among classes, series, and individual shares, etc., etc., endlessly. No one is to be faulted for this pointless expenditure of the energies of intelligent men and women; it is the inevitable, and unresolvable, by-product of the primitiveness and essential irrelevance of the legal capital system.

7. Whether one views it as a blessing or a deficiency of the existing statutory systems, it is at least a fact that the corporation acts do not pursue the implementation of their own scheme with any real seriousness.

—Statutes that provide for nimble dividends admit overtly that companies with heavily impaired legal capital may still make payments to shareholders. The Model Corporation Act goes almost as far when it permits deficits to be written off against capital surplus.

—Where dividend payments may be made to shareholders and charged to paid-in surplus, the statute offers a direct invitation to the lawyer architect to design a capital structure using low par stock and creating large paid-in surplus accounts —an invitation that is usually accepted.

—Many of the statutes permit payments to shareholders to be charged against reduction surplus, a form of surplus that is usually easy for the board to generate. The Model Act through its provisions allowing shareholder distributions to be charged against capital surplus explicitly directs attention to this device.

—The statutes leave an open trap door for corporate assets to go out to shareholders to buy in their stock.

—All of the legal capital statutes vest in the fox the control of the machinery for protecting the chickens.

—The statutes display no interest in providing serious remedies and they are a procedural wasteland. Almost no instances can be found where liability was in fact imposed either on directors or on shareholders for violations of the stated capital scheme.

—When a certificate of dissolution is filed with respect to a corporation, the entire stated capital machinery is instantaneously suspended. Of course it is true that the corporation acts call for payment of creditors during the process of corporate liquidation and impose liability on the directors if that mandate is disregarded. But once the dissolution certificate has been filed, following a dissolution vote by shareholders under the local procedure, asset distributions may be made to the corporation's shareholders with no further regard for the statutory stated capital provisions. It is at least peculiar that a system designed to create a protective cushion to protect creditors against distributions to shareholders should automatically cut out of operation in precisely the situation where massive distributions to shareholders are most likely to occur—in precisely the situation, indeed, of *Wood v. Dummer*, the progenitor of the entire system.

—The most persuasive evidence of the quintessential triviality of the system, however, lies in the fact that any corporation lawyer of moderate skill can nearly always arrange things (perhaps at some expense and after some procedural dance figures) so as to make a lawful shareholder distribution so long as insolvency is not the immediate consequence. Advance planning and precautionary steps by the lawyer can also go very far to prevent the legal capital question from ever arising for his corporate client.

8. It may be, though difficult to prove, that the legal capital system has some unfortunate side effects. It

can operate as a trap. Many lawyers are not sufficiently familiar with the arcana of legal capital to recognize a related problem when it does arise, and warn their client accordingly. Other practitioners, more sensitized but without the experience or ingenuity to design around the system, sometimes feel compelled to advise their clients that a transaction that is economically sensible cannot be lawfully consummated even though no genuine economic risk to creditors exists. In particular, the legal capital system may operate to prevent the performance of stock buy-out agreements in close corporations when one of the partners of the enterprise has died or withdrawn; in such cases the economic consequences upon the estate, upon the surviving widow, upon the withdrawing partner, and upon those remaining in the enterprise can be severe. Finally, while class-voting has its merits, it is also true that a skillful corporate lawyer representing a special stock class in a multiclass corporation can use the legal capital class voting requirement as a stick-up gun at the head of the board of directors and majority holders who are seeking to restructure the corporation's capital accounts to the advantage of the enterprise, its creditors and its community. Stated capital procedures should not facilitate extortion of one class of shares by another but they can.

Altogether, it must be recognized that the machinery of legal capital established by our corporation acts suffers from a number of deficiencies. Is there nothing to be said for it? Do creditors receive from the system some degree of practical protection despite its analytic frailty? To make such a case persuasive is impossible but perhaps something can be put together.

The best argument suggesting that the system has some protective consequence for creditors is the argument historical, cultural, and psychological. For nearly 150 years it has been thought important that an enterprise have something called its "capital" and the concept has acquired its own independent aura of respectability, whatever its actual significance to real creditors in real business situations. Bankers and other businessmen view a "thin" stated capital with suspicion, and it is—in some sense—considered to be a mark of fiscal probity and sound management to have a substantial stated capital on the right-hand side of the corporate balance sheet.[1] Deep in the consciousness

---

1. This point is wholly different from the wise creditor's insistence that there be a substantial exposure of equity assets in the enterprise;

of the American businessman, lawyer, accountant and banker is the general idea that distributions to shareholders are not supposed to be made "out of" capital. Everybody knows that ways are available to design around statutory restrictions; but the restrictions themselves are no more than a reflection of the more general principle. The statutory provisions on stated capital and distributions to equity investors are expressions of a general norm of behavior to which the business community subscribes in principle. For this reason, among others, it is very unlikely that the statutory provisions will be repealed or significantly amended. (But see Part Three).

Perhaps it may be argued that the statutes hang today in precisely the right balance. They announce a general and salutary principle which commands wide assent; but they are so feebly constructed and loosely enforced that a corporation's financial managers, lawyers, and accountants can move as they wish when it is necessary to do so, as everyone agrees one should be able to do. If this line of thought is valid, creditors do, in some general sense, benefit from the statutory scheme to the extent that the stated capital provisions contribute to an atmosphere in which corporate managements psychologically feel themselves inhibited from distributing assets to shareholders indiscriminately.[2]

A second line of speculation, unprovable, is that the statutory provisions may have a degree of actual operating impact upon corporations of the medium size range. Those in control of the incorporated small enterprise typically manage its, and their, economic lives with little or no awareness of or regard for the niceties of procedure spelled out in legal capital provisions. Large public enterprises on the other hand, can draw on lawyers and other professionals who see to it that wide flexibility of corporate financial action and decisions is maintained while scrupulously observing the statutory mandates. But it may be that the managers of a medium sized incorporated enterprise may be sufficiently conscious of statutory and regulatory requirements to be affected in their behavior, and yet not served with sufficient continuity or professionality of advice to enable them to control their own destinies in the legal capital thicket. And perhaps the medium sized corporation is the one that offers

that exposure arises out of the entire equity account, not how it is divided among stated capital and various kinds of surpluses.

2. But at best the argument is terribly thin. Salary payments and other fringe benefit pay-outs to executive shareholders are not affected by the legal capital statutes at all. And the real determinants of dividend payment levels are tax considerations, the board's perception of the corporation's working capital needs, and the estimate of the stock by the market.

the greatest problem for the creditor; there he has not the close personal contact that grounds his extension of credit to the incorporated barbershop nor has he the institutional protections that back up a credit to General Motors.

But whatever may be argued at these general and abstract levels one basic bit of evidence almost compels the conclusion that creditors do not gain very much from the system. That evidence is the almost total lack of interest that creditors show in this subject. Creditors' groups do not try to lobby changes into the corporation acts to tighten up the obvious loopholes. They do not clamor for participation in the procedures by which corporations shuffle about their capital accounts. And, on the affirmative side, creditors have, where they have cared to, gone ahead to develop, negotiate for, and put into practice genuinely effective techniques for achieving the purposes that the statutory legal capital provisions purport to address. The next chapter takes a look at these privately ordered techniques, not only to see how the job is done, but also because they provide light on the question of the efficacy of the statutory machinery. The next chapter shows the kind of control structure that must be constructed if one wishes to pursue seriously the objective of the statutory schemes. It throws into contrasting and visible relief the seismic faults that inhere in the statutory legal capital scheme.

Chapter VI

CREDITOR PROTECTION OUTSIDE THE LEGAL CAPITAL STATUTES

How does the modern creditor of a corporation actually go about protecting himself against the risks outlined in Chapter I?

A. THE GENERAL TRADE CREDITOR

It may happen that a business enterprise may occasionally buy an automobile on an installment payment basis like any other end consumer. But the typical creditor of an incorporated enterprise is not an installment creditor but either a trade creditor who has provided trade goods or services to the corporation or an institutional or finance creditor, such as a bank. The institutional or finance creditor is discussed later.

What does the general trade creditor do to try to maximize the chances that his billings will be paid? The main answer is that he stays alert. Like the price of freedom (and the price of tyranny), eternal vigilance is the price of successful credit management. The credit manager's main protection is to stay close to the situation, to know his debtor, to spot the slow downs in payment that are the telltale signs of drying up of working capital, to put prudent limits on the amount of credit extended to each trade purchaser, to clear checks immediately, to take instantaneous action, perhaps legal action, when a delinquency is spotted, to badger and cajole the delinquent debtor tirelessly, to see to it that when the next payment is made it does not go to other creditors, etc.

The credit manager has a number of things going for him, and a number of tools available to him that upgrade his assignment from the impossible to the merely difficult.

National professional credit agencies, such as Dun & Bradstreet, can provide him much information rapidly and at relatively small cost about a customer's liquidity and record of timely payment. Modern telecommunications and the computer afford the credit manager today almost instantaneous information on check clearances, bank balances, and the like, whether in or out of his own local area. Regionalization, and regionalization of economic interests, were characteristic of nineteenth century America. Much of the development of commercial law, and some of the development of corporation law, in the last century were attributable to regional differentiations. In a rapidly developing, erratic and wide open entrepreneurial economy, shareholder investors, and particularly bank investors, tended to be urban and tended to be Eastern. The inevitable division of interest between the long-term player and the short-term player—between shareholders and bondholders on one hand and trade creditors on the other—often tended to be a division as well between outsiders and locals.

The economic conflict between outside interests and local interests was a major theme in the evolution of American law in the nineteenth century, occurring in many guises and contexts, including the long contest over federal diversity jurisdiction, the concept of federal common law and *Swift v. Tyson*, state legislation providing liberal homestead exemptions for local debtors, struggles over the rights of *bona fide* purchasers of goods and holders in due course of financial paper, the rejection of the English doctrine of the floating charge on inventory and receivables, the federal doctrine of irrebuttable recitations in municipal bonds, and the like. In the 20th century, by contrast, relative homogenization of the national economy, the development of major financial and industrial centers scattered throughout the nation, physical and cultural mobility, and the emergence of instantaneous communications, have virtually eliminated the economic regionalism of America's past. A supplier can do business anywhere in the country and draw upon a nationwide intelligence network to help him assess whether to extend credit to the prospective purchaser.

The relative stability of modern patterns of business and of business enterprises is also of immeasurable help to the credit manager. Except for businesses that do deal primarily with the transient consumer public passing by their doors, most enterprises build up a central core of regular customers with whom they have had experience and about whom they usually know a great deal. In turn, to a regular customer his regular supplier is an important person; the customer is generally satisfied with the supplier's goods or services and with his prices; the customer has some bargaining position with his supplier and can from time to time ask for and be confident of receiving special favors; and the customer knows that if he does not pay his bills to his supplier a valuable resource will be converted into a hostile voice that will pass the word through the commercial intelligence network that the customer is in economic trouble—a report that will almost instantly dry up other sources of credit. The credit manager who is dealing with a newly formed enterprise often does not have this confidence of experience; a new enterprise may therefore find trade credit less readily available to it.

Other institutional arrangements also serve to protect the trade creditor. For example, the creditor may send out bills that are due 30 days after the billing date, but on which a discount will be given if paid within 10 days. In effect, the trade creditor becomes a banker after 10 days and charges interest on his advance to his customer. That interest charge will not make the creditor's fortune; but if his customer is any kind of a businessman, and adequately liquid, he will be moved by the discount incentive to avoid the interest charge by paying his bills promptly. If he does not, the trade creditor has at least passed along to his customer a portion of the creditor's cost of having his capital tied up in the account receivable plus the administrative costs of paying his credit manager to hound the debtor. The discounted bill system also provides the credit manager with a built-in system of small craft warning. Since no rational businessman who has sufficient funds at his disposal will forego the opportunity to take the discount, as soon as the credit manager spots a customer who is not taking his discounts he will smell trouble and start enquiry.

Then there are the tax laws. Business enterprises know that from time to time they will wind up with a sour account and have to absorb the loss for an unpaid bill; their accountants allow for this through the creation of "reserves" for bad debt losses. When a loss is actually sustained, the United States Treasury, and any local jurisdiction that has an income tax law applicable to the creditor, split the loss with him by allowing him to deduct it as a business expense.

As may be seen even from this brief sketch, the real world of the trade creditor and his credit manager stands in remarkable contrast to the overall concept and set of assumptions that underlie the legal capital provisions of corporation acts. The small creditor's real concerns are at very close range and in an immediate time frame. They have nothing to do with stated capital accounts. The trade creditor measures his world in days and hours; his concern with ancient business history is minimal; his regard for subtleties of balance sheet accounting is almost non-existent. He wants cash, he wants it promptly, he does not much care where else the cash may have gone, and he will act immediately in one institutional way or another if he is not paid. Of course the creditor would be pleased if he should be told by a lawyer that he may be able to sue a shareholder of a bankrupt debtor corporation on the ground that the shareholder had at an earlier time received an asset distribution that did not conform with the stated capital provisions of the local corporation act: any port in a storm, and any remedy is better than no remedy.

But the trade creditor is certainly not looking to that resort in his daily business. Usually, too, the creditor would prefer simply to write off the bad debt rather than spend time and money pursuing a "no good" account. It is interesting to recall again that there are virtually no modern cases reported where creditors, or bankruptcy trustees, have successfully pursued the avenue of forcing shareholders to disgorge distributions. Perhaps this is because corporate shareholders and their lawyers are able, almost at will, to design distributions to equity holders in a legal way. Or perhaps the remedy of litigation is usually too complex or expensive for the gains to be achieved. Whatever the facts may be (and we do not really know) it is clear that the stated capital machinery is not in fact a significant part of the trade creditor's armory.

B. THE FINANCE OR INSTITUTIONAL CREDITOR

Finance creditors of incorporated enterprises may for convenience be considered to fall into two general categories: commercial (or short term) creditors and investment (or long term) creditors. Typical of the former are banks that extend revolving lines of short term credit to commercial enterprises; typical of the latter are holders of bond and debenture issues. Under modern practice, a bank might appear in either role, since some long term bank loans and bank loan agreements are functionally almost indistinguishable from short duration bond and debenture issues. The long term creditor investor is considered later in these pages.

1. The Commercial Creditor

How does the short term commercial lender go about the business of protecting himself against the risks of non-payment by his debtor?

Anyone who has ever borrowed money from a bank knows the two major answers. First, the bank insists upon full disclosure of the economic situation of the borrower and conducts an investigation of his economic resources. Unless the bank is satisfied that the borrower has both the resources for repayment and the reputation for repayment, the loan is simply refused, giving rise to the canard that the only people who can borrow money from a bank are those who do not need it. Second, unlike the trade creditor, the bank will often insist upon security or collateral of some kind. The collateral may take the form of a mortgage of real estate, or pledge of securities or other readily saleable chattels, or, under modern statutes and practice a pledge of accounts receivable, the classic collateral of the lending factor. Unsecured open lines of credit are of course provided by banks, too, but the lender reserves these for the well-established and well known enterprise, and to limit the bank's exposure (while shading the interest rate upward) the bank will usually require that the borrowing enterprise maintain substantial balances in its account with the bank—balances that add to the bank's deposits and are at all times available to be set off by the bank against the borrower's indebtedness.

Where the incorporated enterprise is not yet well established, or is lightly funded, or is closely held, the bank will usually insist upon another form of collateral that, in effect, eliminates much of the significance of the corporate form. The bank will insist that the directors, shareholders, or other persons in interest, become co-makers or endorsers of the corporation's note so that their individual assets become liable for payment of the corporation's debt to the bank.

With increase in the amount of the loan, or lengthening of the time for payment, the bank or other commercial lender begins to think of additional commitments it would like to extract from the debtor corporation. As this occurs, the commercial lender begins to act more and more like the long term investor creditor, and a bank loan agreement comes increasingly to resemble an indenture of the kind discussed below.

When to these protective measures taken by the commercial lender there are added the techniques of surveillance used by the trade creditor, the availability of the national credit intelligence network, and the usual strong desire of the borrower to preserve its credit standing formidable arrays of defensive arrangements can be constructed by the lender, and usually are. They do not always work. Like everyone else, banks and other commercial lenders sometimes get stuck on a bad credit. But certainly their protections against bad deals do not lie in the legal capital machinery of the corporation acts, nor do they rely upon those provisions, nor do they seek to enforce them. To the eye of the current lender, it is wholly irrelevant whether shareholders in years past did or did not pay par value for their stock, as is the entire question of the structure of the company's legal capital accounts. And if the commercial lender is worried about the risk of corporate asset distributions to equity investors, it does not look to the corporation statutes for protection but attacks the problem directly and effectively, as discussed below.

2. The Investment Creditor and His Contract—The Corporate Indenture

The investment creditor—one who extends a large amount of credit for a substantial period of time to an incorporated enterprise—wheels into place for his protection the Long Tom of corporate finance, the bond or debenture indenture, or a loan agreement that is substantially equivalent to it. A century of experience has gone into the development of this awesome engine, and though in the process it has become gargantuan and slow footed, its design is subtle, its range is great, its fire power is devastating, and its boiler plate armor is impenetrable.

No attempt can be made here to conduct a full tour through a modern indenture dreadnaught or its more compact or pocket version, the triple riveted bank loan agreement. But it is worth pausing to note what kinds of things are in it and, in particular, to see how it handles the problem of regulating distributions to shareholders.

a. Structure

A corporate indenture is a contract entered into between the corporate borrower and the lender (or many coequal lenders) through their representative, the "trustee". The loan may be a secured loan, in which case the indenture will contain elaborate provisions concerning the management and handling of the properties being pledged or mortgaged. If the security is real property, the pieces of credit paper issued "under" the indenture are called "bonds"; if there is no security pledged, or chattels are pledged, the instruments are called "debentures"; both bonds and debentures are in essence simply promissory notes, but all gussied up.

An indenture has two major parts, divided by a great hinge. The first part spells out all the things that, after much negotiation, the borrowing company has obligated itself to do, and many things it has obligated itself not to do; this part imposes the will of the lender upon many aspects of the conduct of the enterprise. Any substantial breach of any of these covenants by the debtor corporation constitutes, by the terms of the indenture, an "event of default". Upon the occurrence of such an event of default, the lender, or trustee, may, according to the terms of the indenture, accelerate the entire debt, step into control of the enterprise and take all sorts of drastic action to see to its own payment.[1] The section of the indenture specifying the events of de-

---

[1]. In fact, of course, launching of this massive remedial onslaught will likely trigger off counter-action by other creditors or the corporate debtor and precipitate all parties into a corporate reorgan-

fault is the hinge of the document. The balance of the contract relates to the time period following an event of default. The functions of this latter part of the indenture are two. It does what it can to provide the lender as favorable a position as possible vis-a-vis other creditors of the corporation; if there is an event of default and the lender has to step in to protect its loan, it is certain that swarms of other creditors will appear on the scene in a hurry, all clamoring to be paid out of the limited assets and enterprise earnings of the corporate debtor. Following the precise prescriptions of the federal Trust Indenture Act of 1939, this part of the indenture also delineates the relationships between the body of bond holders or debenture holders and their representative, the indenture trustee, and the procedures that the trustee must follow in fulfillment of his fiduciary obligations to them. The indenture provisions that detail what will happen after an event of default are of little interest to the management and shareholders of the borrowing corporation; if the disaster of default and takeover should occur, the game will probably be over for the shareholders (though the management may survive), and the creditors of various types and kinds will be left to fight among themselves over the remains. By contrast, the management and shareholders will be intensely interested in the first part of the indenture, and negotiations between them and the lender over the restrictive covenants will be hard fought.

b. Key Covenants

Chapter I of this book begins with a recitation of the main concerns that a lender will continue to have after he has satisfied himself that the general economic position, character, and income-producing capacity of the prospective borrower is sufficient to induce the lender to go ahead with the transaction. He wishes to be sure that there are equity investors exposed to risk in the enterprise ranking junior to him; he wants assets to stay in the enterprise and not be distributed to junior security holders; he is concerned to keep down the number of other creditor claimants in his own class; and he is even more concerned to keep down the claims of creditors who would rank senior to him. The indenture may contain restrictive covenants on many other aspects of the conduct of the business enterprise, but it will always contain provisions carefully tailored to assuage these particular concerns of the lender.

ization proceeding under Chapter XI of the Bankruptcy Act. But the indenture seeks to do all it can by way of providing contractual protection to the holder of securities issued under the indenture.

(i) Covenant on Secured or Prior Debt

The indenture normally includes a covenant either flatly prohibiting the borrowing company and its subsidiaries from incurring secured or prior debt, or at least narrowly restricting the freedom of the company to do so; exceptions are often made for purchase money mortgages, at least in limited circumstances. As to this risk, it will be recalled, the corporation acts provide the lender no help at all.

(ii) Covenant on Unsecured or Funded Debt

Covenants forbidding the company to incur further long-term unsecured debt are sometimes seen in indentures and bank loan agreements, but absolute prohibitions against such debt are not usual. More often the borrower agrees that it will not incur further debt unless a particular financial formula of some kind can be met. Various approaches to this formula, or combinations of them, are used. The company may be forbidden to incur further debt unless its current assets bear a designated relationship to its liabilities due and payable within a set time, such as a year. Additional debt may be prohibited unless the company's average earnings over a period of years have been a multiple of the amount required to meet carrying charges and installment principal payments of all existing debt, including the debt of the indenture. Or new debt may be permitted but only if certain other steps are taken, such as retirement of existing debt, or sale of stock that produces junior equity proceeds in a certain amount, or subordination of the new debt to the debt of the indenture. (By a provision of this sort, the indenture can exert significant pressure on the borrower to maintain a high proportion of equity or junior debt investment). The indenture will also typically be especially strict in limiting the freedom of subsidiaries of the borrower to incur debt, however junior that debt may be, since the claim of any creditor of the subsidiary against the assets of the subsidiary stands higher in rank than the parent's equity claim to those assets and therefore higher than the claim of the parent's creditor.

(iii) Covenant on Distributions to Shareholders

The indenture invariably carries special provisions designed to carry out the investment creditors' desire to hold down the distribution of corporate assets to shareholders. Set out below is the text of a dividend restriction covenant taken from a modern bond indenture of a public utility. It is somewhat more detailed than many such provisions, but it is quite standard in its structure and technique. A fairly elaborate specimen has been selected to illustrate the subtlety and the range of matters that must be addressed if such a contractual control mechanism is to be effective. Following the quoted excerpt appears some explanatory comment about it. The following indenture text itself should be read before the commentary, however.

Under the indenture agreement, the borrowing corporation (the Company) agrees, in addition to many other things—

"Section 7.12. That, so long as any of the bonds of any of the present series are outstanding, the Company will not

(a) declare or pay any dividends or make any other distribution on any of its capital stock of any class (other than cash dividends on shares of any class of such stock ranking prior to the Common Stock in respect of dividends or assets at the rate applicable to such shares under the Certificate of Incorporation of the Company, as amended, and other than dividends on Common Stock paid solely in shares of Common Stock of the Company), or

(b) purchase, redeem or otherwise retire for a consideration any shares of its capital stock of any class (otherwise than in a transaction involving the purchase, redemption or retirement of shares of capital stock of the Company, other than its Common Stock, in exchange for or from the proceeds of the substantially simultaneous sale of other shares of capital stock of the Company), except any shares of any class of stock ranking prior to the Common Stock in respect of dividends or assets which may be purchased, redeemed or otherwise retired to the extent required to comply with the provisions of any sinking fund applicable to such shares under the Certificate of Incorporation of the Company, as amended,

if

(i) any such dividend is declared to be payable more than 75 days after the date of declaration; or

(ii) after giving effect to such proposed dividend, distribution, purchase or retirement, the aggregate amount so declared or distributed for all such dividends or distributions or expended for all such purchases or retirements after December 31, 1957, plus the amount of any cash dividends paid on any shares of its capital stock of any class ranking prior to its Common Stock (other than amounts so paid which represent the disbursement of sums received by the Company as accrued dividends as a part of the selling price of any such shares) after December 31, 1957 to and including the date of declaration, in the case of a dividend, or the date of payment, in any other case, would exceed the aggregate net earnings of the Company, computed as hereinafter in this Section provided, for said period from December 31, 1957 to and including such date of declaration or date of payment, as the case may be, plus the sum of $30,000,000, less the amount of expenditures for the retirement for sinking fund purposes of any shares of any class of stock of the Company ranking prior to the Common Stock in respect of dividends or assets in any year subsequent to December 31, 1963 in which as of the close of any calendar quarter the Common Stock equity of the Company is less than 25% of the total capitalization of the Company.

"The term 'Common Stock equity of the Company' shall mean, at any date as of which the amount thereof is to be determined, the aggregate of the amount of the Common Stock liability of the Company, plus (or minus in the case of a deficit) the capital surplus applicable to the Common Stock and earned surplus of the Company, plus any premium on Common Stock of the Company, all as determined in accordance with sound accounting practice.

"The term 'total capitalization of the Company' shall mean, at any date as of which the amount thereof is to be determined, the aggregate of (a) the amount of the capital stock liability of the Company, plus (or minus in the case of a deficit) the capital surplus and earned surplus of the Company, plus any premium on capital stock of the Company of any class, all as determined in accordance with sound accounting practice and (b) the aggregate principal amount of all funded debt of the Company outstanding at such date. The term 'funded debt' shall mean all indebtedness of the Company which matures by its terms, or is renewable at the option of the obligor to a date, more than one year after the date of its creation or incurring by the Company.

"[So long as any of the bonds of any of the present series are outstanding, the Company will not at any time after October 1, 1958 issue any shares of any class of stock of the Company ranking prior to the Common Stock in respect of dividends or assets the terms of which shall require the redemption of said stock by the operation of a sinking fund at a rate more rapid than that applicable to any of the Company's Preferred Stock outstanding on October 1, 1958.] [2]

"For the purposes of this Section, the amount of any dividend declared or distribution or payment made in property of the Company shall be deemed to be the book value of such property at the time of declaration in the case of dividends, or at the date of distribution or payment in any other case.

"[The Company will not permit any subsidiary or any controlled corporation to purchase any shares of any class of stock of the Company from any person other than the Company.] [3]

"For purposes of this Section, the term 'net earnings of the Company' shall mean the sum of the operating revenues and other income of the Company, less all proper deductions for operating expenses, taxes (including income taxes or other taxes based upon or measured by or in respect of net earnings or income or based upon or measured by or in respect of undistributed net earnings or income) and interest charges (exclusive of interest or taxes properly capitalized as interest or taxes during construction), appropriations to retirement or depreciation reserves for properties other than gas or oil production properties and provisions for depreciation and depletion of gas and oil production properties (which appropriations to retirement or depreciation reserves with respect to properties referred to in the first paragraph of Section 7.11 and which provisions for depreciation and depletion with respect to gas production properties shall be in amounts not less than those required by the provisions of Section 7.11 as in effect from time to time) and other appropriate items, all determined in accordance with sound accounting practice; provided, however, that in computing the amount of the net earnings of the Company as aforesaid (A) any interest received by the Company on obligations or indebtedness of any subsidiary or controlled corporation may be included in other in-

---

2. See comment at page 104, infra.   3. See comment at page 104, infra.

come of the Company only to the extent that (i) such interest is not in excess of the net earnings available for interest of such subsidiary or controlled corporation, computed in accordance with sound accounting practice, for the period in respect of which such interest was paid (after first deducting from such net earnings available for interest an amount equal to all interest, if any, accrued for such period on obligations or indebtedness of such subsidiary or controlled corporation held by others than the Company and ranking prior to or on a parity with the obligations or indebtedness of such subsidiary or controlled corporation held by the Company in respect of which such interest was received) or (ii) such interest is properly capitalized by such subsidiary or controlled corporation as interest during construction in accordance with sound accounting practice; and any dividends received by the Company on stock of any subsidiaries or controlled corporations may be included in other income of the Company only to the extent that the aggregate amount of such dividends is not in excess of the combined net earnings of all subsidiaries and controlled corporations applicable to the stock interest of the Company in such subsidiaries and controlled corporations, computed as to each subsidiary or controlled corporation, in accordance with sound accounting practice, from the date on which such subsidiary or controlled corporation became a subsidiary or controlled corporation to the date of the most recent payment of a dividend to the Company by any subsidiary or controlled corporation, and (B) no deduction or adjustment shall be made for or on account of (i) any charges for redemption or prepayment premiums or other expenses in connection with the retirement by the Company, by redemption, payment or otherwise, of any of its bonds, debentures, promissory notes or preferred stocks or any charges for the write-off of the unamortized portion of any debt discount and expense applicable to any such retired bonds, debentures, notes or preferred stocks remaining at the time of the retirement thereof, or any expenses in connection with the creation, issuance or sale by the Company of any of its bonds, debentures, promissory notes, preferred stocks or Common Stock, (ii) interest, taxes or other overhead charges during construction to the extent chargeable to fixed property accounts of the Company in accordance with sound accounting practice and so charged, (iii) any profits realized or losses sustained in the sale of fixed properties or securities by the Company, (iv) any earned surplus adjustments properly applicable to any period or periods prior to January 1, 1958, other than adjustments required to give effect to assessments of additional income taxes paid by the Company or refunds of income taxes received by the Company applicable to any fiscal period or periods prior to January 1, 1958, or (v) any charges for amortization or elimination of gas plant adjustment accounts or acquisition adjustment accounts or other intangibles.

"In the event that, at the time of any determination of net earnings of the Company for purposes of this Section, the Company shall be collecting increased rates which have been placed in effect subject to refund by order of the Federal Power Commission or other governmental regulatory authority or any court, in any proceeding relating to such rate increase, the revenues resulting from such rate increase shall be taken into account in such determination to the extent that the inclusion of such revenues does not, in the opinion of independent accountants retained by the Company, result in the Company's earning a rate of return on its business subject to rate regulation (considered as a whole) in excess of the rate of return last allowed to the Company by the Federal Power Commission or other governmental regulatory authority having jurisdiction in the premises."

Beneath the stifling verbiage and detail of this indenture covenant, its underlying skeletal structure can be readily (well—more or less readily) seen. It is quite typical. In general, it sets up a formula restricting asset distributions to the effect that the debtor company may not make any payments specified in sub-paragraph (a) or any payments specified in sub-paragraph (b) if the conditions specified in sub-paragraph (i) exist or if the conditions specified in sub-paragraph (ii) exist. The balance of the Section 7.12 is largely made up of finely honed definitions of the terms, and specifications of circumstances that are referred to in the restriction formula.

Sub-paragraph (a): This sub-paragraph includes within the range of its prohibitions any payment of dividends or any other asset distribution on common stock. So-called "stock dividends" on common stock are permitted, since a stock dividend entails no more than a splitting up of pieces of paper and does not involve the pay out of assets from the corporate treasury. The provision also excludes from its reach dividends paid on the company's preferred stock; this exclusion is usual, since neither the management nor the lender is anxious to create the unfavorable aura that attaches to a company that has fallen into arrears on its preferred stock dividend payments and has perhaps thereby become subject to remedial resorts open to holders of the preferred.

Sub-paragraph (b): This sub-paragraph reaches out beyond dividend payments and similar distributions, to limit purchases, redemptions and retirements by the debtor company of its own shares. The lender forbids the Company to buy in its own stock because such a purchase is a form of distribution of assets to a shareholder. There are two exceptions. The Company is permitted to comply with the sinking fund provisions of its outstanding preferred stock and in so doing to distribute assets to the preferred shareholders in accordance with the requirements of the preferred stock provisions contained in the Company's certificate of incorporation. Sub-paragraph (b) also excludes from its prohibition a refunding or refinancing of the existing preferred stock; this leaves open to the Company, so far as the lenders are concerned, the option of calling in its existing preferred in favor of a new preferred issued on more favorable terms if the general price of the money market should drop. (Incidentally, the terms of the outstanding preferred stock may not be so permissive to the issuer.)

The drafting of sub-paragraph (b) is somewhat wanting in elegance since it contains, buried within the mass of definitional material, two other independent covenants. The brackets that set off these provisions have been added by the present author. In the first bracketed covenant the Company agrees that so long as the bonds are outstanding it will not issue any preferred stock that has a sinking fund that works at a rate more rapid than the existing preferred stock; the lender is willing to see assets go to the preferred shareholders at the rate prescribed at the time of the loan, but no faster. The second bracketed provision forbids a subsidiary to buy in the Company's stock. As a matter of style—and for ease in locating them—these two provisions should be separately numbered as independent covenants in the indenture.

Sub-paragraph (i): This sub-paragraph requires the Company to pay a dividend promptly after its date of declaration, the lender's fear being that the Company could otherwise declare dividends whenever it is in a fiscal position to meet the formula contained in sub-paragraph (ii) and then later pay the money out to the shareholders at a time when the company is in a weakened condition and the lender's position is threatened.

Sub-paragraph (ii): This sub-paragraph contains the financial conditions that must exist whenever the Company declares or pays a dividend or makes any other distribution to shareholders proscribed by section 7.12. The formula begins with the figure $30,000,000, a sum arrived at by negotiation between the borrower and the lender. To this $30,000,000 the formula adds the net earnings of the Company since December 31, 1957, a date roughly coinciding with the issue of the bonds. The formula then provides, in substance, that no restricted distribution may be made unless at the time the sum of the $30,000,000 plus such net earnings is greater than all restricted distributions theretofore paid out plus all cash dividends paid on the preferred stock since that date. Although, as noted, cash dividends on the preferred are not a restricted distribution under subparagraph (a), and may therefore be paid whether the formula is met or not, such cash dividends on preferred *do* count against the Company in computations under sub-paragraph (ii) so that they have the subsequent effect of making it more difficult for the Company to pay dividends on the common stock.

The restriction formula in sub-paragraph (ii) has a somewhat unusual twist regarding sinking fund requirements of the preferred. Such sinking fund requirements are not restricted distributions under sub-paragraph (b), nor do they normally enter into the financial formula of sub-paragraph (ii), but they do count against the Company in the formula after 1963 if they are paid out at a time when the equity of the common stock in the company has become so thin as to drop below 25% of the Company's total capitalization. This special provision says, in effect, that the Company may proceed with its sinking fund retirement on the outstanding preferred, but if in the future the common stock equity exposure in the enterprise drops too low (below 25%) then the sinking fund retirement payments on the preferred stock will be counted against the Company in its formula with the result of further restricting the ability of the Company to pay dividends or make distributions on its common stock. Every dividend restriction like this representative section is individually negotiated by the corporate debtor and the lender in the context of the particular circumstances, and it is quite normal to find special hand-crafted features of this kind.

The lengthy definitional provisions do not require special comment, but they should be read over, for they illustrate what is actually involved in making a real dividend restriction formula work. The whole formula restricting shareholder distributions is based fundamentally on the earnings rate of the borrowing enterprise. The definition of "net earnings of the Company" is thus absolutely critical to its administration and the draftsmen of the indenture have consequently elaborated it in considerable detail. Even so, a careful reading of the definition will reveal that it contains many terms and references that are themselves hardly self-executing and that could in turn have been further refined in the covenant. The question of where the lawyer should stop in the process of specification in the document is a matter for negotiating and drafting judgment in each situation, line-by-line and term-by-term; there are no automatic stopping places; and no matter where one stops, the provision will contain open ended unresolved questions, breeding pools for later dispute.

So much for indenture Section 7.12.

(iv) Covenant on Informing the Trustee

Once a long term loan has been made to the corporate borrower, all the indenture covenants and provisions will be of little help to the lenders (trustee) unless they know what is going on at the borrowing company, and particularly whether the company has violated a covenant and precipitated an event of default. The lenders (trustee) must arrange to have current business information about the company—lots of it. Key provisions in the indenture will therefore require the company to provide the lenders (trustee) with a stream of reports about the company's operations and fiscal condition and grant the trustee freedom to inspect company records and interview executives. Without such an information flow the lenders will have little hope of realizing full benefit from the covenants they negotiated so hard to extract from the borrower.

c. Contract and Statute Compared

It is now possible, and fruitful, to compare the approach of the statutory legal capital machinery with that of the negotiated corporate indenture.

The indenture hits squarely and effectively against the borrowers' incurring additional debt, and especially secured debt, both of which would be to the detriment of the present lender. Corporation acts make no effort to deal with this problem at all.

The lender will not enter into the transaction at all without a close examination of the asset structure, earnings potential, and general economic health of the enterprise. This perspective and attitude is reflected throughout the covenants of the indenture. By contract, the stated capital machinery assumes—or rather simply asserts—that the key premise of concern to the lender has something to do with payments that shareholders did or did not make into the corporate treasury at an earlier day in payment for their stock.

In the indenture's provisions restricting distributions to shareholders, the emphasis is placed upon a particular negotiated figure based upon the economic strength of the enterprise at the time of the borrowing, plus the earnings of the company. Attention is therefore focused on the enterprise's earnings track record, its potential to make a profit, and its capacity to throw off sufficient earnings to cover carrying charges on its debt plus distributions to shareholders. Under the statutory scheme, in states having the balance sheet surplus test, there is no focus at all on the enterprise's earning ability and even in states that putatively use the earned surplus standard under the Model Act, earnings have only a limited role.

The contractual indenture approach permits the lender and borrower to negotiate a platform figure on which to build the restriction formula (in the quoted case $30,000,000)[4] instead of seeking to find a universal answer. In the same way the process of negotiation in the indenture permits the lender to protect himself against particular hazards or possibilities that he sees in his capital situation, as in the cited instance of the preferred stock sinking fund.

The legal capital statutes place the entire control over equity distributions in the hands of the board of directors and shareholders—those who are supposedly to be regulated. The indenture binds the borrower (i. e., its board and shareholders) by contract to the lender, gives the lender an elaborate machinery to protect his position, puts the lender's representative, the trustee, in control of that machinery and assures a flow of information that will enable the lender to proceed intelligently if trouble develops.

Most important of all—and perhaps simply generalizing all of the points just made—however much the prose of the indenture may reek of legalese, it is at heart a businessman's document. In it are reflected the real needs, priorities, interests and worries of a lender who has put large quantities of its capital at risk in an enterprise that is controlled by others. By contrast, the statutory scheme of legal capital is a conceptual structure based mainly upon legalistic doctrines of the 19th century.

---

4. The dollar figure is usually the regular quarterly dividend multiplied by an agreed upon number of quarters, typically four, thus providing the borrower one year's leeway in his dividend payments.

Chapter VII

END QUESTIONS

It now seems fair to ask:

(i) Does the present day statutory legal capital machinery made up of par value, stated capital, and related non-economic concepts—controlled as it is by the shareholders, directors and their lawyers and accountants—effectively perform any significant relevant function in protecting creditors of corporations?

(ii) If the statutory machinery does perform a significant function, is it sufficiently great to warrant the aggregate investment of time, energy and dollars that is now required of thousands of lawyers, accountants, law teachers, law students, and an occasional judge?

(iii) Given the institutional and contractual protections that are available to creditors of corporations today, do they have a real need for special statutory protection?

(iv) If so, is anything more needed than the Massachusetts provision forbidding a distribution to shareholders if the company is insolvent or if it would be rendered insolvent by the distribution?

And it seems fair to answer each of these four questions, "No."

In that case, will the bramble bush of legal capital statutes throughout the nation soon (or ever) be repealed in favor of the simple Massachusetts rule? Until very recently, it seemed sure that the answer to that question, too, would be "No." But it now appears that the answer may be "maybe." Change is now in the wind, and Part Three has been added to this 2nd Edition to discuss these new currents. But for the reasons set out in the Preface, change will be adopted slowly, if at all. And, therefore, for decades to come, a general familiarity with the arcane material surveyed in this book will continue to be a required part of the intellectual equipment of those who work, or aspire to work, in the fields of corporate or commercial law.

PART TWO

THE LEGAL CAPITAL STATUTES

IN ACTION

Introduction

This Part Two illustrates the statutory legal capital scheme at work. It surveys the balance sheets—particularly the owners' equity section—arising from a series of common corporate transactions and reviews the legality of asset distributions to shareholders under different types of laws, given such balance sheets.

Part Three discusses some recent developments in the field, particularly in the Model Business Corporation Act. Since no state has yet, at this writing (fall 1980) adopted the new Model Act provisions, the Model Act referred to in this Part Two is that which is now in the statute books of many states, and for clarity is frequently designated here as "Model Act (1979)."

Three initial observations:

(1) Since the law in this field varies from state to state, and since more than one accounting option is often available, the shorthand legal and accounting entries set out here must be understood to be illustrative only. This Part Two must also be read in context of the discussion in Part One.

(2) As has been developed earlier, the experienced corporation lawyer, working with an experienced accountant, can almost always (absent existing or ensuing insolvency) find a lawful procedural way to design around legal capital restraints, to reconstruct the balance sheet so that a distribution to shareholders would be conformable to the applicable statutory scheme. This fact in no way implies fraud or sharp practice; it merely demonstrates the insubstantiality of the system of legal capital restraints.

Thus, to cite a simple case, the Model Act, which purports to be an "earned surplus" statute, makes it very easy for shareholder distributions to be charged against capital surplus, and also makes it very easy to create capital surplus.[1] Therefore the

---

1. Model Act §§ 46 and 69.

reader must understand that any statement made here that, given a particular balance sheet, a shareholder distribution would be prohibited by a particular kind of legal capital statute must *not* be taken to mean that no way can be found to arrange for a legal distribution to shareholders.

The real factors that determine corporate dividend policy in the absence of insolvency are availability of cash, management's attitude toward profit reinvestment, the directors' appraisal of the effects of dividend policy on the market price of the stock, deference to shareholders' concerns about tax liability, and contractual restraints contained in loan agreements. As should by now be apparent to the reader, the actual effect of statutory legal capital provisions upon corporate distributions to shareholders is minimal.

(3) Finally, as used in the illustrations here, "shareholder distribution" means any form of distribution of corporate assets (in cash or in kind) to shareholders as such, such as dividends, stock repurchases, liquidating distributions, and the like. Correspondingly, the term "shareholder distributions" does not include payments made to persons who happen to be shareholders but who receive the payment in some capacity other than that of shareholders—for example, salary paid to an employee who is a shareholder or interest paid to a lender who is also a shareholder. And a statement here that a "shareholder distribution" is not legally allowable does not apply to a stock dividend or stock split since those transactions involve no distribution of corporate assets. This careful usage of "shareholder distribution" is not followed universally, however, and all too often one may hear persons who should, and do, know better, refer to stock dividends and splits as "distributions.")

The successive transactions considered here proceed from the balance sheet of Laminated Thumbscrew, Inc. immediately after its formation and the issuance at par for cash of 500 shares of common stock with a par value of $100 per share, the simple high par model set out as the first illustration in Chapter II.

Laminated Thumbscrew, Inc.
Immediately Following Organization

ASSETS		LIABILITIES	
Cash	$50,000		$ –0–
		SHAREHOLDERS' EQUITY	
		Capital: $100 par common, 500 sh.	50,000
	$50,000		$50,000

Transaction 1: Loss

During its first year of active business operations, the corporation buys land, builds up inventory, develops some accounts receivable and payable, borrows $10,000 from the bank and incurs an operating loss of $20,000.

(a) *Balance sheet presentation*:

Laminated Thumbscrew, Inc.
Balance Sheet #1 (giving effect to Transaction 1)

ASSETS		LIABILITIES	
Cash	$20,000	Accounts payable	$ 2,000
Accounts receivable	6,000	Bank loan	10,000
Inventory	11,000	Liabilities	$12,000
Land	5,000	**SHAREHOLDERS' EQUITY**	
		Capital: $100 par common, 500 sh.	$50,000
		Earned surplus (deficit)	(20,000)
		Shareholders' equity	$30,000
	$42,000		$42,000

(b) *Legal capital restraints*:

(i) **Insolvency jurisdiction:** shareholder distribution of $30,000 allowable since assets exceed liabilities by $30,000. (This result, and all subsequent references to insolvency restraints, take as assumptions that the local statute uses the bankruptcy rather than the equity definition of insolvency and that the asset figures on the balance sheet reflect the fair market value of the assets if liquidated.)

(ii) **Balance sheet surplus jurisdiction:** no shareholder distribution allowable since there is a negative surplus of $20,000. That is, assets are $20,000 less than liabilities plus legal capital. The balance sheet is said to be "under water" and the capital "impaired".

(iii) **Earned surplus jurisdiction:** no shareholder distribution allowable since earned surplus is a deficit of $20,000.

(iv) **Current earnings jurisdiction:** no shareholder distribution allowable since no current earnings.

Transaction 2: Small Profit

During the second year, the company has a small profit of $5,000, all of which is reflected in further build-up of inventory.

(a) *Balance Sheet presentation:*

Laminated Thumbscrew Inc.
Balance Sheet #2 (giving effect to Transaction 2)

ASSETS		LIABILITIES	
Cash	$20,000	Accounts payable	$ 2,000
Accounts receivable	6,000	Bank loan	10,000
Inventory	16,000	Liabilities	12,000
Land	5,000	**SHAREHOLDERS' EQUITY**	
		Capital: $100 par common, 500 sh.	$50,000
		Earned surplus (deficit)	(15,000)
		Shareholders' equity	$35,000
	$47,000		$47,000

(b) *Legal capital restraints:*

(i) **Insolvency jurisdiction:** shareholder distribution of $35,000 allowable since assets exceed liabilities by $35,000.

(ii) **Balance sheet surplus jurisdiction:** no shareholder distribution allowable since assets are $15,000 less than liabilities plus legal capital.

(iii) **Earned surplus jurisdiction:** no shareholder distribution allowable since earned surplus is a deficit of $15,000.

(iv) **Current earnings jurisdiction:** shareholder distribution of $5,000 allowable since current earnings equal $5,000. These are so-called "nimble dividends"; the company lost money before this year and may lose money after this year, but in a current earnings jurisdiction, wherever in a "current" year there are any earnings they may be quickly paid out to shareholders. If the earnings are not paid out in the current year, (or, in Delaware, the following year) they disappear into the maw of the balance sheet deficit.

Transaction 3: Large Profit

In the third year of operations the company has a large profit of $20,000.

Tr. 4 APPRECIATION SURPLUS 113

(a) *Balance sheet presentation*:

Laminated Thumbscrew, Inc.
Balance Sheet #3 (giving effect to Transaction 3)

ASSETS		LIABILITIES	
Cash	$18,000	Accounts payable	$ 2,000
Accounts receivable	20,000	Bank loan	10,000
Inventory	24,000	Liabilities	$12,000
Land	5,000	**SHAREHOLDERS' EQUITY**	
		Capital: $100 par common, 500 sh.	$50,000
		Earned surplus	5,000
		Shareholders' equity	$55,000
	$67,000		$67,000

Accounting Note: Current usage among accountants is "Retained earnings" rather than "Earned surplus," but the older term is used here throughout because it is still the term generally used in the legal capital statutes and other legal materials.

(b) *Legal capital restraints*:

(i) **Insolvency jurisdiction:** shareholder distribution of $55,000 allowable since assets exceed liabilities by $55,000.

(ii) **Balance sheet surplus jurisdiction:** shareholder distribution of $5,000 allowable since assets are $5,000 more than liabilities plus legal capital.

(iii) **Earned surplus jurisdiction:** shareholder distribution of $5,000 allowable since earned surplus is $5,000.

(iv) **Current earnings jurisdiction:** Where the statute says "current earnings or surplus" may one rely on current earnings only if there is no earned surplus? Under these facts does a current earnings provision allow a distribution of $5,000, $20,000, $25,000, or (taking Transactions 2 and 3 together) $30,000? The current earnings statutes are very unclear in application.

Transaction 4: Asset Write-up—Appreciation Surplus

During the fourth year, the board of directors decides to apply for a bank loan to finance a proposed diversification into the production of laminated thumbtacks. The bank refuses to lend the company the money on the basis of Balance Sheet #3. President Torquemada and the Thumbscrew board feel that this is unfair, and that the enterprise is worth more than its balance sheet shows. The land, for example, has appreciated in value to $10,000. The board decides (in contravention of generally accepted accounting principles) to show the land at its fair market value of $10,000, so land is "written up" by $5,000.

(a) *Balance sheet presentation*:

Laminated Thumbscrew, Inc.
Balance Sheet #4 (giving effect to Transaction 4)

ASSETS		LIABILITIES	
Cash	$18,000	Accounts payable	$ 2,000
Accounts receivable	20,000	Bank loan	10,000
Inventory	24,000	Liabilities	$12,000
Land	10,000	**SHAREHOLDERS' EQUITY**	
		Capital: $100 par common, 500 sh.	50,000
		Appreciation surplus	5,000
		Earned surplus	5,000
		Shareholders' equity	$60,000
	$72,000		$72,000

Accounting Note: By the tenets of today's generally accepted accounting principles, such a write-up would not be approved by an accountant.

(b) *Legal capital restraints*:

(i) **Insolvency jurisdiction:** shareholder distribution of $60,000 allowable since assets exceed liabilities by $60,000.

(ii) **Balance sheet surplus jurisdiction:** a jurisdiction following *Randall v. Bailey*, 23 N.Y.S.2d 173; aff'd without opin. 262 App.D. 844, 29 N.Y.S.2d 512 (1st Dept. 1941), aff'd with opin. 288 N.Y. 280, 43 N.E. 2d 43 (1942), would accept the written-up value for the land and allow a shareholder distribution of $10,000 since assets are then $10,000 more than liabilities plus legal capital. A jurisdiction not following the *Randall* case would, with the accountants, view the write-up of the land as improper, and, valuing the land at its $5,000 cost, allow a shareholder distribution of only $5,000.

(iii) **Earned surplus jurisdiction:** shareholder distribution of $5,000 allowable since earned surplus is $5,000. The "appreciation surplus" is not considered as derived from a profit since it is not yet "realized."

(iv) **Current earnings jurisdiction:** even in a jurisdiction following the *Randall* case, a court might (and an accountant surely would) balk at the idea that the write-up yields "current earnings." And see 2(b)(iv) and 3(b)(iv) supra.

Transaction 5: Elimination of Asset Write-up

During the same year (the fourth) the board of directors decides against expanding into laminated thumbtacks and negotiations for the bank loan are cancelled. At the end of the year, the board also decides it was a bit hasty in writing up the land and decides to write it down to its former book value, a decision no doubt influenced by the remonstrations of its auditors.

(a) *Balance sheet presentation:*

Laminated Thumbscrew, Inc.
Balance Sheet #5 (giving effect to Transaction 5)

ASSETS		LIABILITIES	
Cash	$18,000	Accounts payable	$ 2,000
Accounts receivable	20,000	Bank loan	10,000
Inventory	24,000	Liabilities	$12,000
Land	5,000	**SHAREHOLDERS' EQUITY**	
		Capital: $100 par common, 500 sh.	$50,000
		Earned surplus	5,000
		Shareholders' equity	$55,000
	$67,000		$67,000

(b) *Legal capital restraints:*

(i) **Insolvency jurisdiction:** shareholder distribution of $55,000 allowable since assets exceed liabilities by $55,000.

(ii) **Balance sheet surplus jurisdiction:** shareholder distribution of $5,000 allowable since assets are $5,000 more than liabilities plus legal capital.

(iii) **Earned surplus jurisdiction:** shareholder distribution of $5,000 allowable since earned surplus is $5,000.

(iv) **Current earnings jurisdiction:** see 2(b)(iv) supra.

Transaction 6: Stock Issuance for Secret Process

During the fifth year of operations, Laminated Thumbscrew acquires a secret process for laminate adhesive that is valued by the board at $5,000; it issues 50 shares of $100 par stock to the inventor in payment for the process.

(a) *Balance sheet presentation:*

Laminated Thumbscrew, Inc.
Balance Sheet #6 (giving effect to Transaction 6)

ASSETS		LIABILITIES	
Cash	$18,000	Accounts payable	$ 2,000
Accounts receivable	20,000	Bank loan	10,000
Inventory	24,000	Liabilities	$12,000
Land	5,000	**SHAREHOLDERS' EQUITY**	
Secret process	5,000	Capital: $100 par common, 550 sh.	$55,000
		Earned surplus	5,000
		Shareholders' equity	60,000
	$72,000		$72,000

(b) *Legal capital restraints:*

  (i) **Insolvency jurisdiction:** shareholder distribution of $60,000 allowable since assets exceed liabilities by $60,000.

  (ii) **Balance sheet surplus jurisdiction:** shareholder distribution of $5,000 allowable since assets are $5,000 more than liabilities plus legal capital.

  (iii) **Earned surplus jurisdiction:** shareholder distribution of $5,000 allowable since earned surplus is $5,000.

  (iv) **Current earnings jurisdiction:** see 2(b)(iv) supra.

Transaction 7: Write-down of Asset

At the end of year five the corporation finds it has made a profit from operations of $6,000 during the year. Meanwhile, the accountant questions the valuation of the secret process for the laminate adhesive and suggests that it would be better practice to carry the secret process at a book value of $1. The board of directors grudgingly accepts this write-down.

(a) *Balance sheet presentation:*

Laminated Thumbscrew, Inc.
Balance Sheet #7 (giving effect to Transaction 7)

ASSETS		LIABILITIES	
Cash	$20,000	Accounts payable	$ 2,000
Accounts receivable	22,000	Bank loan	10,000
Inventory	26,000	Liabilities	$12,000
Land	5,000	**SHAREHOLDERS' EQUITY**	
Secret process	1	Capital: $100 par common, 550 sh.	$55,000
		Earned surplus	6,001
		Shareholders' equity	$61,001
	$73,001		$73,001

Accounting Note: The $6,000 profit for the year passes through the company's income statement for that year to increase earned surplus at the end of the year to $11,000. However the secret process write-down of $4,999 may be handled on the current income statement, the $4,999 will be ultimately charged against the earned surplus account, leaving a balance of $6,001.

(b) *Legal capital restraints:*

   (i) **Insolvency jurisdiction:** shareholder distribution of $61,001 allowable since assets exceed liabilities by $61,001.

   (ii) **Balance sheet surplus jurisdiction:** shareholder distribution of $6,001 allowable since assets are $6,001 more than liabilities plus legal capital.

   (iii) **Earned surplus jurisdiction:** shareholder distribution of at least $6,001 allowable.

   Shareholder distribution of $11,000 may be allowable, depending on whether the $4,999 write-down of the secret process is considered a "loss" under the local statutory definition of earned surplus, which typically reads something like "balance of net profits, income, gains, and losses." In most earned surplus jurisdictions it is unclear whether the write-down is to be treated as a "loss." Note that the statutory question is one for a lawyer's decision. Corporate counsel may often have to go behind the accountant's treatment of a transaction on the balance sheet or income statement "in accordance with generally accepted accounting principles" to assess its legal effect on the permissibility of equity distributions.

Note further that the legal decision reached on a transaction like the write-down will have a forward impact into the indefinite future; if the allowable distribution to shareholders is $11,000 in the local earned surplus jurisdiction while at the same time the accountants insist on passing the write-down through the income statement, future balance sheets will continue to carry an accountants' "earned surplus" that is $4,999 less than the legal "earned surplus" used to measure the legality of shareholder distributions.

(iv) **Current earnings jurisdiction:** shareholder distribution of at least $6,000 allowable from current earnings. See 2(b)(iv) and 3(b)(iv) supra.

Transaction 8: Stock Dividend

The company's cash position is low, as inventories and accounts receivable have risen, so the board of directors decides to skip a cash dividend and declare a 10% "stock dividend." The shareholders are informed of the declaration of this "dividend" and shortly thereafter each shareholder is mailed a one-share stock certificate for each 10 that he already has, a total of 55 new shares being thus added to the 550 shares theretofore outstanding.

(a) *Balance sheet presentation:*

Laminated Thumbscrew, Inc.
Balance Sheet # 8 (giving effect to Transaction 8)

ASSETS		LIABILITIES	
Cash	$ 1,000	Accounts payable	$ 2,000
Accounts receivable	37,000	Bank loan	10,000
Inventory	30,000	Liabilities	$12,000
Land	5,000	**SHAREHOLDERS' EQUITY**	
Secret process	1	Capital: $100 par common, 605 sh.	$60,500
		Earned surplus	501
		Shareholders' equity	61,001
	$73,001		$73,001

Accounting Note: A stock dividend is a paper transaction and an accounting transaction only; no assets leave the corporate treasury for distribution to the shareholders.

In the case at hand, it merely leads to an accounting entry increasing the stated capital account by $5,500 (55 shares times $100 par) and reducing the earned surplus account by the same amount.

As a matter of rational analysis, the market price per share should respond to a stock dividend by a drop equal to the dividend percentage, in this case 10%. If, however, the market does not drop the full 10% (as it often does not) the recipient of the stock dividend may be put in a position to realize a gain "from" the stock dividend by selling some or all of his shares, of which he has a 10% greater number than he had before the dividend. Another real economic consequence of a stock dividend may arise in the future. If a company continues to pay out an annual cash dividend per share equal to that which it had been paying out before the stock dividend, the stock dividend will lead to a 10% increase in the assets paid out annually to shareholders as dividends (and reduce correspondingly the cash in the corporate treasury.)

Granting that the stock dividend will increase stated capital, and that a surplus account should be charged, *what* surplus account may be charged under the statutes? It appears that, regardless of the form of the local statute, any surplus account may be charged.[2]

But is it legally necessary that there be *any* surplus account available before the dividend? Why should there be? Notice that if the stock dividend is effected when there is no surplus to charge, the result of the increase in the stated capital will be to create a deficit in the surplus account. That looks bad, and sounds worse if in classical language, it is described as putting the stock "under water." But if the board of directors is willing to create such a deficit and thereby, without distributing corporate assets, further inhibit *future* distributions of assets to shareholders, why should creditors complain or the statute prevent it? Most lawyers would say, however, that, in the nature of things, a stock dividend may not be made if it creates a deficit surplus. Why not then reduce the par? Why not indeed. See Transaction 9.

---

2. Accounting principles require that capital surplus should first be charged before earned surplus for this purpose.

A second accounting question has to do with the *amount* by which stated capital should be written-up and a surplus account charged to reflect the stock dividend. Three answers are analytically possible: (i) stated capital should be increased by the par value of the shares issued through the dividend; (ii) stated capital should be increased by the fair market value of the shares issued, so long as not less than par (after or before giving effect to the dividend itself?); (iii) stated capital should be increased for each share newly issued through the dividend by an amount equal to the average stated capital per share as shown on the books before giving effect to the dividend, so long as it is not less than par. For reasons that may or may not be persuasive to others, accountants have chosen the second option. The statutes are silent as usual. The answer chosen will determine the size of the charge to be made against the surplus account and thereby the future availability or nonavailability of dividend payments. To simplify the balance sheet above, it has been assumed that the entry to be made in the stated capital account, and the charge to earned surplus is the par value of the shares issued through the dividend.

A question for the Scaramouche reader with a sense that the world is mad: Is it not evident that all shares issued by way of stock dividend are illegal and void? On the face of it, these shares are not issued for "goods, services, or labor done" as all the statutes require that they be. May not then the shareholder who receives the stock dividend later be required by a creditor, or someone, to pay in to the corporation an amount of money or property equal to the par value of the shares he received? The only available counterargument to that contention must be that (i) corporate "surplus" is "goods," and that (ii) an accounting entry charging a surplus account and increasing a stated capital account constitutes a "payment" to the corporation that complies with the statutory sections requiring that stock be "paid" up to its par value. It is difficult to think that anyone could advance that two point argument with a straight face. But it is exactly the position that lawyers, accountants, courts and commentators take on the question. Those who work regularly with these materials have become so accustomed to talking about issuing stock "against surplus" that they are no longer sensitive to its manifest non-compliance with the principle that assets are supposed to come into the corporate till when shares of the company are issued. Or perhaps they simply never ask the question, in tacit recognition that the statutory legal capital structure is in such disrepair that it will inevitably produce answers that are inconsistent or palpably unsupportable.

(b) *Legal capital restraints*:

    (i) **Insolvency jurisdiction:** shareholder distribution of $61,001 allowable since assets exceed liabilities by $61,001.

    (ii) **Balance sheet surplus jurisdiction:** shareholder distribution of $501 allowable since assets are $501 more than liabilities plus legal capital.

    (iii) **Earned surplus jurisdiction:** shareholder distribution of $501 allowable since earned surplus is $501. But see the discussion at 7(b)(iii) supra.

    (iv) **Current earnings jurisdiction:** see 2(b)(iv) supra.

Transaction 9: Stock Split

During year six, Laminated Thumbscrew's financial vice president, Mr. Rack, believing that the current market price of Thumbscrew stock ($120 per share) is too high to attract the small investor, proposes and the board decides that a stock split of 2 for 1 is called for. By vote of shareholders and directors the articles of incorporation are amended to reduce par value from $100 to $50 per share, and each shareholder is distributed a certificate or certificates representing 2 shares of common stock with a par value of $50 per share for each share of $100 par stock he theretofore held. The market price per share promptly drops to $62.

(a) *Balance sheet presentation*:

Laminated Thumbscrew, Inc.
Balance Sheet # 9 (giving effect to Transaction 9)

ASSETS		LIABILITIES	
Cash	$ 1,000	Accounts payable	$ 2,000
Accounts receivable	37,000	Bank loan	10,000
Inventory	30,000	Liabilities	$12,000
Land	5,000	**SHAREHOLDERS' EQUITY**	
Secret process	1	Capital: $50 par common, 1,210 sh.	$60,500
		Earned surplus	501
		Shareholders' equity	61,001
	$73,001		$73,001

Accounting Note: Obviously the transaction denominated a "stock dividend" in Transaction 8 could have been effected by reducing par rather than charging surplus, and the transaction denominated a stock split in Transaction 9 could have been effected by charging surplus (assuming there is enough surplus for the purpose) rather than by changing the par. On the whole, lawyers and accountants tend to use the term "stock dividend" where the change in the number of outstanding shares is relatively small and "stock split" when it is relatively large. If par stock is involved and if the transaction is denominated a "split," the lawyer assumes that a reduction of par will be made, since otherwise stated capital will be sharply increased and the company's freedom to declare dividends correspondingly reduced.

(b) *Legal capital restraints*:

No change from 8(b).

Transaction 10: Reduction of Stated Capital

(A) Near the end of year six it appears to the Laminated Thumbscrew management that a loss of $7,000 will occur from operations that year. The loss, plus routine changes in cash

Tr. 10   REDUCTION OF STATED CAPITAL   123

and accounts receivable, would produce the following balance sheet:

Laminated Thumbscrew, Inc.
Trial Balance Sheet # 10A (giving effect to Transaction 10(A))

ASSETS		LIABILITIES	
Cash	$ 6,000	Accounts payable	$ 2,000
Accounts receivable	25,000	Bank loan	10,000
Inventory	30,000	Liabilities	$12,000
Land	5,000	**SHAREHOLDERS' EQUITY**	
Secret process	1	Capital: $50 par common, 1,210 sh.	$60,500
		Earned surplus (deficit)	(6,499)
		Shareholders' equity	$54,001
	$66,001		$66,001

If this were to become the year-end balance sheet, the board of directors would find itself in the position of (i) not having paid a cash dividend in the preceding year; (ii) having enough cash on hand to pay up to $6,000 at the end of year six; but (iii) being prevented (in all but an insolvency jurisdiction) from legally declaring a dividend because of the earned surplus deficit of $6,499.

(B) At the suggestion of the company's counsel, Peine, Forte & Dure, and after consulting its accountants, Raven, Grackle & Co., the board of directors decides to meet its problem by reducing the company's stated capital. It does this by following the local corporation code procedure for "reducing capital." This procedure usually consists of (i) voting at a directors' meeting to take this action, (ii) in some cases, holding a shareholders meeting at which the certificate of incorporation is amended by shareholder vote to reduce the par, (iii) filing a certificate of amendment with the state corporation commissioner, and (iv) filing a statement of capital reduction with the same official. Laminated Thumbscrew's shareholders approve the resolution to reduce par from $50 per share to $40 per share and the necessary papers are filed.

(a) *Balance sheet presentation:*

Laminated Thumbscrew, Inc.
Balance Sheet # 10B (giving effect to Transaction 10(A) and Transaction 10(B))

ASSETS		LIABILITIES	
Cash	$ 6,000	Accounts payable	$ 2,000
Accounts receivable	25,000	Bank loan	10,000
Inventory	30,000	Liabilities	$12,000
Land	5,000	**SHAREHOLDERS' EQUITY**	
Secret process	1	Capital: $40 par common, 1,210 sh.	48,400
		Reduction surplus	12,100
		Earned surplus (deficit)	(6,499)
		Shareholders' equity	$54,001
	$66,001		$66,001

Accounting Note: With the par reduced from $50 to $40 per share, the aggregate stated capital statutorily required drops from $60,500 to $48,400. The balance of $12,100 is declared reduction surplus by the board and so entered on the balance sheet by the accountant.

The reduction of the par is in itself economically meaningless, and, analytically, the market price of the stock should be unaffected. In fact, however, the market may respond; for example, the market may accurately read the par change as a preliminary to a major asset distribution on the stock, and the stock price may rise as a result.

(b) *Legal capital restraints:*

   (i) **Insolvency jurisdiction:** shareholder distribution of $54,001 allowable since assets exceed liabilities by $54,001.

   (ii) **Balance sheet surplus jurisdiction:** shareholder distribution of $5,601 allowable in some jurisdictions since assets are $5,601 more than liabilities plus legal capital. Some balance sheet jurisdictions specifically forbid the use of reduction surplus as a basis for distribution. Others permit the use of the reduction surplus, but only if shareholders are notified with the distribution payment that reduction surplus has been charged for the purpose.

(iii) **Earned surplus jurisdiction:** no shareholder distribution allowable since earned surplus is a deficit and the reduction surplus may not be used directly to support a dividend payment. But under the Model Act (1979), which sets the general pattern for modern earned surplus statutes, a reduction surplus *may* be used to offset an earned surplus deficit up to the extent of the deficit, thus helping to put the company in a position to pay future dividends as soon as it has even $1 of earned surplus. (See Transaction 11).

Further, given the change of par to $40, a distribution of $5,601 to shareholders would be allowed under the Model Act (1979) as a "distribution of capital surplus" so long as shareholders are given notice of the basis for payment and so long as (as here) liquidation preferences of preferred shares are not threatened. Indeed, under the Model Act, the charge reflecting such a distribution can (after appropriate shareholder vote) be made directly to *stated* capital, without going through the double step of creating, then charging the reduction surplus account. And where stands the creditor, for whose protection all this intellectual machinery was built?—once again, so far as the legal capital statutes are concerned, he stands helpless as assets are passed out of the corporate treasury and into the hands of shareholders.

(iv) **Current earnings jurisdiction:** see 2(b)(iv) supra.

Transaction 11: Reduction Surplus as Offset to Deficit

(A) The board of directors declares and pays a cash dividend in the amount of $5,601, charging it to the reduction surplus account.

(a) *Balance sheet presentation:*

Laminated Thumbscrew, Inc.
Trial Balance Sheet # 11A (giving effect to Transaction 11(A))

ASSETS		LIABILITIES	
Cash	$ 399	Accounts payable	$ 2,000
Accounts receivable	25,000	Bank loan	10,000
Inventory	30,000	Liabilities	$12,000
Land	5,000	**SHAREHOLDERS' EQUITY**	
Secret process	1	Capital: $40 par	
		common, 1,210 sh.	48,400
		Reduction surplus	6,499
		Earned surplus (deficit)	(6,499)
		Shareholders' equity	$48,400
	$60,400		$60,400

(B) Both Peine and Raven suggest that the appearance of the company's balance sheet could be measurably improved if the remaining reduction surplus were used to offset the earned surplus deficit. The board votes to do so.

(a) *Balance sheet presentation:*

Laminated Thumbscrew, Inc.
Balance Sheet # 11B (giving effect to Transaction 11(A) and Transaction 11(B))

ASSETS		LIABILITIES	
Cash	$ 399	Accounts payable	$ 2,000
Accounts receivable	25,000	Bank loan	10,000
Inventory	30,000	Liabilities	$12,000
Land	5,000	**SHAREHOLDERS' EQUITY**	
Secret process	1	Capital: $40 par	
		common, 1,210 sh.	48,400
		Earned surplus	–0–
		Shareholders' equity	$48,400
	$60,400		$60,400

Accounting Note: Even in jurisdictions where reduction surplus may not be used directly to charge a shareholder distribution, it may often be used in this manner to offset a deficit, as it may under the Model Act (1979).

(b) *Legal capital restraints:*

  (i) **Insolvency jurisdiction:** shareholder distribution of $48,400 allowable since assets exceed liabilities by $48,400.

(ii) **Balance sheet surplus jurisdiction:** no shareholder distribution allowable since assets do not exceed liabilities plus legal capital.

(iii) **Earned surplus jurisdiction:** no shareholder distribution allowable since no earned surplus.

(iv) **Current earnings jurisdiction:** see 2(b)(iv) supra.

Transaction 12: Paid-in Surplus

At the beginning of year seven, Laminated Thumbscrew sells 100 shares of its $40 par stock at its then market price of $50 per share, receiving cash of $5,000 in the transaction.

(a) *Balance sheet presentation:*

Laminated Thumbscrew, Inc.
Balance Sheet # 12 (giving effect to Transaction 12)

ASSETS		LIABILITIES	
Cash	$ 5,399	Accounts payable	$ 2,000
Accounts receivable	25,000	Bank loan	10,000
Inventory	30,000	Liabilities	$12,000
Land	5,000	**SHAREHOLDERS' EQUITY**	
Secret process	1	Capital: $40 par common, 1,310 sh.	52,400
		Paid-in surplus	1,000
		Earned surplus	–0–
		Shareholders' equity	$53,400
	$65,400		$65,400

Accounting Note: Cash is increased by $5,000, stated capital by $4,000 and a paid-in surplus (or, in more modern accounting terminology, "capital in excess of par") of $1,000 is created.

(b) *Legal capital restraints:*

(i) **Insolvency jurisdiction:** shareholder distribution of $53,400 allowable since assets exceed liabilities by $53,400.

(ii) **Balance sheet surplus jurisdiction:** shareholder distribution of $1,000 allowable since assets are $1,000 more than liabilities plus legal capital.

(iii) **Earned surplus jurisdiction:** no shareholder distribution allowable since no earned surplus. Some statutes permit a capital surplus, such as paid-in surplus shown above, to be used as a basis for a distribution if notice thereof is given to shareholders.

(iv) **Current eanings jurisdiction:** see 2(b)(iv).

Transaction 13: Stock Repurchase Agreement

During the first six months of year seven an unusual spurt in business activity produces a $5,000 profit for the company.

(a) *Balance sheet presentation:*

Laminated Thumbscrew, Inc.
Balance Sheet # 13 (giving effect to Transaction 13)

ASSETS		LIABILITIES	
Cash	$10,399	Accounts payable	$ 2,000
Accounts receivable	25,000	Bank loan	10,000
Inventory	30,000	Liabilities	$12,000
Land	5,000	**SHAREHOLDERS' EQUITY**	
Secret process	1	Capital: $40 par common, 1,310 sh.	52,400
		Paid-in surplus	1,000
		Earned surplus	5,000
		Shareholders' equity	$58,400
	$70,400		$70,400

At this point, one of the original investing shareholders dies. Company counsel, Peine, Forte & Dure, reminds the management that, at the time of the company's formation, the original shareholders, and the company, entered into a stock repurchase agreement under the terms of which the company is given a right of first refusal to buy any or all of the company's shares held in the estate of any deceased shareholder at "the fair market price" of the shares. It is stipulated that the fair market price is $55 per share. Is the company free under the legal capital restrictions to buy in any of the company's outstanding shares, and if so how many?

(b) *Legal capital restraints:*

(i) **Insolvency jurisdiction:** share reacquisition of $58,400 allowable since assets exceed liabilities by $58,400.

(ii) **Balance sheet surplus jurisdiction:** share reacquisition of $6,000 allowable since assets are $6,000 more than liabilities plus legal capital.

(iii) **Earned surplus jurisdiction:** share reacquisition of at least $6,000 allowable, since assets are $6,000 more than liabilities plus legal capital. The "repurchase" is oddly not limited to the $5,000 of earned surplus. In fact, earned surplus jurisdictions will sometimes permit stock repurchases to be made where there is *no* surplus of any kind! Once again, the statutory system fails to block an outpouring of corporate assets into the hands of one or more shareholders, and the creditor's cushion of stated capital proves illusory.

(iv) **Current earnings jurisdiction:** whether, in the absence of surplus, current or recent earnings may be used as a basis for stock reacquisition is not clear.

Legal Note: Stock repurchase agreements are an extremely important device for the closely held corporation. When there is only a handful of shareholders there is usually no market for the stock, but the estate of a deceased shareholder will often need cash to pay death duties. The surviving shareholders will also usually want to protect themselves against an unwelcome stranger as a purchaser of the deceased's shares and would also like, if possible, to take up *pro rata* among themselves the control fraction of the deceased. The surviving shareholders can achieve these objectives by buying the shares themselves, of course, but that takes cash from their own pockets. They would therefore prefer that the same objectives be attained through repurchase of the deceased's shares by the corporation and payment of funds out of the corporate treasury into the estate. Stock repurchase agreements are designed to achieve that purpose.

The stock repurchase agreement often provides only for a right of first refusal to buy the deceased's shares to be extended to the corporation and/or the surviving shareholders, but some agreements purport to *require* the corporation, or surviving shareholders, to buy up the shares from the estate. Stock repurchase agreements display considerable variety in their manner of setting the price for the repurchased shares. It is not uncommon for closely held corporations to carry insurance on the lives of their shareholders to meet the share purchase options or requirements of such agreements.

Share "repurchases" by issuing corporations are not limited to situations where stock repurchase agreements exist. For one reason or another (some unsavory) a corporation's board may wish to have the corporation "buy in" the shares of a particular shareholder. Or a publicly-held corporation's management may be moved to "buy in" some of the company's outstanding shares from time to time because the market price is "low." If the management is successful in "buying in" shares at a price lower than the liquidating value per share, and the company then liquidates and distributes all its net assets to its remaining shareholders, it is obvious that the shareholder who sold his shares "to the corporation" is out of pocket, and the other shareholders are ahead of the game. In principle the same proposition is true if the company's assets are not liquidated but the discounted capitalized future income stream per share proves greater than the price per share paid to the seller shareholder who sold his shares "to the corporation."

It is extraordinary that legal capital restraints on stock reacquisitions are in such a state of disarray and require so much legal guesswork. Older cases and statutes did not recognize at all that a purchase by the corporation of its own stock is a form of shareholder distribution from which the "corporation" receives nothing, which is obnoxious to creditors, and which, depending on price, may prejudice or favor shareholders whose shares were not bought in. Many statutes are silent on the matter; some set up special rules on repurchases; some treat them as a kind of "reduction of capital" or liquidating distribution; others treat the reacquisitions like any other shareholder distribution.

Transaction 14: Purchase of Stock for the Treasury

Laminated Thumbscrew pays out $2,750 in cash to buy in from shareholders 50 shares of its own stock at the market price of $55 per share and the board of directors by resolution designates that the 50 shares shall be held as "treasury stock."

Tr. 14   PURCHASE OF STOCK FOR THE TREASURY   131

(a) *Balance sheet presentation*:

Laminated Thumbscrew, Inc.
Balance Sheet # 14 (giving effect to Transaction 14)

ASSETS		LIABILITIES	
Cash	$ 7,649	Accounts payable	$ 2,000
Accounts receivable	25,000	Bank loan	10,000
Inventory	30,000	Liabilities	$12,000
Land	5,000	**SHAREHOLDERS' EQUITY**	
Secret process	1	Capital: $40 par common, 1,310 sh. (50 sh. in treasury)	52,400
		Paid-in surplus	1,000
		Earned surplus Unrestricted $2,250 Restricted by treasury shares 2,750	5,000
		Less: 50 sh. treasury stock	(2,750)
		Shareholders' equity	$55,650
	$67,650		$67,650

Accounting Note: Modern accounting practice recognizes that a corporation's shares in its own hands are not an asset; corporate assets have been reduced by $2,750 by the reacquisition of the stock. As a legal matter, however, treasury shares have not been "retired" or "cancelled." They are still "outstanding" (at least for some purposes), and they continue to be reflected in the stated capital figure. In the accounting treatment shown here, these elements are recognized. In addition, earned surplus available for shareholder distributions is shown to be restricted by a reserve in the amount of the purchase price of the shares. This accounting treatment conforms to current practice but other accounting treatments are possible; for example, before restricting the earned surplus, it might be permissible to make a first charge against the paid-in surplus account, at least to the extent of $15 for each share acquired, the excess of the purchase price per share over the stated capital per share. The statutes usually offer no specific guidance.

(b) *Legal capital restraints*:

(i) **Insolvency jurisdiction:** shareholder distribution of $55,650 allowable since assets exceed liabilities by $55,650.

THE LEGAL CAPITAL STATUTES IN ACTION Pt. 2

(ii) **Balance sheet surplus jurisdiction:** shareholder distribution of $3,250 allowable since assets are $3,250 more than liabilities plus legal capital.

(iii) **Earned surplus jurisdiction:** shareholder distribution of $2,250 allowable since unrestricted earned surplus is $2,250. (The local statute may not contain the refinement of "restricted earned surplus" in which case perhaps $5,000 is available for dividends since the balance sheet continues to show earned surplus as $5,000.)

(iv) **Current earnings jurisdiction:** see 2(b)(iv) supra.

Transaction 15: Sale of "Treasury Shares"

Three months later, at a time when the market price of Laminated Thumbscrew stock has risen to $60 per share, the board of directors authorizes the sale of 20 shares of the company's 50 shares of treasury stock and the shares are sold by the corporation for $1,200 cash.

(a) *Balance sheet presentation:*

Laminated Thumbscrew, Inc.
Balance Sheet # 15 (giving effect to Transaction 15)

ASSETS		LIABILITIES	
Cash	$ 8,849	Accounts payable	$ 2,000
Accounts receivable	25,000	Bank loan	10,000
Inventory	30,000	Liabilities	$12,000
Land	5,000	**SHAREHOLDERS' EQUITY**	
Secret process	1	Capital: $40 par common, 1,310 sh. (30 sh. in treasury)	52,400
		Paid-in surplus	1,000
		Paid-in surplus— treasury stock sales	100
		Earned surplus Unrestricted $3,350 Restricted by treasury shares 1,650	5,000
		Less: 30 sh. treasury stock	(1,650)
		Shareholders' equity	$56,850
	$68,850		$68,850

Accounting Note: By the accounting treatment shown, cash is increased by the $1,200 sale price of the 20 shares, stated capital is left unaffected, unrestricted earned surplus is restored to the extent of the $1,100 that the company had paid for the 20 shares, the $100 difference between the company's purchase price and the resale price is entered as paid-in surplus, and the two offsetting treasury stock items are reduced from $2,750 (50 shares @ $55 per share) to $1,650 (30 shares @ $55 per share). Modern accounting would not recognize the $100 as a "profit" to be added to earned surplus.

Note that throughout these treasury share transactions, regardless of asset outflows from the corporation's treasury to shareholders, and asset inflows from shareholders to the corporate treasury, the legal stated capital figure remains frozen and wholly unreflective of what is going on.

(b) *Legal capital restraints*:

(i) **Insolvency jurisdiction**: shareholder distribution of $56,850 allowable since assets exceed liabilities by $56,850.

(ii) **Balance sheet surplus jurisdiction**: shareholder distribution of $4,450 allowable since assets are $4,450 more than liabilities plus legal capital.

(iii) **Earned surplus jurisdiction**: shareholder distribution of $3,350 allowable since unrestricted earned surplus is $3,350. See also 14(b)(iii).

Is the $100 paid-in surplus item derived from the purchase and sale of the treasury shares available for dividend purposes? Though accountants maintain that the $100 gain is not an income increment but an increase in paid-in surplus, is it clear that it falls outside the Model Act's definition of earned surplus—"net profits, income, gains and loss"?

(iv) **Current earnings jurisdiction**: No special considerations unless, perhaps, the $100 "gain" is a "current earning" for purposes of these statutes.

Transaction 16: Retirement of "Treasury Shares"

A short time later the board of directors by resolution "retires" the remaining 30 shares of treasury stock to the status of authorized but unissued stock.

(a) *Balance sheet presentation*:

Laminated Thumbscrew, Inc.
Balance Sheet # 16 (giving effect to Transaction 16)

ASSETS		LIABILITIES	
Cash	$ 8,849	Accounts payable	$ 2,000
Accounts receivable	25,000	Bank loan	10,000
Inventory	30,000	Liabilities	$12,000
Land	5,000	**SHAREHOLDERS' EQUITY**	
Secret process	1	Capital: $40 par common, 1,280 sh.	$51,200
		Paid-in surplus	1,000
		Earned surplus	4,650
		Shareholders' equity	$56,850
	$68,850		$68,850

Accounting Note: On retirement of the 30 shares that had been purchased for $1,650, $1,200 (30 shares @ $40 par) is charged against the stated capital account, $100 is charged against "Paid-in surplus—treasury stock sales," eliminating that item, and the remaining $350 is charged against earned surplus; the matching entries restricting earned surplus disappear.

Expressing these entries in another way, the treasury share offset of $1,650 appearing on Balance Sheet #15 is eliminated, $1,200 of it being charged against stated capital, $100 against paid-in surplus, and $350 against earned surplus. In turn, the $1,650 restriction on earned surplus is removed, so that the net effect on unrestricted earned surplus is an increase of $1,300.

Again, alternative accounting treatments might have been possible, such as a charge to the general paid-in surplus account. The statutes give almost no guidance.

Observe carefully the aggregate effect of the acquisition of treasury stock and its retirement. If these transactions are covered by the local legal capital control scheme at all, the end product of the full transaction is a reduction of surplus only to the extent that the purchase price of the reacquired shares exceeds the stated capital attributable to them. *That is to say, if the market price of the shares is equal to or less than the stated capital attributable to them, then any number of shares may, through step transactions, be bought in and retired without reducing the surplus account at all.* The assets flow out of the corporate till to the shareholders as their shares are bought up by the company, but the company's balance sheet capability to make shareholder distributions remains as great as before.[3] This process is a "reduction of capital" in the real economic sense—an actual pay-out of corporate assets to shareholders, not simply a write-down of "stated capital" and concurrent write-up of a surplus account. The legal capital system fails utterly to restrain the outflow of assets to shareholders by this method until the point where further distributions to shareholders would render the company insolvent. In this sense all statutory legal capital schemes are, ultimately, insolvency statutes and nothing more.

Under the corporation laws of many jurisdictions, the legal retirement of the shares is called a "reduction of capital"; it is not legally effectuated until a statement of reduction of capital is duly filed with the commissioner of corporations and perhaps until other procedural steps are taken.

(b) *Legal capital restraints:*

(i) **Insolvency jurisdiction:** shareholder distribution of $56,850 allowable since assets exceed liabilities by $56,850.

(ii) **Balance sheet surplus jurisdiction:** shareholder distribution of $5,650 allowable since assets are $5,650 more than liabilities plus legal capital.

(iii) **Earned surplus jurisdiction:** shareholder distribution of $4,650 allowable since earned surplus is $4,650.

(iv) **Current earnings jurisdiction:** see 2(b)(iv) supra.

Transaction 17: Distribution in Kind

During year eight the board of directors wishes to make a large distribution to shareholders. The company has long held two parcels of land that are carried on the company's books at their initial costs of $350 and $4,650. The latter parcel now has a fair market value of $13,950, and the board, wishing to preserve the corporation's cash, decides to distribute undivided interests in the parcel to the company's shareholders.

---

3. If the purchases of shares from the shareholders are prorated among them in proportion to their holdings, the transactions also leave intact the shareholders' relative equity fraction and voting control.

(a) *Balance sheet presentation:*

Laminated Thumbscrew, Inc.
Balance Sheet # 17 (giving effect to Transaction 17)

ASSETS		LIABILITIES	
Cash	$ 8,849	Accounts payable	$ 2,000
Accounts receivable	25,000	Bank loan	10,000
Inventory	30,000	Liabilities	$12,000
Land	350	**SHAREHOLDERS' EQUITY**	
Secret process	1	Capital: $40 par common, 1,280 sh.	51,200
		Paid-in surplus	1,000
		Earned surplus	–0–
		Shareholders' equity	$52,200
	$64,200		$64,200

Accounting Note: The land account is reduced by $4,650, and the earned surplus account is charged the same amount, reducing it to zero.[4]

This transaction well illustrates the complete dependence of the legal capital system upon the conventions of accounting, and the difference between economic reality and the world of accounting and law. From a creditor's standpoint and an economic perspective, $13,950 in real assets have been taken from the corporate pot and given to shareholders, despite the fact that, as noted at 16(b), the balance sheet would indicate that a shareholder distribution would (except in an insolvency jurisdiction) be limited to $4,650 or $5,650.

(b) *Legal capital restraints:*

  (i) **Insolvency jurisdiction:** shareholder distribution of $52,200 allowable since assets exceed liabilities by $52,200.

  (ii) **Balance sheet surplus jurisdiction:** shareholder distribution of $1,000 allowable since assets are $1,000 more than liabilities plus legal capital.

  (iii) **Earned surplus jurisdiction:** no shareholder distribution allowable since no earned surplus.

  (iv) **Current earnings jurisdiction:** see 2(b)(iv) supra.

---

4. As a result of the distribution, the corporation would, however, have to recognize a $9,300 gain on the parcel for income tax purposes. Would that also be viewed as "earnings" for purposes of a current earnings statute?

Transaction 18: Increase of Stated Capital by Resolution

Later in year eight, the board of directors votes to increase the company's stated capital by transferring $500 of the paid-in surplus to stated capital.

(a) *Balance sheet presentation:*

Laminated Thumbscrew, Inc.
Balance Sheet # 18 (giving effect to Transaction 18)

ASSETS		LIABILITIES	
Cash	$ 8,849	Accounts payable	$ 2,000
Accounts receivable	25,000	Bank loan	10,000
Inventory	30,000	Liabilities	$12,000
Land	350	**SHAREHOLDERS' EQUITY**	
Secret process	1	Capital: $40 par common, 1,280 sh.	$51,700
		Paid-in surplus	500
		Earned surplus	–0–
		Shareholders' equity	$52,200
	$64,200		$64,200

(b) *Legal capital restraints:*

(i) **Insolvency jurisdiction:** shareholder distribution of $52,200 allowable since assets exceed liabilities by $52,200.

(ii) **Balance sheet surplus jurisdiction:** shareholder distribution of $500 allowable since assets are $500 more than liabilities plus legal capital.

(iii) **Earned surplus jurisdiction:** no shareholder distribution allowable since no earned surplus.

(iv) **Current earnings jurisdiction:** no special considerations.

Legal Note: Circumstances are relatively rare in which management may wish to increase stated capital by transfer from other surplus accounts, but they do arise. For present purposes, the key points to note are two. First, an *increase* of the stated capital can be done by a simple vote of the board; reductions of stated capital (except through purchases of shares for the treasury) often require a shareholders' vote in addition to a vote by the board. Second, though it is customary for the stated capital per share of par stock to be equal to the par, the statutes require only that it be equal to, *or greater than,* par; it is not uncommon therefore to find stated capital accounts like that shown in Balance Sheet #18 where the stated capital per share ($40.39) is more than the par.

Transaction 19: Issuance of Preferred Stock

Business improves during year eight, and the company makes $14,000. As its accounts receivable rise, the management feels the need for more capital. Thereupon the board and shareholders vote to amend the certificate of incorporation to create a class of preferred stock with a par of $10, a liquidating preference of $100 and a cumulative dividend of $8 per year; the stock is redeemable by the company at any time at a price of $100. The company sells 100 shares of this preferred stock, and receives for it $80 cash per share.

(a) *Balance sheet presentation*:

Laminated Thumbscrew, Inc.
Balance Sheet # 19 (giving effect to Transaction 19)

ASSETS		LIABILITIES	
Cash	$10,015	Accounts payable	$ 2,000
Accounts receivable	58,334	Bank loan	10,000
Inventory	17,500	Liabilities	$12,000
Land	350	**SHAREHOLDERS' EQUITY**	
Secret process	1	Capital: $40 par common, 1,280 sh.	51,700
		$8 preferred, $10 par 100 sh.	1,000
		Paid-in surplus:	
		Common	500
		Preferred	7,000
		Earned surplus	14,000
		Shareholders' equity	$74,200
	$86,200		$86,200

Accounting Note: The stated capital of the new preferred is entered at $1,000 (100 shares @ $10 par) and the remaining $7,000 received is entered as paid-in surplus; it would have been possible for the board to designate as stated capital for the preferred any number between $1,000 and $8,000. Note that a separate stated capital account is created and shown for each class of stock, as required by modern accounting practice. Less often required by corporation statutes, the accounting treatment above also creates a separate paid-in surplus account for each class; the reason will appear in the next paragraph.

(b) *Legal capital restraints*:

With two classes of stock outstanding, it now becomes necessary to inquire separately for each class whether distributions may be made to the holders.

I. **Preferred**

In general, the statutes on legal capital are more lenient on their restrictions on the distribution of dividends on preferred stock, unless the company would thereby be rendered insolvent. Corporate managements usually insist that the company be free under its bond indentures to pay preferred dividends as they accrue; they do so to preserve the credit image of the company, to give some reality to the putative preferred position of the senior stock, and to head off remedial protective action by the holders of preferred, as by electing directors in the event of non-payment of preferred dividends. The same arguments have led to weakening of the statutes restricting preferred dividends.[5]

If a company under the statute of a particular state cannot legally pay dividends on its common stock because of insufficient earned surplus, but can legally do so on its preferred, may not the board issue some low par or no par preferred shares as a "stock dividend" to common shareholders in proportion to their holdings of common and thereafter merrily pay out corporate assets to them as preferred dividends free of the legal capital statutes?

II. **Common**

All common dividends of the company are now subject to the prior contractual claim of the preferred stock for its dividends.

Otherwise:

(i) **Insolvency jurisdiction:** common shareholder distribution of $74,200 allowable since assets exceed liabilities by $74,200.

(ii) **Balance sheet surplus jurisdiction:** common shareholder distribution of $21,500 allowable since assets are $21,500 more than liabilities plus legal capital.

---

5. See Model Act (1979) § 46 last paragraph.

Legal Note: In accordance with most if not all legal capital statutes, this calculation draws no distinction between the stated capitals and surpluses of the separate classes. If, however, the balance sheet test is applied by class of stock, then one would deduct from the $21,500 an additional $7,000 (the paid-in surplus of the preferred) leaving a total of $14,500 available for common stock dividends.

The implications of this point are of importance. This can be readily seen if the facts above are changed to assume that the *only* surplus on the balance sheet is the $7,000 paid-in surplus created through the issue of the preferred. Would the management then be free to pay out dividends to the common and charge that surplus? If so, the result is that the new preferred holders will have "invested" dollars in the corporate enterprise only to see them paid out to the holders of securities ranking junior to them. That will not make the preferred shareholders happy.

The point also has other facets. When it comes time to pay the annual $8 dividend on the preferred, may (should) that dividend be charged against the earned surplus account, or may the common shareholder now contend that since such a charge will have the effect of reducing the company's future capacity to pay dividends to the common, the preferred dividends should be charged against the preferred's paid-in surplus?[6] And what about the possibility of charging the common's paid-in surplus for the preferred dividends?

No statutory legal capital scheme is sufficiently sophisticated or worked through to deal with such questions, nor indeed can it be without resort to a complexity that far outbalances any gains from it. Yet corporate lawyers and accountants must provide definitive answers to such questions as the company does business in due course.

(iii) **Earned surplus jurisdiction:** shareholder distribution of $14,000 allowable since earned surplus is $14,000.

---

6. Or, if the statute permits, a direct charge against stated capital, to preserve earned surplus for the common.

(iv) **Current earnings jurisdiction:** shareholder distribution of $14,000 allowable because current earnings are $14,000.

Transaction 20: Present and Future Stock Issuance (Issuance of No Par Stock; Convertible Debentures; Stock Subscriptions; Stock Warrants; Stock Options)

As Laminated gains momentum, the board of directors effects a number of financial capital transactions in year nine. The market price of the $40 par common has meantime dropped to $25.

(These five transactions all have elements in common that can profitably be compared with each other. For that reason, and for conciseness in presentation here, the five transactions are grouped together and reflected in the single balance sheet, Balance Sheet #20.)

(1) The company buys for stock all the assets (and assumes all the liabilities) of a small enterprise. Laminated Thumbscrew's certificate of incorporation is amended to provide for a separate class of common stock that is in all respects *pari passu* to the outstanding $40 par common except that it is non-voting and is no par. The board authorizes the issue of 250 shares of the no par stock for the net assets of the selling company; the assets acquired (all real estate) are valued by the Laminated board of directors at a fair market value of $18,000 and the liabilities at $13,000, for a net of $5,000. The board resolves that the stated capital for the 250 outstanding shares of no par stock is to be $2,000 and the balance of $3,000 is to go to paid-in surplus.

Legal Note: If the value of the net assets purchased was in fact $5,000, as the board's resolution asserts, the price paid for the no par common was $20 per share. Under the doctrine of "equitable contribution," was that transaction fair to the holders of the $40 par common which was selling at $25 at the time? What would one need to know to decide? e. g. What would have been the cost to Laminated of alternative capital? Did the real estate purchased have a unique value to Laminated? Are there any risks of additional hidden liabilities? What is the effect on market valuation of the new no par class of the fact it is non-voting stock?

Accounting Note: The accounting entries for this transaction are:

Dr. Land	$18,000	
Cr. Accounts payable		$13,000
Cr. Stated capital, no par common, 250 sh.		2,000
Cr. Paid-in surplus, no par common		3,000

(2) Requiring additional capital, the management of Laminated sells for $20,000 in cash $20,000 face amount of 9¼% ten-year convertible debentures. Under the terms of the debentures, the holder may at any time convert a $1,000 face amount debenture into 30 shares of the company's $40 par common stock.

Legal Note: As a matter of logical analysis (not necessarily true market behavior) a rational holder of one of these $1,000 debentures, which pay interest of $92.50 per annum, will convert it into 30 shares of Laminated $40 par common stock if (a) the market value of the common rises above $33.33 and there is a resale market for it; or (perhaps) if (b) the dividend on a share of common comes to exceed $3.08 ($92.50 divided by 30) per annum and promises to continue to do so; or (c) the average annual growth of the per share value, plus dividends, exceeds $3.08 per share and promises to continue to do so.

Under the doctrine of "equitable contribution," were the terms of the convertible debentures fair to the existing holders of $40 par common, which at the time had a market price of $25?

Accounting Note: When a $1,000 debenture is converted into 30 shares of $40 par common, the company's liabilities will be reduced and its stated capital must be increased to reflect the issue of the new shares. But the figures do not match evenly. On the conversion of a debenture, the company's liabilities will be reduced by $1,000 but stated capital will have to be increased by $1,200 with respect to the 30 newly-issued shares. Arguably nothing need be done about this until the time of conversion. But modern accounting would say that at the time the debentures are first issued, a surplus account should be restricted by $200 for each debenture in anticipation of the ultimate conversion and of the charge that will at that time have to be made to a sur-

Tr. 20   PRESENT AND FUTURE STOCK ISSUANCE   143

plus account to make up the stated capital deficiency. Thus, the accounting entries made on the issue of the convertible debentures are:

Dr. Cash	$20,000	
Cr. 9¼% ten-year debentures		$20,000

and, in addition, enter under a surplus account. "Restricted reserve for conversion of 9¼% debentures to $40 par common stock, $4,000."

(3) The management persuades the holders of the outstanding $40 par common to subscribe to an additional 500 shares of the same class, but they will not agree to a subscription price greater than $25 per share.

Legal Note: If the applicable corporation statute provides for preemptive rights, and the certificate of incorporation of Laminated Thumbscrew does not exclude them, each $40 par common shareholder must be given an opportunity to subscribe to the new issue in proportion to the number of such shares he holds.

This transaction is a subscription agreement to buy stock in the future, and not a present purchase; the subscription price will be required to be paid in and the stock certificates issued whenever the board calls upon the subscribers for payment. For reasons grounded in history, however, stock subscribed is considered to be issued stock for purposes of capital accounting and the legal capital statutes. There are a number of anomolies about this convention, the most bizarre of which is that if (as is not the case here) the subscription price is greater than par, then the effect of the subscription will be to create a corporate receivable, to increase the stated capital to the extent of the par, *and* to create a paid-in surplus (!). In this way a paper transaction, that involves no payment of assets into the corporate treasury, could be used in a balance sheet surplus jurisdiction to provide a surplus basis for legally distributing corporate assets to common shareholders.

In the case given, however, the problem is different. The subscription price of $25—which is dictated by market realities—runs flatly afoul of the arbitrary statutory stated capital requirement that, unless bankruptcy is impending, the purchasers of newly issued stock must pay in an amount equal to or greater than par. The board of directors and shareholders could, of course, simply amend the certificate of incorporation again to reduce the par, as in Transaction 10. But there may be another way to go or at least another argument to run. As noted with regard to Transaction 8, the shares issued in a stock dividend are simply issued "against" surplus. Similarly, in the case of shares issued on conversion of the debentures, as just discussed, part or all of the stated capital can be made up by simply charging a surplus account. Why can this not also be done in the case of "watered stock" (stock that is issued for less than par) where the company has a sufficient surplus to enable it to make up a sufficient stated capital entry by simply charging the surplus account? Laminated Thumbscrew decides to try this in its handling of the new stock subscriptions. The accounting entries are:

> Dr. Subscriptions receivable, $40 par common, 500 sh. @ $25 $12,500
> Dr. Earned surplus   7,500
> Cr. Stated capital, $40 par common, 500 sh. $20,000

(4) Laminated Thumbscrew's management also goes to its preferred shareholders with an offering of stock warrants. Under the terms of these warrants the holder may buy from the company one share of its $8 preferred stock, $10 par value, at any time within the next year at a price of $75. The market price of the preferred at the time of the sale of the warrants is $65. The management succeeds in selling 1,000 of these warrants, but is only able to obtain a price of $1 per warrant.

Accounting Note: In the world of corporate finance, the warrant is a close family relation of the convertible debenture, and at least a cousin of the subscription, but the accounting convention with regard to warrants is different. Sale of these warrants will not lead to a balance sheet entry for the preferred stock that may ultimately be issued on exercise of the warrants; the only balance sheet entry will be a reference to the warrants themselves, with a footnote giving the details of the terms. If the warrant purchase price of the stock were below par, would the answer be different?

Tr. 20   PRESENT AND FUTURE STOCK ISSUANCE   145

And if the price of the preferred reaches, or approaches, $75—the price above which a warrant holder would find it to his economic advantage to exercise his warrant—will the accountants begin to require an entry on the balance sheet for the preferred stock to be sold through the warrants?

The accounting entries (apart from explanatory footnote) are:

    Dr. Cash $1,000
    Cr. Warrants outstanding $1,000

(5) A committee of the board of directors, acting pursuant to a vote of shareholders establishing a management stock option plan, issues a block of incentive stock options to the company's four key executives. Under the terms of these options, each executive may at any time within the ensuing five years, if still in the employ of the company, purchase up to 50 shares of the company's $40 par common stock at a price of $35 per share.

Legal Note: Former Federal tax incentives for executive stock options have lost their allure, but the options mechanism continues to have some appeal as a compensation tool since they increase the executive's equity position in the company and conserve assets of the corporation by rewarding the executive off the balance sheet through dilution of the value of the shares of shareholders.

Accounting Note: Unlike the other transactions involving potential future stock issues, the accounting convention is that the grant of the stock options does not lead to any entry on the balance sheet.

Future exercise by Laminated Thumbscrew's executives of their options to purchase $40 par shares at a price of $35 per share will obviously not comply with the statutory legal capital requirement that no less than par be paid. But the issuance of the option itself is not a violation of the statute. As for the future, it is the hope of the **management that when** an executive option is executed, and a share issued, the accounting entries can be handled in a manner parallel to Transactions 20(2) and (3) supra i. e.:

Dr. Cash	$35	
Dr. Earned surplus	5	
Cr. Stated capital, $40 common		$40

* * * * * * * * *

(a) *Balance sheet presentation*:

The five transactions grouped as Transaction 20 and the correlative accounting entries listed above produce the following balance sheet:

Laminated Thumbscrew, Inc.
Balance Sheet #20 (giving effect to Transaction 20)

ASSETS		LIABILITIES	
Cash	$ 31,015	Accounts payable	$ 15,000
Subscriptions receivable—$40 par common, 500 sh. @ $25	12,500	Bank loan	10,000
		Debentures, cv, 9¼%, 10 yr.	20,000
Accounts receivable	58,334	Liabilities	$ 45,000
Inventory	17,500	**SHAREHOLDERS' EQUITY**	
Land	18,350	Capital:	
Secret process	1	$40 par common, 1,780 sh.	71,700
		No par common, 250 sh.	2,000
		$8 preferred—$10 par, 100 sh.	1,000
		Warrants [1]	1,000
		Paid-in surplus:	
		$40 par common	500
		No par common	3,000
		$8 preferred	7,000
		Earned surplus:	
		Restricted [2] $4,000	
		Unrestricted 2,500	6,500
		Shareholders' equity	$ 92,700
	$137,700		$137,700

1. Outstanding, 1,000 warrants, issued at $1 per warrant, each entitling the holder to purchase 1 share of $8 preferred $10 par value, at $75 at any time within the ensuing year.
2. Appropriated reserve for conversion of 9¼% cv. debentures to $40 par common stock, 600 sh.

(b) *Legal capital restraints*:

I. **Preferred**

See discussion at Transaction 19.

II. Common

Although the no par stock subscribed for is "issued" for technical reasons of legal capital accounting, it is not, of course, "outstanding" for purposes of receiving dividend payments.[7] Considering, therefore, only the outstanding $40 par common:

(i) **Insolvency jurisdiction:** shareholder distribution of $92,700 allowable since assets exceed liabilities by $92,700.[8]

(ii) **Balance sheet surplus jurisdiction:** shareholder distribution of $17,000 allowable since assets are $17,000 more than liabilities plus legal capital. The balance sheet statutes accord no special recognition to the accountants' entry restricting the earned surplus account by $4,000 in anticipation of the future conversion of the debentures. But would a modern court? And should a careful lawyer?

(iii) **Earned surplus jurisdiction:** shareholder distribution of $6,500 is statutorily allowable since earned surplus is $6,500. But of this amount, $4,000 is restricted by the accounting entry anticipating conversion of the convertible debentures. It is

---

7. Is it "outstanding" for purposes of voting rights? computations of shareholder quorums? computations of class voting requirements, etc.?

8. Suppose, as an analytic exercise, that the board now decides in an insolvency jurisdiction to distribute to shareholders all assets except the $45,000 required to pay its creditors —decided, in short, to liquidate. Assume, too, that the conversion privilege of the debentures, the warrants and the stock options all lapse or are cut off. Assume that the subscriptions for the 500 shares of $40 par common are called, and, as agreed, $12,500 is paid in. Assume, finally, that the actual liquidating values of the company's assets are equal to their book value, so there will be $92,700 to be distributed. Of this, $10,000 must go to pay the $100 per share liquidating preference of the 100 shares of preferred. The remaining $82,700 must be divided among the 1,780 shares of $40 par common and the 250 shares of no par common since they rank *pari passu* on liquidation. $82,700 ÷ 2,030 = $40.73 per share. In this circumstance, it will clearly advantage the earlier shareholders for the board not to call the new subscriptions, since the new subscribers will pay in only $25 per share and promptly receive back $40.73. If the subscriptions are not called, this will reduce corporate assets available for distribution by $12,500 to $70,200, but will reduce the common shares outstanding to 1,280, so that the *pro rata* distribution per share will increase to $54.84.

Does this analysis establish that $25 per share was too low a price for the subscriptions, and "unfair" to the existing shareholders under the principle of equitable contribution?

likely that an earned surplus statute would be interpreted to take such restrictions into account and would limit the allowable distribution to $2,500.

(iv) **Current earnings jurisdiction:** see 2(b)(iv) supra.

Legal Note: In the interest of simplicity, it has been assumed that Laminated Thumbscrew's lawyer, accountant and board of directors set up the $4,000 provision for the convertible debentures as a restriction on the earned surplus account. But it is worth considering that the restriction (if made at all) might have been offset against one or more paid-in surplus items. If, for example, the paid-in surplus item for the preferred stock were to be restricted to provide a source of stated capital for the common shares issued on conversion of the debentures, the result will be to preserve earned surplus and thus make it possible to make dollar payments on junior stock that are charged against sources invested by senior stock.

Transaction 21: Transactions between Corporation and Shareholders

In year ten, the fortunes and prospects of Laminated Thumbscrew steadily improve as it makes a profit of $11,000, the $40 par common rises on the market to $36 per share, the no par common rises to $32 and the $8 preferred goes up to $76.

A. The following share transactions then take place:

(1) The board of directors calls the outstanding $40 par common stock subscriptions, the subscribers pay in the $12,500, and the certificates for the 500 shares are issued to the purchasers.

Accounting Note: The entries are:

Dr. Cash	$12,500	
Cr. Stock subscription		$12,500

No entry is needed for stated capital since it was made when the subscriptions were entered into.

(2) The holders of all the convertible debentures convert their $20,000 in debt instruments to 600 shares of common stock.

Accounting Note: The entries are:

Dr. Debentures	$20,000	
Dr. Earned surplus	4,000	
Cr. Stated capital, $40 par common		$24,000

The entry restricting earned surplus by $4,000 is eliminated, and the number of outstanding $40 par common shares is increased to 2,380.

(3) The holders of 100 of the outstanding warrants exercise their right to buy shares of the $8 preferred at a price of $75 per share; the other 900 warrants lapse.

Accounting Note: The entries are:

Dr. Cash	$ 7,500	
Cr. Stated capital, $8 preferred $10 par		$ 1,000
Cr. $8 preferred paid-in surplus		6,500

* * * * * *

Dr. Warrants	$ 1,000	
Cr. $8 preferred paid-in surplus		$ 1,000

The number of outstanding $8 preferred shares is increased to 200.

(4) The president and vice president of Laminated Thumbscrew exercise their options to buy 10 shares of $40 par common for $35 per share.

Accounting Note: The entries are:

Dr. Cash	$ 350	
Dr. Earned surplus	50	
Cr. Stated capital, $40 par common		$ 400

The number of outstanding $40 par common shares is increased to 2,390. See discussion at Transaction 20(5).

Legal Note: In most jurisdictions a careful lawyer would be reluctant to give an opinion that these 10 shares are "fully paid and non-assessable" despite the proper appearance of the stated capital account since each of these shares was clearly issued for less than par. But then so were the shares that were issued on conversion of the debentures, and the shares issued "against surplus" in the stock dividend, etc., etc. There is no relief from internal inconsistencies in the statutory stated capital system. The lawyer could at least assure the purchasing executives that their actual risk of liability is both very remote and narrowly limited.

B. Following on these share transactions, the board of directors makes the following distributions to shareholders:

(1) The company pays the annual dividend of $8 per share on the 200 shares of outstanding $8 preferred stock.

Accounting Note: What surplus should be charged for this $800 distribution? The management would prefer to keep earned surplus available for common stock dividends, it decides to charge the preferred dividend to the paid-in surplus account attributable to the $8 preferred. In a balance sheet surplus jurisdiction, the corporation's lawyer would approve the legality of this action. The accounting entries are:

```
Dr. Paid-in surplus
    $8 preferred        $ 1,600
Cr. Cash                              $ 1,600
```

(2) The company pays a dividend of $5 per share on the 2,390 outstanding shares of $40 par common and the 250 shares of no par common.

Accounting Note: It is assumed that the cash and earned surplus accounts were increased by the $11,000 profit for the year. The accounting entries for the dividends are:

```
Dr. Earned surplus    $13,200
Cr. Cash                              $13,200
```

See Legal Note below with regard to this transaction.

(3) The company redeems 50 of the 200 outstanding shares of $8 preferred stock at the redemption price of $100 per share.

Accounting Note: The accounting entries are:

```
Dr. Stated capital,
    $8 preferred        $  500
Dr. $8 preferred paid-in
    surplus              4,500
Cr. Cash                              $ 5,000
```

How do creditors like this redemption transaction? How do common shareholders like it? How do the preferred shareholders who were redeemed like it? How do preferred shareholders whose shares were not redeemed like it?

(a) *Balance sheet presentation:*

Laminated Thumbscrew, Inc.
Balance Sheet #21 (giving effect to Transaction 21)

ASSETS		LIABILITIES	
Cash	$ 42,565	Accounts payable	$ 15,000
Accounts receivable	58,334	Bank loan	10,000
Inventory	17,500	Liabilities	$ 25,000
Land	18,350	**SHAREHOLDERS' EQUITY**	
Secret process	1	Capital: $40 par common, 2,390 sh.	96,100
		No par common, 250 sh.	2,000
		$8 preferred, $10 par, 150 sh.	1,500
		Paid-in surplus:	
		$40 par common	500
		No par common	3,000
		$8 preferred	8,400
		Earned surplus	250
		Shareholders' equity	$111,750
	$136,750		$136,750

(b) *Legal capital restraints:*

I. **Preferred**

See discussion at Transaction 19.

II. **Common**

(i) **Insolvency jurisdiction:** shareholder distribution of $111,750 allowable, since assets exceed liabilities by $111,750.

(ii) **Balance sheet surplus jurisdiction:** shareholder distribution of $12,650 allowable since assets are $12,650 more than liabilities plus legal capital.

Legal Note: The above distributive transactions illustrate some of the questions that arise regarding which surplus account should be charged when a distribution is made. Laminated Thumbscrew at this stage has two classes of common stock and one of preferred. In a jurisdiction allowing dividends to be charged to paid-in surplus, may dividends on one class be charged to paid-in surplus attributable to the other? If one class has a paid-in surplus account, and another does not, should dividends on the former be charged to its paid-in surplus in order to preserve support for dividends for the class that has no such surplus? Note that the present case is simpler than many in that the two classes of common are *pari passu* in respect of dividends and liquidation; interest conflicts between the holders of the two classes would be much greater if dividends could be paid to one class while being skipped for the other. For ease and clarity in the above example, the common stock dividend was entered as a charge to earned surplus, the most conservative option.

    (iii) **Earned surplus jurisdiction:** shareholder distribution of $250 allowable since earned surplus is $250.

NOTE: Now consider the situation as a practical business matter. Is there any conceivable business reason why common shareholder distributions *should* be limited to an infinitesimal $250 in the case of this successful profitable enterprise that has a gaudy equity/debt ratio of 4.5, cash equal to nearly twice its total liabilities, a current ratio of 7.9, a quick ratio of 3.9, and at least one asset (the secret process) that is probably undervalued on the books?

The most fundamental criticism of the legal capital structure is not that it is shot through with analytic flaws—which it is—but that it operates arbitrarily, wholly unrelated to sensible business considerations, as the above situation illustrates.

    (iv) **Current earnings jurisdiction:** shareholder distribution of $11,000 allowable since the company had earnings of $11,000 in the current year.

Transaction 22: Corporate Combination; Purchase Accounting and Pooling of Interests Accounting

In year eleven, the management of Laminated Thumbscrew learns that it might be possible for the company to acquire another company, Iron Maidenform, Inc. Maidenform is in trouble. After many successful years under the leadership of a strong executive, the recently deceased founder, the company's board has not been able to find or agree upon a successor, and the family shareholders are at sword's point. Maidenform has lost money for the last two years and is cash short. The management of Laminated Thumbscrew believes, however, that Maidenform has some undervalued but developable assets, and that the two enterprises are promisingly complementary. A striking additional feature of Maidenform is that, despite recent losses, its balance sheet carries a substantial earned surplus. Its balance sheet is as follows:

Iron Maidenform, Inc.

ASSETS		LIABILITIES	
Cash	$ 5,000	Accounts payable	$ 17,000
Accounts receivable	20,000	Bank loan	8,000
Inventory	15,000	Liabilities	$ 25,000
		SHAREHOLDERS' EQUITY	
Equipment	25,000	Capital: $50 common, 1,000 sh.	$ 50,000
Land	35,000	Earned surplus	25,000
		Shareholders' equity	$ 75,000
	$100,000		$100,000

Unlike the case of Laminated, there is no public market for the closely held Maidenform stock; as can be seen, Maidenform's book value per share is $75 per share. The book value of Laminated's 2,390 shares of $40 common and 250 shares of no par common (after allotting $15,000 to the liquidation value of the $8 preferred) is $36.65; as its affairs have prospered, its market price has climbed to $50 per share. But many factors go into the negotiation of a stock exchange ratio, predominantly the comparative bargaining power of the parties, and out of the Laminated-Maidenform negotiation emerges a formula under which each shareholder of Maidenform stock will be offered 1.4 shares of Laminated Thumbscrew $40 par common for each share of Maidenform common that he holds. To acquire Maidenform, therefore, Laminated Thumbscrew will have to issue 1,400 additional shares of its $40 par common. All Maidenform shareholders decide that the Laminated offer is less unattractive than the available alternatives, and accept it. Laminated Thumbscrew thereupon issues to them 1,400 shares of its $40 par common which, in effect, is exchanged for their Maidenform stock.

> **Legal Note:** The description of this transaction has been written so as not to characterize or specify the legal means through which combination is effected. There are several ways by which it can be done.

> **Purchase of assets for shares:** As in Transaction 20(1), Laminated Thumbscrew can issue stock to Maidenform

in exchange for all its assets and liabilities.[9] Thereupon the selling corporation might retain the stock; or it might sell it on the market and use the proceeds to continue in some other business; or it might dissolve and distribute in liquidation the Laminated Thumbscrew shares to its own shareholders.

Merger: The two companies might effect a statutory merger. In the merger, upon vote of both boards of directors and both groups of shareholders, one company would be designated as the continuing company (here Laminated Thumbscrew) and the other as the terminating company; by force of the corporation statute, all the assets and liabilities of Maidenform would, upon effectiveness of the merger, become assets and liabilities of the continuing company; at the same time, all assenting shareholders of Maidenform would by force of law immediately become shareholders of the continuing company. Shareholders voting against the merger would be entitled to receive cash in the amount of the "fair value" of their shares.

Exchange of stock: In an exchange of stock, Laminated Thumbscrew would offer to shareholders of Maidenform to exchange Laminated Thumbscrew shares for their Maidenform shares and upon the exchange Maidenform would be a subsidiary of Laminated.

Six structural possibilities exist for this basic economic transaction, since the combined economic enterprise can be lodged inside either of the corporate carapaces.[10]

A. *Accounting Note: Purchase Method*

Transaction 20(1) describes the purchase of the assets and liabilities of another corporation in exchange for an is-

9. For a greater number of shares, Laminated might instead acquire all the assets, leaving the liabilities with the seller, but there are complications to that procedure, including some risk that unpaid creditors of the seller might be able to pursue the purchaser regardless of the contract between seller and buyer.

10. Other avenues exist to achieve the same economic result otherwise than by issue of stock of the existing companies. For example, Laminated could make a cash tender offer to shareholders of Iron Maidenform. Or through the procedure of statutory consolidation, both Laminated Thumbscrew and Iron Maidenform could terminate, their assets and liabilities could be transferred to a newly formed corporation, and assenting shareholders of both terminating companies would automatically become shareholders of the new company; dissenters would be entitled to cash. Or, by a three party combination, Laminated or Maidenform might create a 100% subsidiary, X Company and then combine X Company and the other company by any of the above routes.

sue of stock by Laminated Thumbscrew. The accounting for that kind of transaction is straight-forward. The board of directors of the issuing company determines a fair value for the shares being issued, and fair values for the assets and liabilities acquired. An appropriate entry is made in the stated capital account for the shares issued, and if the net value of the assets and liabilities acquired is determined by the issuer's board to be more than the stated capital entry, the remainder is credited to a paid-in surplus account. Appropriate entries are then made on the balance sheet for the tangible and determinable assets acquired, and if there is a difference between the valuation of the stock issued and the net fair value of assets and liabilities acquired, it is entered on the purchaser's books as "goodwill." [11] Under modern practice, this goodwill item will be amortized against earnings over a reasonable period, not in excess of forty years. The book value of the acquired assets and liabilities as they appeared on the seller's books is often immaterial.

Let it now be assumed that the Thumbscrew-Maidenform combination is to be accounted for as though it were such a purchase. The purchase price for the net assets and liabilities acquired is determined by the Laminated Thumbscrew board to be $70,000, i. e., 1,400 shares times their current market price of $50 per share. The new liabilities assumed are $25,000, so the assets to be added to the Laminated Thumbscrew balance sheet must total to $95,000 if a write-off is to be avoided. In allocating this amount among all assets except cash, the board of directors assesses the value of each item on the Maidenform balance sheet, as it is taken on to Laminated Thumbscrew's books. It finds Maidenform's book values to be inflated. The board concludes that the accounts receivable acquired should be reduced to $15,000; that the inventory is worth only $5,000; that the equipment should be reduced to $20,000; and that the land should be reduced to $30,000; this leaves $20,000 to be entered as goodwill. These figures are considered to be assets on Laminated Thumbscrew's balance sheet. On the liability side of the balance sheet, the newly assumed liabilities are accepted as is and increase the total liabilities by $25,000; stated capital for the $40 par common is increased by $56,000 (1,400 shares times $40 par) and paid-in surplus at-

---

11. Modern accounting practice would prefer the far clearer term "excess of cost over actual assets acquired," but "goodwill" is still in common use.

tributable to $40 par common is increased by the balance of $14,000. The balance sheet then reads as follows:

(a) *Balance sheet presentation*:

Laminated Thumbscrew, Inc.
Balance Sheet #22A (giving effect to Transaction 22)
Accounting by Purchase Method

ASSETS		LIABILITIES	
Cash	$ 47,565	Accounts payable	$ 32,000
Accounts receivable	73,334	Bank loan	18,000
Inventory	22,500	Liabilities	$ 50,000
Equipment	20,000	**SHAREHOLDERS' EQUITY**	
Land	48,350	Capital: $40 par common, 3,790 sh.	$152,100
Goodwill	20,000		
Secret process	1	No par common, 250 sh.	2,000
		$8 preferred, $10 par, 150 sh.	1,500
		Paid-in surplus:	
		$40 par common	14,500
		No par common	3,000
		$8 preferred	8,400
		Earned surplus	250
		Shareholders' equity	$181,750
	$231,750		$231,750

(b) *Legal capital restraints*:

I. **Preferred**

See discussion at Transaction 19.

II. **Common**

(i) **Insolvency jurisdiction**: shareholder distribution of $181,750 allowable, since assets exceed liabilities by $181,750.

(ii) **Balance sheet surplus jurisdiction**: shareholder distribution of $26,150 allowable since assets are $26,150 more than liabilities plus legal capital.

(iii) **Earned surplus jurisdiction**: shareholder distribution of $250 allowable since earned surplus is $250.

(iv) **Current earnings jurisdiction**: no special considerations.

B. *Accounting Note: Pooling of Interests*

An alternative way of looking at the corporate combination leads to an alternative accounting method, the so-called "pooling of interests" method. The combinatory transaction may be regarded as an arrangement between two shareholder groups rather than a transaction between two corporate entities. If a combination is effected by issuing common stock, each stockholder group partially gives up its interest in assets which it formerly held but receives a partial interest in assets formerly held by the other. The shareholders may be said to "pool their interests." From this premise and perspective, it is contended that the financial statements of the component companies in the combination should be "pooled." When the "pooling of interests" method of accounting is used, the recorded assets and liabilities of the constituent companies are carried forward to the combined corporation at their recorded amounts; that is, the transaction is not used as an occasion for placing an accounting value on the shares issued nor for allocating that value on the books among the assets acquired. Correspondingly, no goodwill item is created on the combined balance sheet. Not only are the balance sheets combined in this manner through the use of the "pooling of interests," but current income statements are also combined, and income statements for prior years are restated to show such a combination.

The plausibility of the "pooling of interests" concept can be most easily seen when the formal form of the combination is a "consolidation," that is, a combination in which both shareholder groups surrender their stock and receive in exchange the stock of a new corporation into which the two former corporations are combined. But the fact that one of the corporations usually issues its stock in exchange for that of the other does not alter the substance of the transaction. Thus the pooling of interests technique may apply equally to business combinations in which one or more companies become subsidiary corporations, or one company transfers its net assets to another, or each company transfers its net assets to a newly formed corporation. One or more combining companies may be subsidiaries of the issuing corporation after the combination is consummated. Dissolution of the combining company is not a condition for applying the pooling of interests method; if the newly acquired subsidiary is continued in existence, the pooling of interests method governs the process by which the financial statements of the subsidiary are consolidated with those of the parent.

Let it be assumed that the Thumbscrew-Maidenform combination is to be accounted for by the pooling of interests method. The asset side of the balance sheet of Laminated Thumbscrew is augmented by the recorded values that appeared on the asset side of the Maidenform balance sheet. Similarly the liabilities are transferred. But stated capital on Laminated Thumbscrew's balance sheet must be increased by $56,000 (1,400 shares times $40 par) to reflect the newly issued shares. The Maidenform balance sheet carried a $50,000 stated capital, and this is "transferred" first to make up the required stated capital of the combined enterprise. But what of the other $6,000 needed? To supply this amount, some surplus account or accounts must be charged. It is probably acceptable to charge one or more paid-in surplus accounts for this purpose—whether originally on the balance sheet of the continuing or the terminating company, and whether or not attributable to the class of shares being newly issued. But assuming the most conservative avenue is taken, and the $6,000 is charged to earned surplus, the result is as follows:

(a) *Balance sheet presentation*:

Laminated Thumbscrew, Inc.
Balance Sheet # 22B (giving effect to Transaction 22)
Accounting by Pooling of Interests Method

ASSETS		LIABILITIES	
Cash	$ 47,565	Accounts payable	$ 32,000
Accounts receivable	78,334	Bank loans	18,000
Inventory	32,500	Liabilities	$ 50,000
Equipment	25,000	**SHAREHOLDERS' EQUITY**	
Land	53,350	Capital: $40 par	
		common, 3,790 sh.	152,100
Secret process	1		
		No par common, 250 sh.	2,000
		$8 preferred, $10 par, 150 sh.	1,500
		Paid-in surplus:	
		$40 par common	500
		No par common	3,000
		$8 preferred	8,400
		Earned surplus	19,250
		Shareholders' equity	$186,750
	$236,750		$236,750

Legal Note: Note that whether the $6,000 is charged to paid-in surplus account or an earned surplus account, once more an example is provided where shares are issued "against" surplus. See the discussion at Transaction 19(3).

(b) *Legal capital restraints*:

I. **Preferred**

See Transaction 19.

II. **Common**

(i) **Insolvency jurisdiction:** shareholder distribution of $186,750 allowable since assets exceed liabilities by $186,750.

(ii) **Balance sheet surplus jurisdiction:** shareholder distribution of $31,150 allowable since assets are $31,150 more than liabilities plus legal capital.

(iii) **Earned surplus jurisdiction:** shareholder distribution of $19,250 allowable since earned surplus is $19,250. If the $6,000 required to increase stated capital had been charged to paid-in surplus accounts, the earned surplus account would be $6,000 higher, or $25,250.

(iv) **Current earnings jurisdiction:** no special consideration except that if Iron Maidenform had had current earnings, they would have been "transferred" to Laminated Thumbscrew under the pooling of interests method of accounting and presumably provided an immediate basis for dividends in a current earnings jurisdiction.

NOTE: Balance Sheets #22A and #22B should be carefully compared. They will be found to be quite different, not only as to capital and surplus structure but in the composition of their asset accounts, with consequent impacts on the company's future earnings statements.

For present purposes, the key point to notice from this transaction as accounted for by the pooling of interests method is that Laminated Thumbscrew has succeeded in developing approximately $19,000 (or perhaps $25,000) in earned surplus by doing no more than issuing more shares of its own stock. If Iron Maidenform had had current earnings, Laminated Thumbscrew would have acquired those too. The enterprise acquired by Laminated Thumbscrew is, at least for the present, a money loser with an inflated balance sheet. Nonetheless, the transaction has now put Laminated Thumbscrew in a position where it may, even in the most stringent jurisdiction, pay out to its shareholders a minimum of about $20,000.

Note, too, that the transaction could have been handled so as to transfer earned surplus onto the Laminated balance sheet with no charge to paid-in surplus or earned surplus. If, instead of $40 par stock, no par or low par shares had been issued to the former Iron Maidenform shareholders, stated capital with regard to the shares issued could have been set by the board of directors at say, $50,000, the same as the stated capital of Iron Maidenform, and the $6,000 charge could have thus been avoided. Indeed, if in that transaction the increment required to be made to stated capital had been set at *less* than $50,000 the difference would have gone on to Laminated Thumbscrew's balance sheet as some new form of additional paid-in surplus. Finally, another possibility might have been to run the merger in the opposite direction, leave Iron Maidenform as the surviving corporation and issue no par or low par stock of Maidenform, transferring to its balance sheet the large, stated capital figure on the Laminated Thumbscrew balance sheet.

In many situations, it is evidently advantageous to an acquiring company to account for a corporate combination on the pooling of interests basis. In the heady days of the go-go funds and of high-flying conglomerates in the mid-sixties, a key factor was the flood of acquisitions that were accounted for on this basis, with a resultant pile-up of earnings and earned surplusses bought with newly issued stock and other more elaborate paper. The reasons for these acquisitions were not related to a desire to circumvent legal capital constraints on shareholder distributions. The stacked up earnings emerging from pooling combinations demonstrated to a credulous market that the issuer was, and continued to be, a "growth company" whose stock was deserving of a high price-earnings ratio, whose price per share rose correspondingly, and whose ability was thereby increased to issue more new shares as the medium of exchange to bring into the conglomerate the income and earned surplus of still more corporations that did not enjoy as high a price-earnings ratio.[12] When the reaction came with the market declines of

---

[12]. To be more complete: The active acquisition-minded companies were perceived by the market as "growth companies" and therefore had high price-earnings multiples, but their technologies, or competition, had developed to a point where their growth in earnings was leveling off. In order to sustain the growth image, these companies leveraged their stock prices against companies that had good earnings

the late sixties, closer attention was brought to bear on the practice of pooling of interests accounting, and a great debate raged among accountants, lawyers, and other interested parties on the question whether the pooling of interests method should ever be allowable, and, if so, under what conditions. The publication in 1970 of Opinion 16 (Business Combinations) by the Accounting Principles Board of the American Institute of Certified Public Accountants has, for the time being, put the matter at rest.[13] This is not a proper place to review the 47-page Opin-

but low price-earnings multiples. Thus, if Company X had 1,000,000 shares outstanding, earned $1,000,000 per year and sold on the market for 40 times earnings, while Company Y was earning $100,000 per year but was valued on the market at 20 times earnings, or $2,000,000, Company X could negotiate to acquire Company Y for approximately 50,000 of X's shares (leaving out the dilution factor). The newly issued 50,000 shares would, after the transaction, generate for Company X $100,000 per year in new earnings, or $2 per new share issued. In general, the $100,000 in new earnings added $4,000,000 to the market value of the shares of Company X. Thus, after the acquisition, Company X could expect its market value to rise to $44,000,000 and, with 1,050,000 shares outstanding, the stock would rise from $40 to around $42. Meanwhile, the former shareholders of Company Y would have received a listed, marketable, "growth" security on a tax-free exchange basis to replace what, typically, had been a non-growth, closely-held stock. Hence, everyone was happy. But the transaction had done nothing to alleviate the basic non-growth character of the acquirer, and there was usually no reason to suppose that the newly acquired $100,000 of earnings flow would grow substantially either. Indeed, as acquisition followed acquisition, it often happened that the newly acquired earnings dropped, for the managements of the conglomerates found that they were unable to manage properly the diverse businesses they had acquired and that they were also unable to enlist dedicated, continuous and enthusiastic management efforts from the former owners and managers of the businesses acquired.

The acquiring conglomerate had to have pooling of interest accounting to avoid the goodwill factor on its balance sheet. Usually the price for the selling company had to be sweetened somewhat to consummate the deal; thus, in the example above, 60,000 shares of Company X would have been a more typical price. In that case, even if the fair value of the assets of Company Y transferred to the books of Company X had been equal to $2,000,000, an additional $400,000 (10,000 shares at $40 per share) would have to be accounted for as goodwill. If, in addition, the fair value of the assets of the acquired company was relatively low, an even larger goodwill item would have had to be entered on the books of the acquiring company if the pooling of interest accounting method had not been available for use. The goodwill item looks bad on the acquirer's balance sheet since it implies that the issuer's stock is not really worth $40, or that the selling company is overpriced; the accountants will require the goodwill to be amortized over time, thereby reducing the earnings of the acquirer; the amortization is not deductible for tax purposes; the result would be that the newly acquired earnings would be depressed, and the whole purpose of the deal would be frustrated.

13. But just barely: Opinions of the Board require a two-thirds vote; in the case of Opinion 16, twelve members assented and six dissented.

ion 16, though language from it has been drawn on *passim* in summary form here. But it may be said that the Board drew a great line, like the Pope in the Treaty of Tordesillas, holding that both the purchase method and the pooling of interests method have their places, but that there can never be a choice between them—if in a particular transaction one is right then the other is wrong. That approach required the Board to specify in detail which kinds of transactions fall on which side of the line, and that is why the Opinion reads like 47 pages of Internal Revenue Service Regulations. (To satisfy the curious reader, the Laminated Thumbscrew-Iron Maidenform transaction falls in the class of transactions that under Opinion 16 must be accounted for by the pooling of interests method.)

As a final observation about merger, it should be noted that under the merger statutes of all states, shareholders of the terminating company (and perhaps of the continuing company) who voted against the merger have the right to insist through a meticulous procedure, that the continuing company pay them in cash the fair market value of their shares.[14] This payment of dissenters' rights is a distribution of corporate assets to shareholders and may entail very large sums; but once again the statutory legal capital constraints do not constrain, since payments of dissenters rights in a merger are everywhere exempt from them and creditors are again left to watch as dollars flow out of the corporate treasury to junior security holders.

Transaction 23: Dissolution and Liquidation

During year eleven, a small syndicate of investors acquires virtually all the shares of Laminated Thumbscrew, and for a number of business and tax reasons decides to dissolve the corporation, sell off its assets, and distribute the proceeds to the shareholders. This is voted by the board of directors and shareholders and a certificate of corporate dissolution is thereupon filed with the corporation commissioner.

(a) *Balance sheet presentation*:

Same as Balance Sheet #22B. The filing of the dissolution certificate does not affect the balance sheet, though the fact of its filing may be footnoted.

---

14. See Manning, "The Shareholder's Appraisal Remedy: An Essay for Frank Coker," 72 Yale Law Journal 223–265 (1962).

(b) *Legal capital constraints*:

All jurisdictions: shareholder distributions are allowable in an amount equal to the net market value of the net assets of the company, as they are liquidated. The dollar amount cannot be taken from the book figures since the total value of the assets distributed will usually be determined by the real market value of the corporate assets as they are sold off and turned into liquid proceeds.[15] For example, what value, if any, will the secret process have in liquidation?

Upon the filing of the certificate of dissolution every jurisdiction becomes an insolvency jurisdiction and nothing more. Dissolution automatically renders the local legal capital statute irrelevant. The board of directors, as it officiates in the liquidation and distribution of the enterprise assets, is of course mandated to pay off the corporation's creditors. And if the board distributes assets to the shareholders without paying the corporation's creditors, the board members themselves may be held liable by the creditors. But so long as the board meets that requirement, it is no longer inhibited by legal capital constraints from making asset distributions to shareholders. Note, too, that though the creditors come "first" in their claim the board is not required to pay them all first chronologically before making distributions to shareholders.

And so, when all is done, and it is the end of the day, and just as the company's situation becomes the very one that gave rise to the doctrine of legal capital—just as most of the assets are being distributed to the shareholders as the creditors wait in line, as in *Wood v. Dummer*—the modern legal capital statutes become inoperative by their own terms.

---

15. This sentence is qualified by "usually" because occasionally a corporate asset will be distributed in undivided interests to the shareholders, or securities held by the corporation will be divided and distributed; in these instances there is no realization of a market value for the assets distributed.

Part Three

FRESH WINDS BLOWING

Fresh winds appear to be blowing in the field of legal capital. Most important are the 1980 changes in the Model Business Corporation Act. But signs of real change first appeared in the General Corporation Law of California, adopted in 1975.

I. CALIFORNIA, 1975

In 1975 California struck out into new territory in the financial provisions of its new General Corporation Law. The draftsmen of the new Law and the accompanying legislative report obviously concurred with the general thesis developed here—that the traditional doctrinal edifice of par and legal capital is ineffective. They did not demolish the structure, but they did subject it to substantial reconstruction.

The new California Corporation Law continues the usual requirement that a corporation's articles of incorporation must set forth the total number of shares of each class of stock which the corporation is authorized to issue. But the statute omits the further provision found in all other state statutes that the articles must also specify whether the stock is par or no par.[1] The subscriber or purchaser must still pay for his stock, and the consideration must meet the conventional statutory standards; but the practical effect of the new California statute is to convert all stock issued by California corporations after the statute's effective date into no par shares.[2]

Treasury shares are given short shrift in the 1975 California Law. The concept is eliminated in its entirety with the comment, "Treasury shares are merely a historical curiosity."[3]

As for controlling distributions to shareholders, the new California statute permits a shareholder distribution

    (i) to the extent of retained earnings; or

    (ii) if, after the distribution, "assets" (as statutorily defined) are 125% of liabilities (as defined) and if other de-

---

[1]. Cal.Gen.Corp.Law § 202(d)(e).

[2]. The California draftsmen say that "a statement of 'par value' is not prohibited; it will simply have no legal significance . . . ."

[3]. Cal.Gen.Corp.Law § 510, revisers' comment.

tailed criteria are met regarding the ratio of current assets and current liabilities.[4]

These changes are a sensible move away from the conceptual and toward the realities of economic and business analysis. At the same time, one must entertain a certain skepticism as to whether the introduction of indenture-like ratio provisions is warranted in a general corporation statute or will prove administrable. The most likely outcome, one fears, is that the new provisions will prove too technical for many purposes and too primitive for others. And it is hard to muster confidence in a future role of California state courts as accounting tribunals.

In any case, the lawyer and accountant today must recall that in matters of legal capital, as in many other matters, California is different.

II. MODEL BUSINESS CORPORATION ACT, 1980 CHANGES

In 1980 the financial provisions for the Model Business Corporation Act were revamped in their entirety. The Model Act provides the basis for the corporation laws of a majority of the states (approximately 35) and although as of this writing no state has yet adopted the revised financial provisions, eventually some or all of these states will. It is therefore necessary to gain an acquaintance with these new provisions, particularly since they embody a dramatic break with the past.

For 30 years, the progenitor and custodian of the evolution of the Model Business Corporation Act has been the Committee on Corporate Laws of the American Bar Association's Section of Corporation, Banking and Business Law. A special joint subcommittee, drawn equally from the Committee on Corporate Laws and from the Section's Committee on Accounting, did the spade work on the revision of the financial provisions of the Act over a period of two years. Their work product then went through the usual Model Act procedure of three readings, national publication for comments in the Section's organ, *The Business Lawyer*, and ultimate adoption by the Committee.

The Report of the Committee on Corporate Laws accompanying the 1980 changes is printed in Volume 34 of *The Business Lawyer* at pages 1867–1889 (July, 1979); page references cited here refer to that source.

The Committee's Report comes right to the point in its opening sentence and boldly takes its stand.

---

4. Cal.Gen.Corp.Law § 500.

"The amendments to the financial provisions of the Model Business Corporation Act (the 'Model Act') reflect a complete modernization of all provisions of the Model Act concerning financial matters, including (a) the elimination of the outmoded concepts of stated capital and par value, (b) the definition of 'distribution' as a broad term governing dividends, share repurchases and similar actions that should be governed by the same standard, (c) the reformulation of the statutory standards governing the making of distributions, (d) the elimination of the concept of treasury stock, and (e) the making of a number of technical and conforming changes which are necessary or advisable in connection with the basic revisions.

"It has long been recognized by practitioners and legal scholars that the pervasive statutory structure in which 'par value' and 'stated capital' are basic to the state corporation statutes does not today serve the original purpose of protecting creditors and senior security holders from payments to junior security holders, and may, to the extent security holders are led to believe that it provides some protection, tend to be misleading. In light of this recognized fact, the Committee on Corporate Laws has, as part of a fundamental revision of the financial provisions of the Model Act, deleted the mandatory concepts of stated capital and par value . . . .

. . .

"The Committee also concluded that the concept of treasury stock should be eliminated, and that reacquired shares should automatically be restored to the status of authorized but unissued stock, unless the articles prohibit reissuance. This is based upon the judgment that treasury stock should have no meaningful or valid status of any substance, particularly in view of the elimination of par value, and stated capital, and of surplus as a measuring limitation . . . ."
(pp. 1867–9)

As can be seen, these are no small tinkerings. The 1980 revisions of the Model Act yank out by the roots every tendril of the doctrines discussed earlier in this book. As revised, the Model Act, like a Soviet encyclopedia dealing with a political "unperson," eliminates almost every reference to par, and eradicates all references to stated capital, treasury shares, surpluses, and all their fearsome progeny. The changes required to achieve this result were extensive. Definitions of these concepts, years in the making, have been deleted. Whole blocks of regulatory sections have simply vanished.[5] And very little new text has been put in their places. One can only conclude that the regulatory system in the revised Act has been radically simplified. And it has.

Following is a review of the revised Model Act, proceeding generally in the sequence of the discussion in Chapters III and IV of Part One of this Book.

A. The Shareholder's Pay-in Obligation

1. *Consideration required*

As before, no minimum amount of assets is required to be paid in to the corporate pot by the shareholders.

The revised Act remains traditional in declaring that promissory notes and future services are not acceptable consideration for the issuance of shares.[6] Perhaps the next round of revision can bring this requirement more into line with business reality.

The central proposition as to the shareholders' pay-in obligation under the revised Act is that shares "may be issued for such consideration as shall be authorized by the board of directors, establishing a price (in money or other consideration) or a minimum price or general formula or method by which the price will be determined."[7] And that is it. The purchasing shareholder's sole obligation to the corporation and to its creditors is to pay whatever he agreed to pay for the shares.[8]

Since many corporations will of course continue to carry old par provisions in existing charter documents, Section 54 of the revised Act specifically authorizes such provisions to be included as optional elements in articles of incorporation. The Committee Report says of that Section:

> "In the revision, there is a specific reference to the permissible inclusion of provisions concerning par value. This new paragraph implicitly recognizes that all existing corporate charter documents have provisions concerning shares with par value, and these provisions will continue to exist. Under the revisions, the current legal effect of 'par value' or 'stated capital' with respect to dividends, redemption of stock, payments for stock and the like is eliminated, whether

---

5. One will now look in vain for the familiar texts of Model Act (1979) §§ 2(h) through 2(n), 45, 46, 66, 67, 68, 69 and 70, plus substantial blocks of other sections.

6. Model Act (1980) § 19.

7. Model Act (1980) § 18(a).

8. Model Act § 25 is unchanged in this respect. See also § 23 regarding issuance of share certificates only upon receipt of the consideration.

or not the corporate charter documents continue to contain references thereto. It will, however, be permissible under the Model Act as revised to include special provisions which as a matter of contract give effect or meaning to 'par value' but such provisions would only have whatever effect any permissible contractual provisions have in the absence of a prohibition by statute. (In this regard, it should be noted that subparagraph (d) of the first paragraph, which contains references to par value, has been retained, since it refers simply to a statement within the articles of incorporation as to the existence or non-existence of par value.) The retention of optional par value is also designed to permit corporations which are to be qualified in foreign jurisdictions in which the franchise or other taxes are computed upon the basis of par value to have (and therefore use) par value for those purposes, if so desired." (p. 1887)

One can only admire the straightforward way in which the revised Act deals with the point noted in earlier pages that stock dividends and similar transactions never have in fact complied with the statutory requirement that for all shares issued the corporation must receive money, property or labor done. Section 18(b) as revised simply says that *pro rata* stock issues, such as stock dividends and conversions, shall not require consideration.

2. *Equitable contribution*

The revised Act makes no new effort to protect the interest of each shareholder in an equitable contribution into the corporate pot by every other shareholder. But the Act as revised continues to impose upon directors a duty of good faith and "such care as an ordinarily prudent person in a like position would use under similar circumstances," and the board must be careful to comply with this standard when it sets the consideration for the issuance of new shares, as in all other transactions.[9]

3. *Procedural remedies*

The revised Model Act makes no changes with regard to procedural enforcement of the shareholder's obligation under Section 25 to pay the agreed upon consideration. But unlike many statutes, the Model Act states clearly that the obligation runs not to creditors but to the corporation, and that any payment required is to be made to the corporation itself—propositions that

---

[9]. Model Act (1980) § 35; see Committee Report, Comments regarding § 18.

in themselves answer many of the procedural questions adverted to earlier.[10]

B. Regulating Distributions to Shareholders

1. *"Distribution"*

The major revisions in the 1980 Model Act begin with a new definition of distribution to shareholders in Subsection 2(i).[11] This is a key provision both in what it excludes (e. g., stock dividends) and what it includes. The Committee Report says in regard to this provision:

> "In new subsection 2(i) the term 'distribution' is introduced and defined as a fundamental part of the series of amendments that have the effect of eliminating the traditional concepts of stated capital and surplus and restating the statutory restrictions on dividends and other distributions to shareholders. In subsection 2(i) 'distribution' is broadly defined to include all transfers of money or other property made by a corporation to any shareholder in respect of the corporation's shares, except mere changes in the unit of interest such as stock dividends and stock splits. Thus, the definition encompasses dividends, purchases by a corporation of its own shares, and distributions in liquidation. Where a corporation incurs indebtedness in a distribution (as in the case of a distribution of a debt instrument or an installment purchase of shares), the creation or incurrence of the indebtedness is the event which constitutes the distribution rather than the subsequent payment of the debt by the corporation, and the tests of Section 45 must be met at that time. The inclusion of the term 'indirect' in the definition is intended to embrace such transactions as the repurchase of parent company stock by a subsidiary whose actions are controlled by the parent, and makes the definition apply to any other transaction in which the substance is clearly the same as a typical dividend of stock repurchase. The Committee did not believe that it was possible to define the full scope of this concept in the statute." [12]

10. See pages 49–57, supra.

11. As revised, § 2(i) reads: "Distribution means a direct or indirect transfer of money or other property (except its own shares) or incurrence of indebtedness by a corporation to or for the benefit of any of its shareholders in respect of any of its shares, whether by dividend or by purchase, redemption or other acquisition of its shares or otherwise."

12. Committee Report, Comments regarding Subsection 2(i), p. 1878.

2. *Insolvency*

The revised Model Act makes no substantive change in the traditional rule that no distribution may be made to shareholders that would render the corporation insolvent, nor does it change its commitment to the equity sense of "insolvency" or alter its definition—the inability to pay debts as they become due in the ordinary course of business.[13] The Committee Report, however, examines the content and scope of this proposition with unusual care and specificity and is worthy of attentive reading:

> "Old section 45 prohibited the payment of dividends if the corporation is, or as a result of the payment would be, insolvent in the equity sense. The Committee concluded that this test was the most important and fundamental test for the permissibility of distributions, and the amendments preserve it in new section 45(a).
>
> "In determining whether or not a corporation is, or as a result of a proposed distribution would be rendered, insolvent, the board of directors must exercise its collective business judgment as to whether making the distribution in question will render the corporation unable to pay its debts as they become due in the ordinary course of its business operations. In making this determination, the directors are required and entitled to make certain judgments as to the future course of the corporation's business, including the likelihood that, based on existing and contemplated demand for the corporation's products or services, it will be able to generate funds over a period of time from its operations or from any contemplated orderly disposition of its assets sufficient to satisfy its existing and reasonably anticipated obligations as they mature. The directors are entitled to expect that substantial indebtedness which matures in the near-term will be refinanced where, on the basis of the corporation's financial condition and future prospects, and the general availability of credit to businesses similarly situated, it is reasonable to assume that such refinancing may be accomplished. To the extent that the corporation may be subject to asserted or unasserted contingent liabilities, the directors are required and entitled to make judgments as to the likelihood, amount and time of any recovery against the corporation, after giving consideration to the extent to which the corporation is insured or otherwise protected by others against loss.

---

13. Model Act (1980) § 45(a).

"What is appropriate for an on-going business enterprise is a cash flow analysis based on a business forecast and budget for a sufficient period of time to permit a conclusion that known obligations of the corporation can reasonably be expected to be satisfied over the period of time that they will mature rather than a simple measurement of current assets against current liabilities, or a determination that the present estimated 'liquidation' value of the corporation's assets would produce sufficient funds to satisfy the corporation's existing liabilities. In exercising their judgment, the directors are entitled to rely on information, opinions, reports and statements prepared by others, as contemplated by section 35. Judgments must of necessity be made on the basis of information in the hands of the directors when a distribution is authorized, and it is not expected that they will be held responsible as a matter of hindsight for unforeseen developments. This is particularly true with respect to assumptions as to the ability of the corporation's business to repay longterm obligations which do not mature for several years, since the primary focus of the directors' decision to make a distribution should normally be on the corporation's prospects and obligations in the shorter term, unless special factors concerning the corporation's prospects require the taking of a longer-term prospective.

"The directors' decision as to whether to authorize a distribution is to be judged on the basis of the business judgment rule; that is, whether the directors acted in good faith and with a reasonable basis for believing that the distribution authorized was permitted by the statute, after due consideration of what they reasonably believed to be the relevant factors." [14]

3. *Balance sheet test*

Revised Subsection 45(b) contains the big bomb. All provisions relating to legal capital having been surgically excised from the Act, the revisers have substituted a single substantive proposition in their place (assuming, of course, no insolvency):

". . . [N]o distribution may be made if, after giving effect thereto, . . . the corporation's total assets would be less than the sum of its total liabilities and . . . the maximum amount that then would be payable, in any liquidation, in respect of all outstanding shares having preferential rights in liquidation." [15]

---

14. Committee Report, Comments regarding § 45(a), pp. 1881–2.

15. Model Act (1980) § 45(b).

While the central idea of this new rule for regulating distributions to shareholders is both sensible and clear, the Committee recognized that retention of a balance sheet test of any kind entails the perpetuation of certain obvious sub-issues that have been troublesome in the past. The Committee felt that, having decided not to rely exclusively on the equity solvency test as a regulatory standard, it should, by legislative language and by legislative history, address some of the more important sub-issues that inhere in any standard that is based on the corporation balance sheet. This material is of sufficient importance to merit presentation here in full, despite its relatively technical character.

(a) Valuation

For purposes of applying the new balance sheet test, how shall valuation be determined?

The second paragraph of revised Section 45 reads:

"Determination under subparagraph (b) may be based upon (i) financial statements prepared on the basis of accounting practices and principles that are reasonable in the circumstances, or (ii) a fair valuation or other method that is reasonable in the circumstances."

As to this provision, the Committee's comments are extensive and important:

"New section 45(b) also requires that, after giving effect to any distribution, the corporation's assets equal or exceed its liabilities and liquidation preferences on senior equity. In an effort to clarify uncertainties that have prevailed in many jurisdictions concerning the permissible way to determine assets and liabilities, section 45(b) authorizes asset and liability determinations to be made on the basis of either (a) financial statements prepared on the basis of accounting practices and principles that are reasonable in the circumstances, or (b) a fair valuation or other method that is reasonable in the circumstances. The determination of a corporation's assets and liabilities and the choice of the permissible basis on which to do so are left to the judgment of its board of directors. This is consistent with other authority granted a corporation's board of directors. In making a judgment under new section 45(b), the board may rely under section 35 upon opinions, reports or statements including financial statements and other financial data prepared or presented by public accountants or others, as provided in section 35. Assuming the assets equal or exceed the liabilities plus any liquidation preferences of senior equity on either a financial statement basis or a fair value basis, and that the other tests provided by section 45 are met, then the board of directors may lawfully authorize and make a distribution.

"*Financial Statement Basis.* Incorporating technical accounting terminology and specific accounting concepts into new section 45 was rejected, principally because such terminology and concepts are constantly under review and subject to revision by the Financial Accounting Standards Board, the American Institute of Certified Public Accountants, the Securities and Exchange Commission and others. The Committee concluded that the Model Act should leave such determinations and resolutions of accounting matters to the judgment of the board of directors, taking into account its right to rely upon professional or expert competence and its obligation to be reasonably informed as to pertinent standards of importance that bear upon the subject at issue.

"Normally, a board of directors would use the corporation's separate 'parent company' financial statements for such determinations of distributions. In the view of the Committee, a board of directors could properly use the equity method of accounting as set forth in APB No. 18 as to all of the corporation's investee corporations, including corporate joint ventures and subsidiaries, in the case of unconsolidated parent financial statements, although other evidence would be relevant in the total determination. Consolidated retained earnings (or 'earned surplus') are usually the same as the parent company's retained earnings following such equity method of accounting under current accounting standards.

"While the directors will normally be entitled to use generally accepted accounting principles and to give presumptive weight to the advice of professional accountants with respect thereto, it is important to recognize that the new Section requires the use of accounting practices and principles that are reasonable in the circumstances, and does not constitute a statutory enactment of generally accepted accounting principles. In the view of the Committee, the widespread controversy concerning various accounting principles, and their constant reevaluation, requires a statutory standard of reasonableness, as a matter of law, recognizing that there may be equally acceptable alternative solutions to specific issues as well as areas requiring judgment in interpreting such principles. This does not mean that the statute is intended to reject the use and reliance upon generally accepted accounting principles; on the contrary, it is expected that their use would be the basic rule in most cases. The statutory language does, however, require informed business judgment in the entire circumstances in applying particular accounting principles to the circumstances that exist at the time, for purposes of the ultimate legal measurement of the validity of distributions.

"If a corporation's financial statements are not presented in accordance with generally accepted accounting principles, however, a board of directors should normally carefully consider the extent to which the assets may not be fairly stated or the liabilities may be understated, to determine the fairness of the aggregate amount of assets and the aggregate amount of liabilities.

"*Fair Valuation Basis.* New section 45 also gives specific authority for determinations on the basis of a fair valuation or other method that is reasonable in the circumstances. The statute accordingly specifically authorizes departures from historical cost accounting and sanctions the utilization of appraisal methods for the purpose of determining the fund available for distributions. In the view of the Committee, the prescription in the statute of a particular method or methods of valuation would be inadvisable, since different methods may have equal validity depending upon the circumstances, including the type of enterprise and the purpose for which the determination is made. For example, it is inappropriate to apply a 'quick sale' liquidation value to an enterprise in most cases, particularly with respect to the payment of normal dividends. On the other hand, a quick sale valuation might be appropriate in certain circumstances, for example, for an enterprise in the course of liquidation or course of reducing its asset or business base to a material degree. In most cases, a fair valuation method on a going concern basis would likely be appropriate, if expectations are that the enterprise will continue as a viable going concern. In determining the value of assets, all of the assets of a corporation, whether or not reflected in the financial statements (e. g., a valuable executory contract), should be considered. Ordinarily a corporation should not selectively revalue assets. Likewise, all of a corporation's obligations and commitments should be considered and quantified to the extent appropriate and possible. In any event, new section 45(b) imposes upon the board of directors the responsibility of applying a method of determining the aggregate amounts of assets and liabilities that is reasonable in the circumstances.

"Clause (ii) of the second paragraph of section 45 also refers to another method that is reasonable in the circumstances. This phrase was inserted to comprehend the wide variety of possibilities that might not be deemed to fall under a 'fair valuation' but would be reasonable in the circumstances of a particular case.

"Recognition is given under section 45(b) to the preference rights of senior equity holders. The preference amount is the contractually stated maximum preference rights of senior equity holders in a liquidation (including if so provided in the articles, any arrearages in cumulative dividends) that would be payable at the time of the distribution." (pp. 1883–5)

(b) Time of measurement

As of what time should a determination be made as to compliance with the statutory standard for a shareholder distribution? The third paragraph of Section 45, as revised, reads:

"In the case of a purchase, redemption or other acquisition of a corporation's shares, the effect of a distribution shall be measured as of the date money or other property is transferred or debt is incurred by the corporation, or as of the date the shareholder ceases to be a shareholder of the corporation with respect to such shares, whichever is earlier. In all other cases, the effect of a distribution shall be measured as of the date of its authorization if payment occurs 120 days or less following the date of authorization, or as of the date of payment if payment occurs more than 120 days following the date of authorization."

As to this provision, the Committee comments:

"The Committee recognized the need to specify the time at which the two tests imposed by section 45 should be measured. Accordingly, where shares of the corporation are acquired by it, a date approximating the earlier of the payment date or the date the shareholder ceases to be a shareholder with respect to such shares is to be used as the measuring date. In all other cases, if payment occurs 120 days or less following the date of authorization, the date of authorization is to be used; if payment occurs more than 120 days following the date of authorization, then a date approximating the payment date is to be used." (pp. 1885–6)

(c) Redemption related debt

What if a corporation distributes instruments of indebtedness to its shareholders? The final paragraph of Section 45, as revised reads:

"Indebtedness of a corporation incurred or issued to a shareholder in a distribution in accordance with this Section shall be on a parity with the indebtedness of the corporation to its general unsecured creditors except to the extent subordinated by agreement."

As to this provision, the Committee explains:

"In an acquisition of its shares, a corporation may pay out property or incur a debt to the former holder of the shares. The case law on the status of such debt has developed in a conflicting and confusing way, making it difficult to know what standards apply in drafting stock repurchase agreements, which are of special importance in closely-held corporate enterprises. Section 45 therefore makes two points clear where indebtedness of a corporation is incurred or issued to a shareholder in a distribution.

"First, such indebtedness is on a parity with the indebtedness of the corporation to its general unsecured creditors, except to the extent subordinated by agreement. General creditors are better off in such a situation than they would have been if cash or other property had been paid out for the shares, and no worse off than if assets had been paid out to the shareholder, who had then promptly loaned the same to the corporation and thereby become a creditor.

"Second, in applying each of the tests of section 45, the legality of the distribution must be measured at the time of the issuance or incurrence of the debt, not at a later date when the debt is actually paid—though of course in some circumstances, such payment could constitute a preferential payment among creditors. In any later challenge arising out of the corporation's subsequent insolvency, if the test of section 45 was properly met at the time of the incurrence or issuance of the debt, the directors would be entitled to rely fully upon the good faith business judgment rule of section 35, as discussed above." (p. 1886)

(d) Liability for improper distribution

While effecting no substantial change in content, Section 48 as revised makes clear that a director who votes for or assents to an improper distribution to shareholders is liable to the corporation to the extent that the distribution was in excess of the amount permitted by Section 45, unless he complied with the standard of care prescribed in Section 35 referred to earlier.

An awkward question regarding the Uniform Fraudulent Conveyance Act has sometimes been raised in connection with restrictions on distributions to shareholders. That question was also addressed by the draftsmen of the 1980 revision. As they observe in their Report:

"The definition of 'insolvent' now contained in old subsection 2(n), namely, the inability of a corporation to pay its debts as they become due in the usual course of its business, is consistent with the objectives of section 45(a) discussed above, and accordingly no change has been made in that definition except to transfer it to section 45(a). On the other hand, the definition of 'insolvency' in section 2 of the Uniform Fraudulent Conveyance Act is different, and may not be consistent with those objectives, since—if it is considered applicable to distributions and not superseded by the corporation statute—it appears to require the directors to determine whether the present liquidation value of the corporation's existing assets will be sufficient to satisfy the corporation's existing obligations as they mature. The Committee believes that the Uniform Fraudulent Conveyance Act, or similar statutes in states where that act is not in force, should be reconsidered in the context of its application to corporate distributions. The new amendments therefore provide an optional provision (new section 152) under which a jurisdiction might choose expressly to supplant the application of other statutes to the subject of corporate distributions. The Committee does not believe, however, that it is appropriate for the Model Act to attempt directly to deal with a different uniform statute. In addition, if a corporation should become involved in proceedings under the federal bankruptcy laws following a distribution, the fraudulent conveyance provisions of section 67d (§ 548 effective October 1, 1979) of the federal Bankruptcy Act could become applicable to the transaction. It should be recognized that, while the Committee questions the desirability of inconsistency between the Model Act, on the one hand, and the Uniform Fraudulent Conveyance Act and the Bankruptcy Act, on the other, the Model Act deals fundamentally with the responsibility of directors, and failure to follow the standard of the Model Act results in potential liability for directors under section 48. In contrast, there is no provision in either the Uniform Fraudulent Conveyance Act or in the federal Bankruptcy Act for liability of directors; rather, the effect of those acts is to enable the trustee or other representative to recapture for the benefit of creditors funds distributed to others in some circumstances. Accordingly, considerations of public policy may justify the application of different standards in these two different sets of statutes." (pp. 1882–3)

Under the new optional provision, Section 152, Section 45 and any other relevant sections of the Model Act are declared to supersede the applicability of any other state statute of jurisdiction with respect to shareholder distributions (particularly the UFCA).

4. Abolition of treasury shares

As noted earlier, the 1980 revision deletes all reference to treasury shares throughout the Act. The relevant Section, Section 6, as revised, reads:

> "A corporation shall have the power to acquire its own shares. All of its own shares acquired by a corporation shall, upon acquisition, constitute authorized but unissued shares, unless the articles of incorporation provide that they shall not be reissued, in which case the authorized shares shall be reduced by the number of shares acquired."

The pay-out of assets by the corporation to acquire its shares is, of course, a "distribution" under Section 2(i) and must comply with the restrictions of Section 45. Section 6 also contains new material providing a simplified means of public filing if the authorized number of shares has been reduced by acquisition.

It would appear that these new provisions on treasury shares may in one sense have more legal bite than the other 1980 changes in the Act, though the latter are substantively more important. The elimination of the requirements relating to par, stated capital and the like are all steps in the direction of relaxing earlier forms of statutory restriction; they do not mandate. Further corporations may under the Act perpetuate par provisions in their articles of incorporation and, with regard to such matters, the statute does not dictate to accountants what to put on their balance sheets.

But the new provisions on treasury shares are different. Under the Act as revised, there simply is no such thing as a treasury share. Further, the legal consequences of acquisition of shares by the issuing corporation is explicitly mandated. In these circumstances, the accountants would not appear to have a choice as to the balance sheet treatment of a share acquisition by the issuer.

Further, as will be recalled from earlier discussion here, it was classical doctrine that treasury shares could be sold for any price regardless of their par. By false extension, some practitioners, or even courts, may have believed—may still believe—that that proposition also means that a board of directors may sell treasury shares for any consideration it wishes, in disregard of the principles of equitable contribution among shareholders. That never was sound doctrine. In any case, a consequence of the Model Act's new provisions on treasury shares is to make it totally clear that the same rules as to the adequacy of consideration received will govern uniformly whenever a corporation puts out additional shares, regardless of past history of share acquisitions, and regardless of verbal distinctions as between "new issue" and "resale."

C. Some Concluding Comments

Whether many states will follow the sudden turn of the ABA's Committee on Corporate Laws and adopt the 1980 revisions to the Model Business Corporation Act remains to be seen. These changes may well strike many practitioners and legislators as so conceptually radical that they may balk. It is conceivable, even, that the proposed changes may lead some persons for the first time to examine the degree of protection afforded to creditors by the present legal capital system and to discover that it is a Swiss cheese made up mainly of holes; some persons might be moved by that observation to move in exactly the opposite legislative direction in an effort to put a new statutory system in place that would seek to give creditors a stronger position.

It will not surprise the reader to learn that, for the reasons developed in this book at length, this author believes that those responses would be regrettable.[16]

The 1980 revision of the Model Act represents a balanced approach to the problems it addresses, carefully hammered out by a large committee of experienced practitioners and scholars over a two year period. Undoubtedly the new financial provisions of the Act will in time give rise to new difficulties and new perceptions of possible improvements, and it is a safe bet that some unforeseen problems will come up in the transition from the old system to the new. But the revisions provide a significant improvement over the present Act, and are worthy of adoption.

The more interesting question is just how the legal and accounting professions—and ultimately the courts—will adapt to the revised Act where it is enacted into law. The Act cannot prevent lawyers, accountants, and corporate financial officers from thinking in traditional terms of "stated capital." [17]

---

16. Let it here be again disclosed that the author was one of those who served on the joint sub-committee that worked on the 1980 revisions.

17. See the Preface to this Edition.

To many experienced readers of corporate balance sheets it will come as a distinct shock to discover suddenly that the southeast corner may henceforth carry only an entry for shareholder's equity—with no distinctions drawn between "stated capital" accounts and surpluses of myriad kinds, and with no elaborate entries for "treasury shares." Indeed, one may predict with some confidence that the shock will be so great that many practitioners will simply keep on in their old ways for many years to come. But in the long run that will not really matter. For, in those states which adopt them, the 1980 revisions of the Model Act, will, in time, at last put to rest the legal effectiveness of the antique and discredited concepts surrounding "legal capital".

INDEX

References are to Pages

ACCOUNTING
General, 33, Part Two, *passim*
Law and accounting, 61, 71, 77, 84

CALIFORNIA, 164

CAPITAL
Different meanings, 21, 27, 28

CAPITAL SURPLUS
See Surplus

CORPORATE COMBINATIONS
Accounting for combinations, 154–162
    Pooling of interests method, 157–159
    Purchase and pooling methods compared, 159–162
    Purchase method, 154–156
Consolidation, 154
Dissenters' appraisal remedy, 162
Exchange of stock, 154
Merger, 154
Stock for assets, 141, 154

CORPORATE INDENTURE
Compared to statutes, 106–107
Debentures, 141, 143
Key covenants, 97–106
Structure, 96

CREDITORS
Commercial creditor, 94
Corporation, 5–8
Finance creditor, 91
General, 2
Investment creditor, 96
Partnership, 4
Perspective of, 1–3, 13–15, 91, 97
Proprietorship, 4
Secured, 2
Trade creditor, 91

DEBENTURES
    See also, Corporate Indenture
Convertible, 141, 143, 148
Interest of holders, 96

DISSOLUTION
Generally, 87, 162–163

DISTRIBUTIONS TO SHAREHOLDERS
    See also, Repurchase of Shares by Issuer; Restraints on Distributions to Shareholders
California, 164
Charged to various types of surplus, Part Two, *passim*
Defined, 110
Dividends in kind, 33, 135, 163
Model Business Corporation Act, 1980 changes, 169
Nimble dividends, 76, Part Two, *passim*
Not paid "out of" surplus, 33
Preferred stock dividend, 104, 150
Redemption of preferred, 105, 150
Stock "dividend", 103, 118
Stock split, 121

EARNED SURPLUS
See Surplus

ENFORCING THE PAY-IN OBLIGATION
    See also, Shareholder's Pay-in Obligation
Procedural problems,
    Generally, 50–52, 168
    Corporation as plaintiff, 56
    Creditor as plaintiff, 46–53
    Shareholder as plaintiff, 53
Theory of action,
    Balance sheet misrepresentation, 48
    Holding-out, 46
    Hybrid theories, 49
    Statutory obligation, 48
    Stock subscription, 48
    Trust fund theory, 46

EQUITABLE CONTRIBUTION
See Shareholder's Pay-in Obligation

HANDLEY v. STUTZ, 23, 45

INDEX
References are to Pages

HOSPES v. NORTHWESTERN MFG. & CAR CO., 46

INSOLVENCY
See also, Legal Capital Statutes
Defined, 59, 170

LEGAL CAPITAL
See Legal Capital Statutes
Basic concepts, 29–32, 34–35
Changes in, 38, Part Two, *passim*
Computation, 34, 64, Part Two, *passim*
History, 16, 21
Impairment of capital, 30, 32, 121, Part Two, *passim*
Reducing capital, see Reducing Capital

LEGAL CAPITAL STATUTES
Applications, Part Two, *passim*
Balance sheet surplus statutes, 60, Part Two, *passim*
California, 164
Corporate indenture, compared, 106–107
Current earnings statutes, 76, Part Two, *passim*
Earned surplus statutes, 72, Part Two, *passim*
Evaluation, 84–90, 106–108, 152
Insolvency statutes, 59, 108, Part Two, *passim*
Model Business Corporation Act, 1980 changes, 165
Surplus or net profit statutes, 75

LEGAL COUNSEL'S ROLE
Opinions of counsel, 35
Preventive measures, 57

MODEL BUSINESS CORPORATION ACT, 1980 CHANGES
Distributions to shareholders, 169
Insolvency, 170
Pay-in requirement, 167
Treasury shares, 178

NO PAR STOCK
Generally, 25, 37, 44, 141

OLD DOMINION COPPER MINING & SMELTING CO v. LEWISOHN, 55

PAID-IN SURPLUS
See Capital Surplus

PAR VALUE
California, 164
History and definition, 18–22
Low par, 24, 35
Model Business Corporation Act, 1980 changes, 165
Reducing par, see Reducing Capital

PROMOTERS
History, 18
Liability, 54

QUASI-REORGANIZATION, 74

RANDALL v. BAILEY, 71, 114

REDUCING CAPITAL
See also, Surplus
Generally, 67, 121–122, 135

REPURCHASE OF SHARES BY ISSUER
See also, Distributions to Shareholders
Generally, 45, 77, 130, 132, 164, 178
Retirement of treasury shares, 133
Sale of treasury shares, 132
Stock repurchase agreement, 128–30

RESTRAINTS ON DISTRIBUTIONS TO SHAREHOLDERS
See also, Legal Capital Statutes
Application of statutes, Part Two, *passim*
Corporate indenture provisions, 98
Factors determining distributions, 109
Liabilities for illegal distribution, 80–82
Uniform Fraudulent Conveyances Act, 59, 176

RETAINED EARNINGS
See Earned Surplus

SCULLY v. AUTOMOBILE FINANCE CO., 53

SHAREHOLDER
Perspective of, 8, 13

SHAREHOLDER'S PAY-IN OBLIGATION
See also, Enforcing the Pay-in Obligation; Handley v. Stutz; Legal Capital; No Par Stock; Par Value
Equitable contribution doctrine, 12, 53–56, 142., 147

INDEX

References are to Pages

SHAREHOLDER'S PAY-IN OBLIGATION—Cont'd
Inapplicable to sale by shareholder, 20
Inapplicable to transferee, 45
Kind of assets, 40
Minimum pay-in required to commence business, 17, 40
Model Business Corporation Act, 1980 changes, 167
Resale by issuer of treasury shares, 45, 77, 130, 132, 164, 178
Stock issued "against surplus", 43, 120, 144, 149, 159, 168
Undercapitalization, 17 n. 2
Valuation of assets paid in, 43

STATED CAPITAL
See Legal Capital

STOCK
See also, No Par Stock; Par Value; Shareholder's Pay-in Obligation
Classes, 79, 144, 151
Early meaning as "assets," 28, 76
Options, 145, 149
Outstanding, 147
Preferred, 104–105, 138, 150

STOCK—Cont'd
Subscriptions, 18, 48, 143, 148
Warrants, 144, 149
Watered, 20

SURPLUS
Appreciation surplus, 71, 113
Earned surplus, 72, Part Two, *passim*
Balance sheet surplus, 60, Part Two, *passim*
Capital (paid-in) surplus, 36–37, 69, 127, Part Two, *passim*
Defined, 68, Part Two, *passim*
Earned surplus, 72, Part Two, *passim*
Equalization surplus, 70
For different classes, 140
Issuing stock "against", 43, 120, 144, 149, 159
Paid-in (capital) surplus, 36–37, 69, 127, Part Two, *passim*
Payment "out of", 33
Reduction surplus, 70, 122, 135

TREASURY SHARES, 45. 66, 130, 132, 164, 178

UNIFORM FRAUDULENT CONVEYANCES ACT, 59, 176

WOOD v. DUMMER, 27, 46, 163